Muslims in Eastern Europe

The New Edinburgh Islamic Surveys
Series Editor: Carole Hillenbrand

www.edinburghuniversitypress.com/series/isur

Muslims in Eastern Europe

Egdūnas Račius

EDINBURGH
University Press

Edinburgh University Press is one of the leading university presses in the
UK. We publish academic books and journals in our selected subject
areas across the humanities and social sciences, combining cutting-edge
scholarship with high editorial and production values to produce academic
works of lasting importance. For more information visit our website:
edinburghuniversitypress.com

Edinburgh University Press Ltd
The Tun – Holyrood Road
12 (2f) Jackson's Entry
Edinburgh EH8 8PJ

Typeset in 11/13pt Baskerville MT Pro by
Servis Filmsetting Ltd, Stockport, Cheshire
and printed and bound in Great Britain by
CPI Group (UK) Ltd, Croydon CR0 4YY

A CIP record for this book is available from the British Library

ISBN 978 1 4744 1578 1 (hardback)
ISBN 978 1 4744 1579 8 (paperback)
ISBN 978 1 4744 1580 4 (webready PDF)
ISBN 978 1 4744 1581 1 (epub)

Contents

Tables, boxes and maps

Tables

Boxes

Maps

Glossary of Islamic terms

'ishq   'longing', a seminal category in Sufi Islam, denoting the mutual longing for each other of God and man

da'wa   'invitation', 'calling', missionary activities aimed at either converting non-Muslims to Islam or attracting Muslims to a particular interpretation of it

dar al-harb   'abode of war', the territory ruled by non-Muslims

dar al-islam   'abode of Islam', the territory ruled by Muslims in accordance with the Islamic law

dervish   a mystic, member of a Sufi brotherhood

dhikr   'remembrance', as a rule, collective meditative devotional ritual in Sufism aimed at bringing believers closer to God

dhimmi   'protected', non-Muslim inhabitant of a Muslim-ruled polity who is obliged to pay a poll tax for which she/he is granted (physical/military) protection by the Muslim polity

fiqh   jurisprudence, theoretical and practical explication of the Divine Law of Shari'a

fuqaha   legal scholars and jurists, theoreticians and practitioners of *fiqh*

hijab   head-covering worn by Muslim women, usually in the form of a scarf

hijra   'emigration', relocation from a non-Muslim ruled land (*dar al-harb*) to a land ruled according to Islamic law (*dar al-islam*)

jamaat   'collective', formal or informal group, congregation or community of like-minded or otherwise bound Muslims

jami'   cathedral mosque, a purpose-built mosque with a dome and a minaret, where Friday communal prayer complete with sermon takes place

khalifa   viceroy (of God), the supreme administrative leader of the Muslim commonwealth (*umma*)

khanaqa   Sufi lodge, 'convent'

khilafa   'viceroyship', political system and form of governance of Muslim polity; also 'Islamic polity'

madhahib   classical Islamic legal schools of thought, originally comprising four Sunni, three Shi'i and one Khariji *madrasa*   religious high school, historically the traditional system of secondary education

majlis   'assembly', council, a collective body of religious or lay officials

maktab   religious primary or prep school, usually mosque-based and informal

masjid   'place for bowing', prayer space, mosque, a converted or purpose-built building without a dome and without or only a symbolical minaret

meshihat   branch office of the collective body of religious officials

mihrab   niche in a wall of a mosque facing Kaaba in Mecca

mufti   in the classical understanding, a legal adviser who, upon usually written request, issues non-binding legal opinions, *fatwas*; the modern usage of the term denotes the top rank in the Islamic spiritual-administrative institution, formally or informally called the 'muftiate'

muhajir   one who has made a religious emigration, *hijra*, from a non-Muslim ruled land (*dar al-harb*) to a land ruled according to Islamic law (*dar al-islam*)

mujahid   one who engages in *jihad*, spiritual and physical efforts to protect, augment, strengthen and spread Islam

murid   'seeker', adept, follower of a shaykh, member of a Sufi brotherhood

musalla   'place for prayer', prayer hall, prayer space in a non-designated building

nikah   Islamic religious marriage ceremony presided over by a religious official

niqab   face-covering female attire worn by conservative Muslim women and attire of choice among Wahhabis and Salafis

qadi   judge, judicial official, usually state-employed, issuing binding legal verdicts

reis ul-ulama   'head of the learned men', chairman of the collective body of religious officials

rijaset   'headship', executive branch of the collective body of religious officials

sadaqa   voluntary alms-giving

shaykh   elder ('abbot') of a Sufi convent (*tekke, khanaqa, zawiya*)/brotherhood (*tariqa*)

Sufi   person or aspect (belief, practice, and so on) of the mystical dimension of Islam, Sufism

tabligh   'conveying', spreading of Islam by missionary activities encompassing both converting non-Muslims to Islam and attracting Muslims to a particular interpretation of it

taqwa   'fear of God', piety

tarbiyya	(religious) education, both formal and informal
tariqa	'path', Sufi brotherhood with its distinct chain of leadership and regulations
tasawwuf	Sufism, the mystical dimension of Islam
tekke	Sufi lodge, 'convent'
umma	'community', 'group', commonly used to collectively refer to the commonwealth of the world's Muslims
waqf	property or business set off for charitable purposes
zawiya	Sufi lodge, 'convent'

Foreword and acknowledgements

Though the study of Islam and Muslims in contemporary Europe is a relatively new subfield of religious studies – the first research results appeared in the 1980s – one cannot claim that there is a lack of scholarly investigation of the presence and development of Muslim communities in the Old Continent. However, with a closer look, it immediately becomes evident that the Europe whose Muslim communities are studied is mainly, if not exclusively, Western Europe, with Southern Europe also having received some of the scholarly attention. Eastern Europe, comprised of what during the Cold War used to be communist-ruled countries, to date has seen far less investigation into its Muslim communities.

Although some might explain this away by suggesting that the Muslim communities in Eastern Europe are less numerous, both in absolute numbers and percentage-wise (and in many cases it is so), or less 'problematic' (however this word is understood), it might be argued that research on Muslim communities in post-communist Eastern Europe lags behind first of all because of the dire lack of scholarly tradition in social sciences in general and religious studies in particular. This is particularly true in the case of research on heterodox Muslim groups; as Stoyanov points out, 'local anthropological and folklorist research on these groups was developing slowly and erratically, as research on the spiritual and mystical aspects of Balkan heterodox Islam was variously deemphasized, discouraged or marginalized during the communist period' (Stoyanov 2013: 164). In most countries of Eastern Europe to this day, local guilds of scholars of religious studies are miniscule with only a handful of them engaged in Islamic studies and even fewer in research on local Muslim communities. The results of the research, as a rule, are published almost exclusively in local languages, making them difficult to access for outsiders. Moreover, until less than three decades ago, most of Eastern Europe was behind what was called the 'Iron Curtain' and Western scholars had a hard time accessing target groups for their research and, even when lucky, due to religious policies and censorship of the then authorities – which sought to marginalise if not altogether get rid of the religious practices of the local populations – had as difficult a time doing fieldwork research.

With the Cold War over and the Iron Curtain gone, since the early 1990s, Eastern Europe opened itself to the world and became available to scholars of practically all fields. However, even with this technical opening, Eastern

European Muslim communities have remained on the periphery of scholarly interests of both local and outside researchers of religion. This in part might have happened due to language constraints – a lack of a common language between outside researchers and the local target groups. Unlike in Asia and Africa and certainly Western Europe, where English and French are widely spoken by local populations, Eastern Europeans, and Muslims among them, usually do not speak any of the major languages, with the exception of Russian, which unfortunately is spoken by only a few in the West. The language barrier apparently became a formidable obstacle not only for Western academics who might have had an interest in Muslim communities of Eastern Europe, but also for others in the West wishing to familiarise themselves with the development of post-communist societies in general and the local Muslim communities in particular. The Western media, also mainly due to language constraints but also for other reasons, failed to report on the Muslim communities in Eastern Europe in such a way that these communities would be perceived by Western audiences as both part and parcel of local wider societies and Europe as a whole.

Even so, it would be unfair not to recognise the media's reporting of numerous armed conflicts both in what used to be the Socialist Federal Republic of Yugoslavia (SFRY) and its successor states, as well as in the Russian Federation, where one side of the conflict would generally be publicly presented as 'Muslims', be it ethnic Bosniaks, Chechens or Albanians. However, in reports on such conflicts, the 'normal life' of Muslim communities was inevitably obscured, giving way to extraordinary activities, mainly related to violence. Even worse, as some of the local Muslims in their armed struggle did use religious rhetoric and symbols, religion and warfare were entangled, sometimes to a point beyond separation. And as a number of armed groups operating in the Balkans and particularly Russia had a bent on hard-line revivalist Islam, local state authorities used this as a propaganda tool to present local Muslim populations in such pejorative terms as 'fundamentalists' and 'Islamists', that bordered on the more generic term 'terrorists'. This all might have contributed to the creation of an image of Muslims in some parts of Eastern Europe as conflictual and problematic, if not the perpetrators, then at least victims, of politically motivated violence. In sum, if Eastern European Muslims are at all known to wider publics in the West, they are mainly known through (at times selective and biased) reporting on their struggle against local (non-Muslim) state authorities; in other words, in exceptional and abnormal situations. The mundane (including religious) life of these communities has until now remained little exposed. The present book seeks to remedy this shortcoming and to present a comprehensive, yet concise, picture of the development of Muslim communities in Eastern Europe.

The Muslim presence in Eastern Europe has hitherto been only occasionally addressed in academic publications on Islam in Europe or the wider world. Apart from country and sub-region (like the former USSR or Yugoslavia/the

Balkans) studies in the form of articles, edited volumes and monographs (see Bibliography at the end of this book), to the best of the author's knowledge, there is just one publication in English which aspires to be comprehensive by addressing the situation and development of Muslim communities in a wide range of Eastern European countries. It is Katarzyna Górak-Sosnowska's edited volume *Muslims in Poland and Eastern Europe: Widening the European discourse on Islam*, published in 2011 in Poland by the University of Warsaw. However, as an edited volume, it is a collection of individual contributions with no aim of providing a coherent picture or a comparative perspective of the situation of Muslim communities in the entire Eastern European region.

The present book covers twenty-one post-communist Eastern European countries and presents the development of the centuries-old Muslim communities in Eastern Europe through a prism of emergence and survival, which tells of the resilience of these Muslim communities in the face of often restrictive state policies and hostile social environments, especially during the half-century communist period, their subsequent revival in the aftermath of the Cold War, finally complimented by the profound changes currently taking place in the demographic composition of the communities but also, and more importantly, in the forms of Islam practised by them. The reader is provided with a picture of the general trends common to the Muslim communities of Eastern Europe, something not previously given, as well as the peculiarities pertaining to clusters of states, like the Baltics, the Balkans, the Višegrad Four and the European states of the Commonwealth of Independent States (CIS). By doing so, the book places the centuries-long Muslim presence in Eastern Europe within a broader European context and so does justice to local Muslim communities, which until recently were made up primarily of indigenous Turkic-, Albanian- and Slavic-speaking groups, as having belonged in and to Europe.

Structurally, the book consists of an introductory chapter of a religious/ Islamic studies nature, a chapter on the history of the Muslim presence in Eastern Europe, four sub-region (country-cluster) -based chapters on contemporary developments, and a final chapter assessing the most recent trends related to the development of Islam and Muslim communities common to most if not all Eastern European countries – conversion, migration, radicalisation and securitisation. The concluding section addresses the perception and view of Islam in the non-Muslim majorities with the focus on trends in populist politics and of Muslimophobia. Division of the book into parts dealing with the historical and contemporary presence may also be understood as a division between Islam 'in' and 'of' the country – for instance, while the Islamic presence 'in' Lithuania dates back to the fourteenth century, it became 'of' Lithuania only with the establishment of a Lithuanian nation (ethnic) state in the aftermath of the First World War. The four core chapters each cover the common trends observable in the distinguished sub-regions and then identify particular aspects peculiar to individual countries, addressing such areas as demographic trends in the Muslim population, regime of governance of religion and juridical status of Islam, organisational structures of and internal divisions in Muslim communities, forms of Islamic religiosity common to the country, and Muslims' participation in national politics, where relevant.

The four identified sub-regions are (1) North-eastern Europe: the European states of the CIS (Russia, Ukraine, Belarus, Moldova) and the Baltic States (Estonia, Latvia, Lithuania); South-eastern Europe, commonly called 'the Balkans', encompassing (2) the former Yugoslav republics (Bosnia and Herzegovina, Serbia, Montenegro, Former Yugoslav Republic of Macedonia, Croatia and Slovenia) and Kosovo, as well as (3) the sovereign states of Romania, Bulgaria and Albania; and (4) Central Europe, or the Višegrad Four, consisting of Poland, The Czech Republic, Slovakia and Hungary. Though the division into sub-regions is naturally geography-based, it also directly corresponds to the realms of influence of three former major empires in the identified sub-regions of the eastern part of Europe: the Russian Empire (to be followed by the USSR) with its significant Muslim minority and centuries-long policies of governance of Islam in the first sub-region, the Muslim Ottoman Empire in the second and third sub-regions, and finally, the Austro-Hungarian Empire with both few Muslims and too short an experience in governance of Islam in the fourth sub-region (with the exception of Poland). The book, however, omits Armenia, Georgia and Azerbaijan (and also Cyprus and Greece), due to the specific historical and contemporary developments in Muslim communities in these countries facilitated by their proximity to the Middle East and diasporic dynamics binding them to the kin communities in the Eastern Mediterranean.

The discrepancy in the availability of publications with research results on the historical development and contemporary situation of Muslims in the respective Eastern European countries in either English or even national languages has been one of the major obstacles to material gathering for the present book – while the Muslim populations of some countries have received a fairly comprehensive share of scholarly attention, others remain almost *terra incognita*. Though in some cases this may be explained away by suggesting that the less developed, less numerous and more recent Muslim communities or forms of Islamic religiosity do not call for elaborate and complex research, one may however firmly state that in many cases the reality on the ground, even if in quantitative terms insignificant, is much more complex (and therefore worthy of research) than the available research findings suggest. This unevenness in accessible research results has inevitably led to the book also being uneven in its treatment of the individual countries covered – some chapters are more of an overview nature just covering the institutionalised side of Islam in the country, usually represented by an officially recognised Islamic administration, while others contain much more detailed and rich material also covering other, non-institutionalised structures, informal authorities and forms of Islamic religiosity.

Methodologically, the book falls into two distinct parts – the historical, where the author had to rely exclusively on secondary and even tertiary sources, and the contemporary, where the primary (like paper and online publications and other information from Muslim communities) and secondary (primarily scholarly texts, but also media and think tank reports and analysis) sources are supplemented, and often in this way verified, by such research methods as participant observation, interviews, informal live and online communication and the like. During fieldwork trips, three quarters of the countries covered in the book were visited, including Albania, Bosnia and Herzegovina, Bulgaria, Croatia, Estonia, Hungary, Kosovo, Latvia, Lithuania, Macedonia, Moldova, Montenegro, Poland, Serbia, Slovenia and the Ukraine.

The author of this book is particularly indebted to the Center for Advanced Studies (Sarajevo, Bosnia and Herzegovina) – to all its staff and especially its Director, Dr Ahmet Alibašić, whose brotherly spiritual and other assistance is not only much appreciated by the author but recognised as having enabled him to conduct the very research on the Balkan part in the first place. The author is also exceptionally grateful to Kęstutis Jaskutėlis for his understanding of the worth of academic research and generous support for it. Davide Calzoni created the maps for which the author is deeply grateful. Thanks also to Sue Dalgleish for her painstaking editing of the manuscript and making it into a reader-friendly text.

As in most cases, though the writing of the text is done by the author, the research material at his or her disposal is often made available by and through other people who empathise with the research done by the author and not only share their insights but also devote time and efforts to facilitate further gathering of fieldwork material. In all the places the author went to gather material for the book, he had old and new colleagues-turned-friends who served in a number of capacities ranging from fixers and go-betweens, through guides and respondents, to first readers of the relevant parts of the manuscript. The list includes but is not limited to Dr Ahmet Alibašić (Bosnia and Herzegovina), Dr Oleg Yarosh (Ukraine), Srđan Barišić (Serbia), Dr Antonina Zhelyazkova (Bulgaria), Dr Ringo Ringve (Estonia), Dr Aurelia Felea (Moldova), Daniel Vekony (Hungary), Dr Agata Nalborzcyk (Poland), Sabina Pačariz (Serbia), Ivan Kostić (Serbia), Omer Kajoshi (Montenegro), Dr Erzsebet N. Rozsa (Hungary), Dr Konrad Pędziwiatr (Poland), and many others. Many sincere thanks go to Dr Jørgen S. Nielsen, whom the author considers his spiritual mentor. The success of his acclaimed *Muslims in Western Europe* (with the fourth edition having appeared in 2016) indirectly opened the possibility for the appearance of the present book as a complimentary volume to cover the development and situation of Muslim communities in practically the whole of

Europe. The author remains indebted to him for his fatherly care in this and other instances.

Finally, the author needs to publicly acknowledge the indirect input of his life partner Aušra, herself a dedicated and accomplished academic, to the project – without her tacit support it would have been much more difficult to pull through the research for and writing of the book. Next to her, our two daughters, Rachelė Elžbieta and Magdalena Veronika, need to be asked to forgive the author's failure to serve as a full-time member of the family throughout the period of procuring the material for and producing the text of the book.

CHAPTER 1

Autochthonous Islam of Eastern Europe – populations, practices, institutions

Eastern Europe as such and particularly its eastern edges have long been on the ever-shifting dividing line between the classically understood *dar al-islam* – 'abode' or lands of Islam, where Muslims, though not necessarily a numerical majority, held political power and presumably governed the land according to Islamic prescripts – and *dar al-harb* – the 'abode of war', where the laws of Islam were not only not followed but where Muslims might even have been oppressed. Retrospectively, there are many fewer lands in Eastern Europe that in the course of history have not had a Muslim presence than those that have. However, due to the uneven spread of Muslim communities, many of which have historically been rural, compact and relatively closed, many (and in some areas even most) local non-Muslims would not encounter Muslims on a daily basis or would not even be aware of their presence in the vicinity.

The two major autochthonous groups, namely, primarily Turkic-speaking Muslims of the north-eastern parts of Europe and Slavic-, Albanian- and Turkish-speaking Muslims of the south-eastern parts, differ significantly in their nature and, historically, this has had repercussions for the development of these groups internally (their identities, feelings of belonging, and also religious practices) but equally so for their relations with non-Muslim communities and state authorities. The historical but also the contemporary role of the powerful Christian churches, particularly the Orthodox, in engaging (both positively and negatively) with the local Muslim communities also needs to be taken into account.

Statistics

Before going into a discussion of the Muslim presence in Eastern Europe, it is worth pausing on the question of who should count as a Muslim. Counting Muslims in Eastern Europe poses certain challenges, not least of which is the juxtaposing of ethnicity and religious belonging. So, for instance, in socialist Yugoslavia (and in fact in some successor states today) 'Muslim' could mean either ethnicity or religious belonging, or both. Likewise, designations of 'Bosniak', 'Pomak', 'Torbeshi', 'Gorani' and the like are sometimes taken to mean both ethnicity and religious belonging so that a Pomak is perceived to be a Slavic- (Bulgarian-) speaking Muslim. The problem, as elsewhere in Europe and the wider world, when counting religious groups, extends into the distinction of self-identification versus ascribed identity and also nominal identification versus active implementation of that identification through religious practices. In other words, the question is not only about whether the person holds herself or himself or is held by others (either of the 'in' group or 'out' group) to be a member of the believer commonwealth, but also of what she or he makes of it in practical terms.

National censuses could be of help here but only if they explicitly include questions on religious identity. But even in such cases, the recorded numbers may reflect only part of the otherwise possibly larger constituency of inhabitants of Muslim (cultural) background. If there is no question on religious identity, and this is arguably a frequent case in Eastern Europe, the used extrapolations of the numbers of inhabitants of Muslim background in a particular country fall back on the basis of ethnicity, which is way too often taken to be directly tied to religious belonging. This way, for instance, Chechens or Turks would en masse be accorded the status of 'Muslim'; the ethnicity-based extrapolations, however, would fail to include converts who would as a rule be counted as belonging to the 'traditional' (read, Christian) faith group of their ethnicity – Hungarians, Lithuanians and Poles as Catholic; Serbs, Ukrainians, Moldovans and Russians as Orthodox; Latvians and Estonians as Protestant. Furthermore, in some of the countries the official census results are questioned, if not outright rejected, by interested groups. So, for instance, in several Eastern European countries, like Macedonia, Bulgaria, Moldova and Serbia, the Muslim leadership has contested census results and argued that the official figures are far below the community-held numbers. In some cases, the governments have even been accused of having tampered with the results, resulting in corrections of the official census. Macedonia is a case in point.

In view of this arguable unreliability of official statistics (common not only to Eastern Europe), where available, it makes sense to look at the figures alongside estimates done by, if not the Muslim communities themselves (who due to vested interests might be tempted to raise the figures), then independent and hopefully unbiased researchers. Though the reliability of these estimates may also be questioned, they at least give an arguably more objective perspective and the upper limit of the number of nominal Muslims (or people of Muslim background) in the given country. Therefore, Table 1.1 includes both the official figures (rounded to hundreds), where available, and the unofficial estimates – which in some cases differ rather significantly.

Table 1.1 reveals that at least two countries in Eastern Europe – Kosovo and Albania, both overwhelmingly Albanian-speaking – have a clear statistical Muslim majority. In Bosnia and Herzegovina, Muslims make up just over half of the country's population. Other Eastern European countries with significant Muslim minorities are Macedonia, whose Muslim population exceeds one

Table 1.1 Muslim populations in Eastern Europe

Country	Muslims (official)	Muslims (estimated)	Muslim, % of population	Muslim ethnicity
Albania	1,650,000[a] (2011)	2,300,000	59–65	Albanian
Belarus	n/a	20,000	0.2	Tatar, Azeri, Turkmen
Bosnia and Herzegovina	1,790,000 (2013)	n/a	51	Bosniak, Roma, Albanian
Bulgaria	577,000 (2011)	600,000	7.8–8	Turkish, Pomak, Roma
Croatia	63,000 (2011)	n/a	1.5	Bosniak, Croat, Albanian
Czech Republic	3,400 (2011)	11,200–20,000	0.1–0.3	Arab
Estonia	1,500 (2011)	2,000	0.14–0.2	Tatar, Azeri, Estonian
Hungary	5,600 (2011)	25,000–32,000	0.06–0.3	Arab, Hungarian
Kosovo	1,750,000 (2013)	n/a	96	Albanian, Bosniak
Latvia	n/a	5,000–6,000	0.2	Tatar, Azeri
Lithuania	2,700 (2011)	4,000	0.1–0.15	Tatar, Lithuanian
Macedonia, FYR of	660,500 (2002)	730,000	31–35	Albanian, Turkish, Roma
Moldova	1,700 (2004)	5,000	0.05–0.2	Arab, Tatar, Azeri, Moldovan
Montenegro	118,500 (2011)	n/a	19	Bosniak, Albanian

Table 1.1 (cont.)

Country	Muslims (official)	Muslims (estimated)	Muslim, % of population	Muslim ethnicity
Poland	n/a	25,000–35,000	0.07–0.09	Tatar, Arab, Chechen, Turkish
Romania	64,300	65,000	0.3	Turkish, Tatar, Romanian
Russia	n/a	16,000,000–20,000,000[b]	12–15	Tatar, Bashkir, Chechen
Serbia	223,000 (2011)	350,000	3.1–4	Bosniak, Albanian, Roma
Slovakia	1,900	4,000–5,000	0.3–0.9	Arab, Macedonian
Slovenia	47,500 (2002)	60,000	2.4–3	Bosniak, Albanian
Ukraine	n/a	200,000–400,000[c]	0.5–1.1	Tatar, Azeri, Arab
TOTAL (up to)		28,355,500		
TOTAL (up to, excl. Russia)		8,355,500		

Notes:
[a] Including over 58,600 (2.09 per cent of the total population), who identified under the category 'Bektashi', which in the census questionnaire was separate from 'Muslim'.
[b] The figure of up to 20 million represents the Muslim population of the entire Russian Federation. The European part of it is estimated to house 12–15 million Muslims.
[c] Excluding 200,000 or so Crimean Muslims, who, as of 2014, after the annexation of Crimea, live under Russian jurisdiction.
Sources: Scharbrodt 2016 and other sources. Compiled by the author.

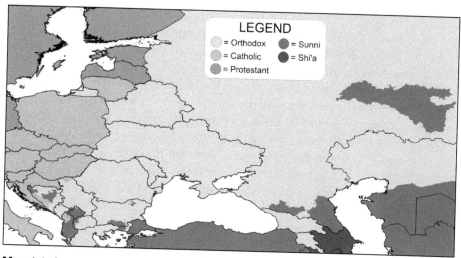

Map 1.1 Current confessional distribution in Eastern Europe
Compiled by Davide Calzoni

third of the total population; Montenegro's Muslims make up one fifth of its population, Russia's one seventh and that of Bulgaria's one twelfth. However, the remaining fourteen countries in Eastern Europe host much smaller Muslim populations, with ten below 1 per cent.

Consecutive official censuses, when measured against each other, reveal some telling dynamics in the Muslim population in the countries of Eastern Europe. While the first censuses after the fall of communist rule showed high (increased) levels of identification with Islam among ethnic groups historically regarded as Muslim, like Tatars, Bosniaks, Albanians and the like, recent censuses indicate that an increasing number of them no longer self-identify as Muslim. Though in some individual cases this may imply a change of religion from Islam to any other, in most cases this signals a move in the direction of categories such as 'non-religious', 'agnostic', 'atheist' or 'undecided'. Tentatively, this may be called the 'return of the secular' (as opposed to the 'return of the religious' in the first years after the fall of the communist system).

The censuses in some Eastern European countries likewise record a steady decrease in absolute numbers of the so-called indigenous/autochthonous 'ethnic' Muslims, this being due to migration, negative birth-death rates in the communities or changes in ethnic identity. As a side effect, migration of Eastern European Muslims to Western Europe since the fall of the Iron Curtain, and especially since the joining of the EU by many of the former communist countries in Eastern Europe, has already led to the emergence of new nascent Eastern European Muslim groups in diaspora (the old ones being those in the Middle East that date back to the Ottoman era or immediately following the empire's collapse), comprised not only of 'ethnic' Eastern European Muslims, like Albanians, Tatars or Bosniaks, but also converts to Islam from among the historically non-Muslim Eastern European ethnic groups, like Poles, Lithuanians, Slovaks and others.

The demographic distribution of Muslims in Eastern Europe, being uneven as it is, reveals some other peculiarities. In the countries with historical autochthonous Muslim populations, until very recently, most of the local Muslim populations (a notable exception being Bosnian Muslims) had been rural settlers and small-town dwellers. However, with the processes of modernisation (and particularly industrialisation and urbanisation), many rural Muslims started migrating to urban centres so that by the end of the twentieth century, the cities and in particular capitals, that previously might have had little to no Muslim presence, had become host to sizeable Muslim populations. Although the demographic balance has not necessarily yet tipped over in favour of urban communities, the observable trends of both internal migration to cities and emigration abroad from rural areas show signs not only of depopulation of rural areas but also of loss of forms of local (folk and other) Islamic practices. On the other hand, in countries with Muslim populations of predominantly immigrant and convert background, the Muslims have always lived in the urban areas. There, new and previously unheard of imported and synthetic forms of Islamic religiosity have emerged adding to the diversity of lifestyles in the respective cities. However, in both cases, the appearance of sizeable and diverse Muslim communities in the cities causes new tensions and adds new pressures as the expectations of the two sides – the Muslims, on the one hand, and the non-Muslim urbanites and municipal authorities, on the other – often diverge. These tensions are very evident in the issue of mosque-building, addressed in more detail in Chapter 7.

The indirect (implied) appearance of Eastern European converts to Islam in the census results is another development; while there were hardly any converts (in the form of those who self-identified as Muslim and as of titular or other traditionally non-Muslim ethnicity) in the first censuses, their numbers have increased remarkably, sometimes several-fold. Finally, many of the Eastern European countries over the years have had to expand ethnic/national categories in the census questionnaires to record inhabitants of immigrant background, many of whom identify as Muslim. However, very few of the Eastern European states have recorded any significant increase in immigrant population, and particularly the Muslim segment of it. Official statistics suggest that post-communist Eastern Europe is still relatively unattractive to migrants (among them refugees) from Asia or Africa. As a result, with all these factors at play, some Eastern European countries have witnessed, at least, an official decrease in the absolute number and/or percentage of Muslims in the country, with Bulgaria being probably the most notorious case, where the number of those inhabitants who

Table 1.2 Largest East European ethnic groups of Muslim background

Ethnic group	Size	Territorial distribution
Volga-Ural Tatars	more than 5,500,000	Russia, Ukraine
Albanians	up to 4,500,000	Albania, Kosovo, Macedonia, Montenegro, Serbia
Bosniaks	more than 2,000,000	Bosnia, Serbia, Montenegro, Croatia, Slovenia
Turks	close to 2,000,000	Bulgaria, Russia, Romania, Macedonia
Bashkirs	1,600,000	Russia
Chechens	1,400,000	Russia

Various sources; compiled by the author

self-identified as Muslims in a ten-year period between two censuses (2001 and 2011) dropped by a staggering more than 40 per cent!

Ethnicity-wise, Turkic-speaking Tatars of the Volga-Urals, amounting to 5.5 million, make up the biggest ethno-linguistic group of Eastern Europeans of Muslim cultural background, followed by Albanian-speaking Muslims with around 4.5 million. Turks and Slavic-speaking Bosniaks are the next largest ethnic groups with around 2 million each. Chechens and Turkic-speaking Bashkirs each number around 1.5 million (see Table 1.2). Together, members of these six ethnic groups alone in Eastern Europe number 17 million souls – some 60 per cent of all the region's people of Muslim cultural background.

Among Muslims of immigrant background, Azeris (or, as they are routinely called in the post-Soviet era, 'Azerbaijanis') are claimed by some researchers (Malashenko 2009: 321) to be the biggest ethnic group – amounting to or possibly even surpassing a full million people, chiefly in Russia. The official statistics for 2010 show that there were over 600,000 Azerbaijanis legally residing in Russia at that time. The numbers of immigrants from Central Asia – particularly Uzbeks, Kazakhs and Tajiks – run into hundreds of thousands, mostly also in Russia. Arabs and Turks are the other two largest ethno-linguistic groups of immigrant background, each also numbering several hundreds of thousands. The numbers of immigrants of Muslim background from South and South-East Asia as well as Africa in Eastern Europe have been and remain miniscule.

Additionally, the number of converts and their progeny, though not forming a single ethno-linguistic group, probably runs into tens of thousands and is another category of Muslims in Eastern Europe. Since many of the converts have their own children who very likely are identified by their mothers as being at least partially of their Eastern European ethnicity and are conceivably nationals of the country of their Eastern European parent, the 'actual' number of Muslim citizens may be even higher. Unfortunately, converts and their progeny, as well as those of mixed parentage (when a non-Muslim mother is married to a Muslim father), as a rule fall through the statistical net. They are hardly ever accounted for in the results of national censuses, even if questions on religious belonging are asked, but especially in the countries where the census does not include such a question and the numbers of Muslims are extrapolated based on ethnicity. The numbers of converts in some Eastern European countries – particularly in the Balkans – remain very modest, to say the least, and their role is rather limited, albeit ever growing. For more about the place and role of European converts to Islam, see Chapter 7.

Ethnicity and its relation to religious identity appears to be a contested issue in parts of Eastern Europe. As argued by Bougarel,

> national identities have undergone various changes over time and important regional differences exist: for example, the links between Albanian national identity and Muslim religious identity are particularly strong in Kosovo and Macedonia, where Islam serves as an 'ethnic marker' against Orthodox Serbs and Macedonians and facilitates the 'Albanisation' of smaller Muslim populations. (Bougarel 2005: 8–9)

The most telling case, however, is of course that of Bosniaks, who until the beginning of the 1990s were mainly identified as Serbo-Croatian-speaking ethnic Muslims. With the birth of the independent state of Bosnia and Herzegovina, a new ethnicity, Bosniaks, speaking a distinct language, Bosnian, was born, with '[t]he national identity of the Muslims/Bosniaks of Bosnia Herzegovina and the Sandjak . . . develop[ing] on the basis of their religious identity, and despite the fact that they spoke the same language as Orthodox Serbs and Catholic Croats' (Bougarel 2005: 8).

If the ethnonym 'Bosniak' does not raise discussions any more, others are still shrouded with deliberations. For instance, are Pomak, Torbeshi and Gorani ethnonyms to be treated as identifying distinct ethnic groups or merely as synonyms used in different countries referring to one and the same group of people? Or maybe there are neither Pomaks nor Torbeshis but simply Bulgarian-speaking Muslims and Macedonian-speaking Muslims respectively? But then, also, many among those called Pomaks and Torbeshis by outsiders identify themselves as Turks (though they do not speak Turkish) and are often identified as such by majority non-Muslim populations, who often use the generic term 'Turk' for 'Muslim' and even anything related to Ottoman heritage.

Finally, even if the numbers of nominal Muslims were known, what do they tell us about the actual religiosity of the people identified (or even self-identifying) as Muslims? The census figures, if at all reliable, provide at best the picture of nominal self-ascriptions and divisions, like 'Sunni', 'Shi'i', 'Bektashi', 'Alevi' and the like, but do not allow us to speculate on the distribution of Muslims on the scale of religiosity between the two extremes of 'nominal/cultural' (that is, hardly, if at all, practising) and 'canonical' (that is, practising on a daily basis; however, here one immediately would encounter the problem of the content of Islam practised). So, apart from the numbers, the content and intensity of Islam practised are other major aspects to be taken into account when talking about Muslim 'communities' in Eastern Europe (as, in practice, anywhere else).

Practices

In most world religions, and certainly so in the monotheistic among them, the sacred texts are of paramount importance. For Muslims, it is foremost the Quran, the reading of which (particularly, in its original Arabic, even without comprehending the contents) has been held of high importance among Muslims worldwide. Until the coming of the popular press, the Quran, like other texts, circulated in the local Muslim communities in Eastern Europe in manuscript form. Translations of the Quran into local languages – either Turkic, Slavic or Albanian – were late in coming. Though the local *ulama* (or at least the most learned among them) must have understood Arabic to some degree (areas with larger concentrations of Muslims had a tradition of religious education in establishments of higher education like madrasas), the majority of even the most devout local members of the communities had no knowledge of Arabic and thus could at best read the text without comprehending the meanings of its verses. Therefore, for centuries, alongside the Quran there have been supplementary texts in local languages, albeit sometimes written in Arabic script – commentaries on the Quranic text (*tafsir*, locally spelt as *tefsir*), prayer books (*hamail*) and the like, all in manuscript form. These supplementary texts reveal the wealth of religious beliefs and practices, sometimes going well beyond the Islamic beliefs and norms held by the custodians of what, in scholarly parlance, has been labelled 'high' or legalist/normativist Islam.

Generally speaking, the commonwealth of the world's Muslims may be tentatively divided into five broad categories, three of which – legalists/ normativists, mystics and folk practitioners – are classical dimensions of Islam, and the remaining two – modernists and revivalists – relatively recent appearances. It goes without saying that these are ideal types and individuals, as a rule, would hold views within a number of these categories, sometimes even those that appear to be contradictory; a person might be conservative on certain issues yet rather liberal on others.

The legalists/normativists, as adherents of legalist/normative Islam,[1] are those who subscribe to and seek to abide by Islamic jurisprudence, which itself is based on and closely follows the Quranic injunctions and verbal heritage of Muhammad found in Hadith/Akhbar collections. Normativists, guided by *ulama* and the foremost *fuqaha* among them, are the true adherents of the legal traditions, the schools of thought known as *madhahib* (like the classical four Sunni, three Shi'i and an Ibadi, which started forming very soon after Muhammad's death in 632 and took definite shape around the ninth–tenth centuries). Though the legal schools of thought differ in both theoretical and practical matters (that is, in the matters of positive law, *furu' al-fiqh*), they all agree on the fundamentals of the law (*usul al-fiqh*). The *raison d'être* of normative Islam is its claim to pave the way to salvation through strict submission (*islam*) to God's will – not only through meticulous performance of rituals but also ethical requirements. The overwhelming majority of historical Eastern European Muslim communities have been nominally Sunni Hanafi – the tradition preferred by Ottomans and followed by practically all Turkic-speaking Muslims – though in the Caucasus, fairly sizeable communities have been Sunni Shafii. Russia has also had its Shi'is of the Jaafari legal tradition, mainly on its southern borders with Persia/Iran, where this has been the official legal tradition since the sixteenth century.

In today's post-communist states in Eastern Europe, normative Islam has not only been institutionalised but also prioritised in the public discourse. However, as argued by Elbasani, in reality,

> [r]ituals and living practices often function as a means of de-authorising hegem-
> onic 'national' perspectives that privilege selected memories and collective
> identities. Believers, moreover, encounter different sources of identification, and
> actively select and weigh the value of each according to the surrounding circum-
> stances and personal experiences. Mixed 'identities' are frequent, particularly in
> peripheral settings where ecclesiastical organizations and state institutions are
> less powerful in terms of how they reach and determine believers' preferences.
> Hence, the more one moves out of and away from centrally controlled religious
> machinery, the more one observes Muslim 'anomalies' – ethno-religious fusion,
> heterodox practices, cultural diffusion and plural forms of belonging and believ-
> ing. (Elbasani 2015: 5)

Therefore, one is always to be cautious in regarding legalist/normative Islam as the sole representative of the forms of Muslim religiosity, both in history and today.

For instance, Islamic mysticism, *tasawwuf* – in the West known as Sufism[2] – has been a very pronounced dimension of non-legalist Islam among Eastern European Muslims of practically all ethnic backgrounds, with a number of brotherhoods holding sway in some regions of Eastern Europe. Though it would be incorrect to claim that Sufis disregard the Quranic injunctions and Muhammad's heritage, their perception of some of the injunctions is certainly at variance with that of legalists. In Islamic mysticism, formal adherence to duties and conduct is often substituted with practices permeated by a rather different feeling from that prevailing in legalist Islam, with God-fearing (*taqwa*) giving way to love and longing (*'ishq*). And while in normative Islam, God the Creator and humanity the creation may never unite in one, the *raison d'être* of mystical Islam is to facilitate the moving closer or even uniting of the two through particular meditative practices, generically called *dhikr* (remembrance, recollection). Mystical Islam emerged several hundred years after Muhammad's death, though still in ephemeral forms of individualist meditations, and by the thirteenth century had developed into a set of parallel networks of distinct brotherhoods. With the arrival of the Ottomans in the Balkans, brotherhoods (*tariqas*) such as the Helvetiyya, Qadiriyya, Tijaniyya, Bektashiyya (see Box 1.1) and several others soon became widespread and in fact were instrumental in luring locals into conversion to (often mystical forms of) Islam. Likewise, Sufism, and particularly the Naqshbandiyya and Qadiriyya brotherhoods, played a prominent role in the conversion to Islam of some Caucasian groups.

Box 1.1 Bektashism

The origins of Bektashism go back to the mystical dimension of Islam – Sufism. The Bektashi brotherhood (Bektashiyya *tariqa*) takes its name from the thirteenth-century mystic Haji Bektash Veli but it was formed in the fifteenth–sixteenth centuries. Bektashis today are mainly found throughout Anatolia and the Southern Balkans. Apart from Turkey, the brotherhood has been particularly strong in Albania and adjacent lands and prevailed chiefly among Albanians. In 1826, banned by Ottoman authorities, it nonetheless survived into modern times and, with the banning of all Sufi brotherhoods in the Turkish Republic, in 1925 it moved its headquarters to Albania, where since 1945 Bektashis have been officially recognised as a distinct religious community separate from Muslims, with their own religious doctrine, dogmas, liturgy and spiritual authority and hierarchy.

Bektashism is generally seen as a form of heterodox Islam (an 'Islamic sect'), comprising not only a Sufi nature with features of Shi'ism but also folk Islam with elements from other religions, thus making it very syncretic. Bektashism has a particularly venerable attitude toward Ali and members of his family to the point where Ali is seen almost like a God-figure. Due to its syncretic doctrine, tolerance and even inclusion of beliefs and practices of other faiths, Bektashism was particularly attractive to the indigenous inhabitants of the Balkans and facilitated conversion of part of them to Bektashi Islam.

Finally, historically many Muslims in Eastern Europe, as elsewhere, adopted religious practices and rituals that not only had little to do with normative Islam but were also distinct from the more universal practices of Sufis. This category of practices came to be referred to in the scholarly parlance as 'folk' (some – Gellner 1992 – would say 'low' as opposed to the 'high' Islam of legalists).[3] Forms of folk Islam are even more diverse than those of mystical Islam as they are representative of truly local cultural milieus – they reflect the habitual life of local Muslims, which might contain elements that would be seen from the perspective of normative Islam as non-Islamic or even anti-Islamic, like engaging in sorcery and divinations. Being open to outside influences, folk Islam is in essence susceptible to syncretism and one thus might find quazi- or crypto-Christian practices among practitioners of folk Islam in Eastern Europe. Furthermore, folk Islam is permeated by superstitious beliefs and related practices where the supernatural in the form of jinns, devils and evil spirits play a prominent role.

Adherents of folk Islam and normative Islam would find themselves at the extreme ends of the spectrum of classical forms of Islamic religiosity and therefore very often at odds with each other, with Sufis falling in-between. However, evidence abounds in Eastern Europe of situations where followers of two or all three categories not only lived in peace with each other but could in fact be found in one and the same congregation – and not only ordinary members but also the leadership. Thus, one should be careful about viewing these classical dimensions of Islam as opposing each other.

Since the end of the nineteenth century, these three classical dimensions of Islam have been supplemented with the appearance in the midst of Muslim societies (particularly in the Middle East and South Asia) of novel ways of being a Muslim. One of them has a direct relation to the general modernising trends, which among other things relegate religion to the private sphere, thus while modernising societies at the same time secularising them. Though there had always been individual agnostics or even atheists among Muslims, their ranks increasingly swelled, particularly with the aftermath of the Second World War, when, in addition to the organic processes of modernisation, local authorities increasingly directed their rhetoric and policies against religion. As Eastern European countries came under communist rule, atheism became the official stance of the states and was to be instilled into local societies, citizens of Muslim background included.

However, even before the advent of communism in Eastern Europe, and certainly with its demise, another novel dimension to Islam started creeping into local Muslim communities. The generic term for this new direction is 'Islamic revivalism' or 'revivalist Islam', which is comprised of a number of sub-divisions – (neo)fundamentalism, Islamism and jihadism, to which post-Islamism and neo-traditionalism are sometimes added. In general, Islamic revivalism is seen by researchers (Demant 2006) as a reaction to both the modernisation of Muslim societies and polities in the nineteenth century and the older processes of what revivalists themselves deem to be spiritual and social deviations from 'true', original, pristine Islam. The declared aim of Muslim revivalists is bringing about (or back) a holistic Islamic system that would govern both the public and private life of citizens. The ways to attain this, however, differ significantly among revivalists belonging to the different categories.

There have always been fundamentalism-inclined Muslim groups in Islam's one and a half millennium history, some of whom would occasionally turn violent. However, the phenomenon of (neo)fundamentalism is associated in academic circles with the person of Muhammad ibn Abd al-Wahhab (1702/3–1791/2) and the movement he paved the way for, popularly known as Wahhabism.[4] Initiated in Najd in the Arabian Peninsula, in what today is the Kingdom of Saudi Arabia, in the course of a century it spread beyond the Peninsula's borders and acquired different shapes and disguises. By the end of the twentieth century, (neo)fundamentalism had become epitomised by the Salafi movement (see Box 1.2),[5] which had gained followers from all over Europe, including Eastern Europe. The chosen instrument for seeking the return of Muslims to the perceived authentic Islamic state (understood here as spiritual and social rather than political) for fundamentalists has been outreach (dawa, tabligh) and education (tarbiyya), that is, a 'bottom up' approach.

Islamism,[6] though also a reaction to the socio-political processes that had been taking place in Muslim-majority lands since the nineteenth century, is in its nature political – it was born out of frustrations with the (neo)fundamentalist approach which was seen by some revivalists not to be bringing the desired results. Such revivalists turned political – they started believing that re-Islamisation of Muslim societies and communities could only be brought about through a change of the political system and elite. Only if (or when) the Islamically minded individuals and groups started ruling Muslim lands and introduced laws complying with the Islamic injunctions (hence, 'the return of Shari'a') was a true revival of Islam all the way down to individual citizens possible. Thus, the Islamist approach may be called 'top-down'. Generally, Islamists can be divided into moderates – those who operate within legal boundaries, thus peacefully – and radicals – those who, either by choice or because of being pushed into it, resort to armed struggle, often termed 'jihad'. Radical Islamist groups among indigenous local Muslim populations in Eastern Europe have been few (the North Caucasus, particularly in the late 1990s and the early 2000s being a notable exception) but there certainly are pockets of moderate Islamists, clustering around such movements and organisations as Hizb at-Tahrir[7] and Muslim Brotherhood[8]-related or inspired local groupings.

A relatively new offspring of Islamic revivalism and certainly its most radical version is jihadism, which is invariably violent. The first blossoms of jihadism in

Box 1.2 Salafism

The term Salafism (Salafiyya) takes its root from the classical Islamic notion of *as-salaf as-salih* – 'the righteous predecessors'/'pious forefathers', the first three generations of Muslims as the most authentic followers of the Prophet Muhammad's message. Though known and used for a millennium, the term *as-salaf as-salih* gained new currency at the end of the nineteenth century, when reform-minded Muslim intellectuals in the Middle East called on their co-religionists to turn to *as-salaf as-salih* as the role models to be closely emulated in Muslims' daily life.

Since then, the ideas and movements based on this basic preconception of *as-salaf as-salih* as the 'ideal' Muslims have proliferated to encompass at times seemingly contradictory or even mutually exclusive visions of how Muslim societies and communities were to re-Islamise themselves and maintain their Islamicity. However, though the ways and techniques to attain the desired result may vary among different groups of Salafis, the underlining idea of purifying the Islamic way of life of all perceived anti-Islamic accretions and innovations has remained the same, uniting Salafis the world over. Thus, in its nature, Salafism is universalist, as it is essentially anti-cultural – that is, against not only any forms of folk Islam but also Sufism, and even critical of the classical legal traditions.

By the end of the twentieth century, Salafism in effect had become a wide-ranging stream of revivalist Islam, comprised of at least three broad categories of Salafis: those who are primarily concerned with personal and communal piety (and as a rule shun politics), those who actively engage in politics and those who use violence to advance their vision. Today, Salafis of one or more types may be found in practically all Muslim communities, including those in Eastern Europe. The overwhelming majority of Eastern European Salafis are of a pietistic nature though the other two types are also present.

Eastern Europe appeared in the Bosnian war in the mid-1990s and more forcefully in Chechnya later the same decade where the local indigenous Muslim communities were engaged in the (independence) fight against what was seen by them as imperial powers – the Yugoslavian and the Russian Federations, respectively. Some of the brothers-in-faith from abroad, who became brothers-in-arms of the local fighting Muslims, had radical inclinations and, with the global advent of jihadism epitomised in al-Qaida, gravitated towards it, drawing some of the locals with them (Li 2014). In the first decade of the twenty-first century, some of the most radicalised Eastern European Muslims would find themselves on the battlefields of the Middle East (Iraq) and Central and South Asia (Afghanistan, Pakistan), and most recently in Syria – it is estimated (The Soufan Group 2015) that no less than 3,600 (and possibly as many as 5,000) Eastern Europeans (arguably, Muslims), with 2,400 from Russia alone, had travelled in the course of five years (2011–15) to Syria to join a plethora of armed groups there. For more on the Eastern European Muslim *muhajirun* to the Middle East, see Chapter 7.

Finally, like elsewhere in the world, there are Muslim individuals and groups in Eastern Europe whose beliefs and practices set them apart from the above-described categories of revivalists and the rest of the co-believers. Examples are the so-called post-Islamists and neo-traditionalists, who, though sharing some features with Islamists and (neo)fundamentalists, are nonetheless quite distinct from them.

To sum up, one needs to realise and acknowledge that the spectrum of forms of Islamic religiosity among Eastern European Muslims (see Table 1.3) is no narrower than the one found in Muslim-majority lands, though the distribution of the groups of different categories may, and in fact does, differ from that found elsewhere in the world, not least because of broader, at times even forced, secularisation processes in Eastern Europe. Though ethnographic or other evidence is hard to come by, based on recent research by the Pew Research Center (Pew 2012), it might be tentatively suggested that the percentage of agnostics and even atheists among Eastern Europeans of Muslim background is relatively high compared to Middle Easterners or Muslim communities elsewhere in Asia or Africa.

The spectrum of religious practices, or forms of religiosity, reveals not only diversity within the Muslim communities in Eastern Europe but very often puts into question the very notion of those 'communities' as unified national entities. As will be shown in subsequent chapters in this book, too often adherents of different strains of Islam, and particularly their leadership, do not recognise each other as 'good enough' Muslims and there is as much, if not more, antagonism as mutual support and cooperation between different Muslim congregations in practically all Eastern European countries. In most cases, the responsibility for intra-communal (as well as extra-communal) relations falls on the shoulders of the respective groups' leadership, that is, their formal and informal institutions.

Institutions and authorities

All the groups on the identified spectrum of Islamic beliefs and practices (see Table 1.3) have their authorities, if not formal institutions. As a rule, they would be housed in premises, which, apart from other spaces, would include those for communal prayer. In popular parlance such spaces are referred to as 'mosques', though in Arabic they could fall into one of at least three categories – *jami'*, *masjid* or *musalla*. The first one implies not only a purpose-built structure with a minaret but also that it serves as Friday mosque where communal Friday prayer complete with a sermon is held; *musalla* is understood as an adapted space in a nondescript building with no minaret. *Masjid*, then, falls in between the two extremes – it may be a small purpose-built mosque, an adapted building or

Table 1.3 Spectrum of forms of Islamic religiosity in Eastern Europe

Classical			Revivalist			
Legalism	Mysticism	Folk Islam	(Neo) Fundamentalism	Islamism	Post-Islamism and neo-traditionalism	Jihadism
Hanafism Shafiism	Naqshabndiyya Qadiriyya Bektashiyya Mawlawiyya Shadhiliyya	Different local practices	Salafism Tablighi Jamaat	Muslim Brotherhood Hizb at-Tahrir	Individuals, various informal groups and NGOs	Al-Qaida Islamic State

Compiled by the author.

its part, with or without a minaret. As argued by Aid Smajić and Muhamed Fazlović, '[in] the Bosnian context, a mosque (*džamija*) is usually expected to have a minaret and a full-time imam. A *masjid* (*mesdžid*) is a smaller place for prayer, usually with part-time service and in most cases without a minaret' (Smajić and Fazlović 2015: 126). Though in South-eastern Europe, and particularly in the Balkans, most of mosques are of *jamiʿ* and *masjid* type, in central and north-eastern parts of Europe many prayer spaces are in fact just *musallas*. Generally, the latter are run and attended by Muslims of immigrant and convert background, while *jamiʿs* and *masjids* are in the hands of historical autochthonous Muslim communities. Consequently, the more the Muslim populations in Eastern European countries are made up of Muslims of immigrant and convert background the higher the percentage of *musallas*.

The financial independence and sustainability of the Islamic infrastructure, particularly mosques, has traditionally depended on *waqf* – pious foundations financing building, upkeep and even daily costs of the Islamic religious infrastructure. The *waqf* system was transplanted to Eastern Europe and functioned more or less intact into the communist period when most *waqf* properties were seized and nationalised by the states. Since the collapse of the communist system in Eastern Europe, in some countries *waqf* property has been returned to Muslim communities and the system has reconstituted itself, but in most cases financing of Islamic infrastructure and activities today comes from membership fees, *sadaqa al-fitr* (voluntary alms-giving) and donations by foreign donors, with the state's financial support to Muslim communities directly depending on the regime of governance of religion and the legal status of Islam in the respective country.

Table 1.4 is an attempt at mapping the distribution of Islamic prayer facilities in Eastern Europe. As seen from the table, Russia has not only the largest number of Islamic prayer facilities but also around a half of all estimated Islamic prayer facilities in Eastern Europe. Table 1.4 also reveals that half a dozen Eastern European countries (still) do not have *jamiʿ*-type mosques – purpose-built premises with typical architectural features, including a minaret and possibly a dome. On the other hand, all Eastern European capitals host at least one 'Islamic centre', most of which are of *masjid*-type – either purpose-built or converted buildings, some of them even with small minarets – and unknown numbers of *musallas*, most of which, however, remain unaccounted for as they are neither registered nor visible from the outside. Therefore, the estimates provided in Table 1.4, and particularly in the *musalla* column, are to be treated with caution – there may in reality be many more *musallas* and even *masjids* thus making the overall figure for prayer facilities in Eastern Europe higher than that provided in Table 1.4. One also needs to realise that *musallas* and *masjids* may spring up as quickly as they close down, for economic, security or other reasons, and their legal status in different countries of the region varies greatly.

Table 1.4 Mosques and other prayer facilities in Eastern Europe, estimates

Country	Purpose-built mosques (*jamiʿ*)	Converted mosques (*masjid*)	Prayer halls (*musalla*)	Total, at least
Albania	660	not known	not known	**700**
Belarus	9	3	not known	**12**
Bosnia and Herzegovina	1,700	740	not known	**2,440**
Bulgaria	1,500	240	not known	**1,740**
Croatia	3	15	10	**28**
Czech Republic	0	2	10	**12**
Estonia	0	1	3	**4**
Hungary	0	3	7	**10**
Kosovo	660	140	not known	**800**
Latvia	0	0	4	**4**
Lithuania	4	1	3	**8**
Macedonia, FYR of	600	not known	not known	**800**
Moldova	0	2	2	**4**
Montenegro	136	4	not known	**140**
Poland	3	7	2	**12**
Romania	78	not known	17	**95**
Russia	7,200	not known	not known	**7,200[a]**
Serbia	195	not known	2	**197**
Slovakia	0	1	7	**8**
Slovenia	0	1	not known	**10**
Ukraine	4	15	not known	**132[b]**

Table 1.4 (cont.)				
Country	Purpose-built mosques (*jami'*)	Converted mosques (*masjid*)	Prayer halls (*musalla*)	Total, at least
TOTAL				14,364
TOTAL, excl. Russia				7,164

Notes:
[a] The figure includes prayer facilities in the entire territory of the Russian Federation. As the overwhelming majority of Russia's Muslims live on the European side, the bulk of Islamic prayer facilities may be expected to also be located there; however, there are no available detailed figures.
[b] Excluding some 300 mosques in the territory of Crimea, which, as of 2014, after its annexation, is under Russian jurisdiction.

Sources: Scharbrodt 2016 and other sources; compiled by the author.

Arguably, the number of mosques may indicate the numbers and religiosity of local Muslims, though assuming a direct link may be questionable, especially when many of the *musallas* are not accounted for as they are not registered as mosques. And, to the contrary, registered *jami's* and *masjids* may not always be full, even on Fridays. Therefore, the visual landscape – the visibility (and statistical number) or not of mosques – may sometimes be misleading when trying to assess local Muslims' current level of religiosity. In any case, Eastern Europe is the part of the Old Continent that has not only some of the oldest mosque buildings in Europe but also the longest-functioning – some have been serving believers since the fifteenth century.

Mosques would traditionally be the bastions of normative Islam; together with the adjacent madrasas they would uphold the traditions of the legal schools of thought, the *madhahib*. In the Balkans, until the formation of nation states, legalist Islam was closely tied to institutions in the Ottoman state with the religious establishment in the persons of judges and jurist consuls (muftis) being appointed/sent by the supreme Islamic authorities in Constantinople. With the rise of sovereign states, the local communities were entrusted to newly founded administrative bodies – the *riyaset* and *meshihat*.

In the Russian realm, mosques would be under the control of lay non-Muslim authorities – the Russian imperial government – which would exercise its control through government-established 'spiritual boards', also known as muftiates. Post-communist Russia has inherited this tradition of muftiates, though now formally independent of the state authorities, and in several other post-Soviet states (Lithuania, Belarus) muftiates have also been established and recognised by the state as the representative institutions of the country's Muslims.

In the rest of the Eastern European countries, there are Muslim religio-administrative institutions which aspire to be recognised by the state as representatives of both the country's Muslims and 'correct and true' Islam. In many cases, they have rival organisations they have to fend off. In some of the countries (like Moldova, Latvia, Hungary and Slovakia), these organisations had to first fight the very state apparatus to be legally registered.

Next to mosques, institutions of religious education are the most important places of preservation and perpetuation of legalist Islam, although in some cases non-legalist (non-Orthodox) forms of Islamic religiosity are included. Institutions of higher religious education in Eastern Europe (see Table 1.5) first of all include Faculties of Shari'a/Islamic Studies, some of which function as independent institutions akin to specialised colleges, while others serve in the capacity of university departments. There are also 'Islamic universities', which next to strictly religious programmes/courses include lay subjects in their curricula. Religious secondary education is provided in high school-type madrasas, while on the primary level it is *kutab*, which often serve as 'weekend schools'. As many mosques (including *musallas*) have such 'weekend schools', their number in countries with significant numbers of mosques may run into dozens or even hundreds (and in the case of Bosnia and Hezegovina approaches 2,000). Furthermore, Muslim pupils in a number of Eastern European countries are (or may be) provided with religious instruction in the state schooling system provided the state recognises Islam as one of the traditional faiths and religious education is foreseen in state school curricula.

However, direct control of institutions such as formal muftiates, and through them the mosques, at no time in history meant that the governments or the formal Muslim institutions themselves had the tools to control the entire masses of their Muslim subjects. Alternative and parallel spiritual leadership developed outside the mosque-centred institutions, chiefly in *tekkes/zawiyas*, *khanaqas* and mausoleums of numerous Sufi brotherhoods, supervised by local shaykhs. Though less institutionalised, mystical Islam should not be seen as less formalised – the brotherhoods as a rule functioned as highly structured and internally well-controlled corporate bodies with clear hierarchies with ensuing duties. Most Sufi brotherhoods operating in Eastern Europe, being mainly of transnational nature, maintained close links to spiritual centres in the Middle East, where the top authorities usually resided. Nonetheless, the living shaykh of the brotherhood's local chapter would be the immediate supreme authority for the adepts. The local non-initiated, who would take part in the weekly *dhikr* rituals, would form the outer circle of the shaykh's influence – some of the lay would revere him as a living saint. In the post-socialist era, in some countries in Eastern Europe, and particularly the Balkans (Bosnia and Herzegovina,

Table 1.5 Institutions of Islamic religious education in Eastern Europe

Country	Estimated number of Muslims	Faculty of Islamic Sciences/Shariʿa, Islamic University	Madrasa/ high school
Albania	1,650,000–2,300,000	1	7
Belarus	20,000	0	0
Bosnia and Herzegovina	1,790,000	3	6
Bulgaria	577,000–600,000	1	3
Croatia	63,000	0	1
Czech Republic	3,400–20,000	0	0
Estonia	1,500–2,000	0	0
Hungary	5,600–32,000	0	0
Kosovo	1,750,000	1	1
Latvia	5,000–6,000	0	0
Lithuania	2,700–4,000	0	0
Macedonia, FYR of	660,500–730,000	1	1
Moldova	1,700–5,000	0	0
Montenegro	118,500	0	1
Poland	25,000–35,000	0	0
Romania	64,300–65,000	0	1
Russia[a]	16,000,000–20,000,000	4	4
Serbia	223,000–350,000	2	3
Slovakia	4,000–5,000	0	0
Slovenia	47,500–50,000	0	0
Ukraine	200,000–400,000	1	3

Note:
[a] Russia has a number of institutions of both higher and secondary religious education, which are not officially recognised/registered by the state. Therefore, the total number of such institutions will be much higher than the one provided here.
Source: Scharbrodt 2016; compiled by the author.

Macedonia), the mystical dimension of Islam is part of the official Muslim religious institution, though in others Sufi brotherhoods continue (or rather resumed) to function independently of official (read, treated by the state as or aspiring to the status of 'representative') Muslim organisations.

Folk Islam, being by its nature local, usually had local informal authorities, the most prominent of whom would be healers and soothsayers. Unlike the male-dominated institutions and authorities of normative and mystical Islam, folk Islam did not shy away from spiritual, albeit informal, female leadership (Bringa 1996: 213–216). These informal leaders of practices of folk Islam survived the communist period with its aggressive atheist policies but in the face of seminal demographic changes – the movement of villagers, the historical custodians of folk Islam practices, to urban areas; increased educational level in villages; overall secularisation trends; but also a growing revivalist backlash to their practices – have been left with an ever shrinking following and pushed on the defensive.

The presence of diverse forms of Islamic religiosity headed and defended by their own institutions and authorities had repercussions not only for intra-communal development; it spilled over into relations between the respective groups of Muslims and the states-that-be, particularly their governments but also other actors, like Christian churches, and the wider public. In connection with longevity of the respective Muslim community in the territory of a concerned country but also due to other, particularly political, considerations, the legal status of Muslim communities (and their institutions) in the Eastern European states varies greatly – from recognised traditional confessional, ethno-confessional or ethnic communities through disregarded to unrecognised or even outlawed. For instance, the historical absence of Shi'is in most parts of Eastern Europe has created conditions for unintended legal discrimination of followers of this branch of Islam who are often seen by the Eastern European states as 'non-traditional' Muslims and therefore are not accorded the same rights as 'traditional' (aka Sunni) Muslims. A case in point is Lithuania, where Sunni Muslims are recognised by law as one of the nine traditional faith communities while Shi'is are legally treated on a par with New Age religious movements.

CHAPTER 2

Historical overview

There is historical evidence suggesting that the first Muslims, in the person of Arabs conquering lands for the then rapidly expanding Caliphate, set foot on what today is the south-easternmost corner of Eastern Europe, namely, Daghestan in the Russian Federation, as early as the mid-seventh century (Akhmetova 2010: 436). A sequence of invasions (the ancient chronicle of Derbend conveys the story of a 24,000-strong Arab Muslim army sweeping into Daghestan in 733) and the subsequent occupation of Daghestan by Arabs from the Middle East led to gradual Islamisation of the area with numerous mosques being built from the eighth century onwards (Shikhsaidov 2009). There is also evidence of Muslim settlements in eastern Ukraine (around Donetsk and Lugansk) dating back to the ninth–tenth centuries (Brylov 2016: 194–6).

In the Volga-Urals region, on the eastern edge of the European part of today's Russia, Islam also started spreading as early as the eighth century and in the state of Volga Bulgars (roughly coinciding with the territory of contemporary Tatarstan), as an outcome of intensive trade and other relations with the Muslim lands to the south, it became the official religion in 922 (Arapov 2001: 16; Yemelianova 2002: 7–8). This Muslim state survived until its conquering by invading Mongols in 1236. Yemelianova (2002: 8), based on earlier Russian researchers, even argues that '[b]y the end of the tenth century, Volga Bulgaria and its capital Biliar, in particular, had become one of the renowned centres of Islamic learning and scholarship. It had a wide Islamic educational network represented by mektebs and medresses.' In this way, Islam became a common religion of indigenous inhabitants of some of the areas on the fringes of Eastern Europe well before those areas were reached by Christianity.

Likewise, a Muslim presence on the north-eastern coast of the Mediterranean, namely, on the shores of the contemporary Albanian, Montenegrin and Croatian states, is also recorded as early as the ninth century: '[i]n the 9th century, the Arabians were aiming at, in addition to conquering Southern Italy, occupying Dalmatian seaside cities: they were trying hard for 15 years to conquer the town known today as Dubrovnik, but they did not succeed' (Császár 2010: 64).

Finally, Muslims are reported to have started immigrating to the Central European lands in the ninth century, first with migrating Hungarian tribes. The migration waves continued until the twelfth century resulting in the formation of a sizeable Muslim community in the territory of today's Hungary. The presence a of Muslim (referred to as Ismaelite) community in Hungarian lands in the Middle Ages is well attested to by historical sources (Berend 2001, 2014; Stojkovski 2010; Štulrajterova 2013). Romanian territory is also reported to have received its first Muslims in the thirteenth century (Kozák 2009: 11). It is also reported that

> part of the Muslims living in the south-eastern part of the Hungarian Kingdom migrated to the Balkan peninsula to settle down as early as in the 13th century. Other regions, too, were sources of Muslims arriving in the Balkan, such as the Al-Aga dynasty moving in from Syria and building the first mosque in Kosovo. The Muslims in Vardar-valley, called 'Turks' arrived in the Balkan from Asia Minor. (Császár 2010: 64)

Though for several hundred years Muslims in this part of Europe appear to have been able to lead a fairly comfortable life with little to no restrictions on their practice of Islam, by the mid-thirteenth century, their situation had deteriorated dramatically. A number of restrictive and discriminating measures were introduced by consecutive rulers of Hungary (arguably, under pressure from the Catholic Church), which led to the virtual disappearance of Muslims by the end of the fourteenth century from Hungarian lands, either through assimilation into the local Hungarian society or migration eastwards to the Muslim-majority Golden Horde. Nonetheless, the first large-scale encounter between the by then Christian Eastern Europeans and Muslims occurred in the fourteenth century, when the advancing conquering Mongols converted to Islam in 1312.

Mongol-Tatar invasion of Eastern Europe and its consequences

Though the advance of the Mongols westwards started as early as the twelfth century, they first reached Eastern Europe in the thirteenth century – by 1240, they had invaded Moscow and Kiev and had come to 'the borders of modern Poland, the Czech Republic, Hungary, Serbia and Bulgaria. Only Novgorod, Pskov and the adjacent territories of northern Eurasia escaped the Mongol conquest' (Yemelianova 2002: 16). With their formal conversion en masse to Islam under Khan Uzbek (1312–42), from 1312 Mongols of the Goldon Horde (*Altyn Urda*, founded in 1242 after the conquering of the Bulgar state and surrounding territories) and its successor states (after the Horde's break-up in 1437) first became sovereigns and later neighbours of Eastern Europeans for several centuries – until the expanding Russian Empire, from the sixteenth century onwards, swallowed them all one by one.

The Golden Horde becoming a Muslim state breathed new life into Islamic culture in the Volga-Urals region. A social stratum of men of religion, of both legalist Islam (in the form of different ranks of *ulama*) and its mystical dimension (in the form of Sufi shaykhs, *murids* and dervishes) re-emerged to provide the faithful, now of both Turkic and Mongolic origin, with spiritual guidance. The Golden Horde adopted the Sunni Hanafi legal tradition as its official legal system and lasted for over a century as a vast Muslim empire stretching from what is today Russia's European part in the west to Siberia in the east, before disintegrating into several successor Muslim states – hordes and khanates – in the first part of the fifteenth century, when

> [b]y the 1420s the Golden Horde had split into the Great Horde, situated upon the ruins of Saray, the eastern part, comprising the Nogay Horde and Siberian khanate, and the western part consisting of the Astrakhan, Crimean and Kazan khanates and various Rus principalities. (Yemelianova 2002: 22)

Thus, on the European side of the Urals, Crimean, Kazan and Astrakhan khanates and partially Nogay (also spelt Nogai, Noghay) Horde were the biggest state formations ruled by Muslim dynasties and inhabited by Muslim majorities (see Map 2.1).

The Nogay state (later Kalmyk khanate) was founded in the 1390s, on the territory between the Volga and Irtysh rivers with its seat of power in the town of Saraychik situated in the delta of the Ural river. It is reported (Yemelianova

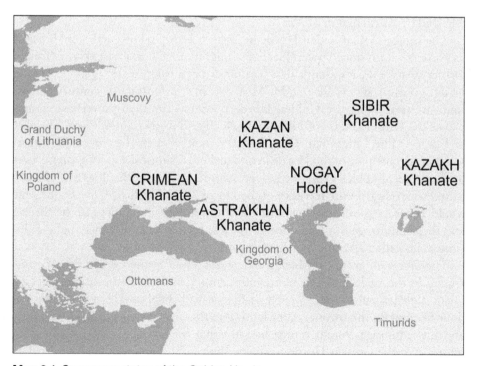

Map 2.1 Successor states of the Golden Horde
Compiled by Davide Calzoni

2002: 24) to have 'extended its political influence from the northern parts of the Kipchak steppe to Siberia and the Bashkir lands.' The Kazan khanate started life as a princedom in the very beginning of the fifteenth century and, by the 1430s, it 'had turned into a powerful state comprising half the territory of former Bulgaria' (Yemelianova 2002: 22). The Crimean khanate, based on the Crimean Peninsula and the surrounding mainland to the north-east of it, split from the Golden Horde in 1443. The Astrakhan khanate followed suit by breaking away from the Golden Horde in 1459. All these new regional players 'clashed over the right of succession to the Golden Horde and forged changing alliances against the crumbling centre and each other' (Yemelianova 2002: 24).

The animosity and competition among the co-religionists was soon to be skilfully used by Russia, another regional, but this time non-Muslim, power, which would go into pragmatic alliances with one Muslim state in order to subjugate another. As Yemelianova (2002: 24) argues, '[f]rom the very beginning, there was a rapprochement between Moscow and Crimea against both the Golden Horde and the Kazan khanate, as the religious factor was subordinated to political and pragmatic considerations.' Ultimately, from the sixteenth century onwards, all of these previously sovereign states were conquered and subsequently incorporated into the emerging regional power – the centralised Russian Empire ruled from Moscow. Kazan was the first to fall in 1552, soon followed by Astrakhan in 1556.

The legacy of the Golden Horde in Eastern Europe, however, went beyond its borders – it produced several waves of migration of Turkic-speaking Muslims further westwards, into lands that had never been ruled by the Golden Horde or its successor states, that is, by Muslims. In the fourteenth century, on its south-western flank, the Golden Horde bordered the then-powerful regional player the Grand Duchy of Lithuania, which had its own interests in that part of Europe. The Lithuanian Grand Dukes took sides in the internal political squabbles in the part of the Horde in and around Crimea by actively supporting preferred local nobles vying for power, who in times of difficulties and defeats would seek refuge in the territory of the Duchy. Usually, the refugee contingent would encompass not only the families of the fleeing contenders to the throne and their entourage but also numerous loyal fighters and servants, making the companies rather sizeable, possibly well into several hundreds.

The first such group of Muslim refugees made it to the safety of the Grand Duchy in the middle of the fourteenth century, when the then-ruling Grand Duke Algirdas (ruled 1345–77) chose to side with Jalal ad-Deen in his aspirations to come to the throne. After loosing in the armed struggle, Jalal ad-Deen and his entourage sought refuge in Lithuania. However, most of them later returned to the Golden Horde to renew their fight for power. The next ruler, Algirdas' nephew Vytautas (ruled 1392–1430), continued Algridas' practice of supporting a chosen rival in the internal fights among princes of the Golden

Horde. Furthermore, Vytautas himself led several expeditions to the Kipchak Steppes and brought home with him both captives and mercenaries, followed by their entire families – 1396 is conventionally regarded as the symbolic year of what was destined to be the permanent settlement of Muslims in what today are the territories of Lithuania, Belarus and Poland. Some of the transported Muslims (arguably, the freed captives) later returned to their homelands but the bulk stayed behind and settled permanently, being joined later (upto and into the sixteenth century) by voluntary migrants, primarily from the Crimean khanate. The Muslims mainly settled on royal estates in western parts of the Grand Duchy of Lithuania (GDL), south and south-east of the capital Vilnius. The choice of settlement points is regarded to have been deliberate on Vytautas' side – he wanted mercenary Muslim troops to always be at hand wherever he moved in the state and particularly around his residences.

From the onset of their immigration and settlement, the political, legal and social situation of Muslims in the GDL has been of peculiar character, constituting a unique phenomenon in respect to the history of Muslim–Christian relations and the presence of Islam in Europe. First of all, the very coming of Islam to the GDL sharply contrasts the arrival of Muslims at almost the same time in Southern and South-eastern Europe: while the latter came to fight and impose their rule, the former were invited and welcomed to peacefully settle in a land that was ruled by non-Muslims (in fact, the GDL was still officially pagan when the first Muslims came to stay in its territory, even if only temporarily – Lithuania only adopted Christianity in 1387). Despite or because of the fact that Muslims have only ever been a tiny minority (though precise data are not available, it can be safely assumed that at no time in history did the Muslim population of the GDL exceed 100,000 souls) of the citizenry of the GDL, they enjoyed almost all rights and freedoms that their Christian fellow citizens did. Upon settlement, Tatar elite were granted the nobility rank and given tracts of land as their personal possession. In return for privileges, Tatar nobility were required to raise their own corps for the state troops in times of military encounters in which the GDL took part. This ultimately meant that occasionally Muslims of the GDL would engage in fighting against adversary Muslims, chiefly Ottomans.

Secondly, Muslims in the GDL (and later, post 1569, the Republic of Two Nations – *Rzeczpospolita*) were never forced to abandon their faith either through coerced conversion or because of artificially created obstacles in practising their religion (such as bans, prohibitions, segregationist decrees, and so on). In the GDL/*Rzeczpospolita*, Muslims throughout the centuries were allowed to publicly observe all Islamic duties and rituals. It is believed that mosques in the territory of the then GDL were being built as early as the late fourteenth or beginning of the fifteenth century (Kričinskis 1993: 158). In the times of *Rzeczpospolita* (that is until the final partition of *Rzeczpospolita* in 1795) there might have been up to two dozen mosques (Kričinskis 1993: 161), as a rule with adjacent cemeteries.

Muslims of the *Rzeczpospolita* were organisationally independent of any foreign religious authorities though they enjoyed a degree of care from the Sublime Porte.

Russian possessions in Eastern Europe and its Muslim population

Though Russia as a state had an early beginning in the ninth and tenth centuries in the form of Slavic city-statelets, its independent development was interrupted in the thirteenth century by the onslaught of the Mongols coming from the Far East, when the eastern Slavic lands were subjected to what was known locally as the 'Mongol yoke'. Until the disintegration of the Golden Horde in the fifteenth century, much of the Slavic lands, later to become the core of the Russian Empire, were under Mongol (and from 1312, Muslim) control. In Russian historiography, this period is portrayed as one of the darkest ages in the history of Russia and Russians. Though the Slavic population was not forced by its Mongol masters to convert to Islam, and the Orthodox Church is reported to have been allowed to function virtually unhampered, dislike of Mongols (and Tatars) as Muslim overlords was ingrained in the popular Russian mind and particularly the Russian Orthodox Church stance vis-à-vis Muslims for centuries to come.

With fortunes changed – the disintegration of the Golden Horde and the re-emergence and continuous expansion of the Russian state centred on Moscow – since the middle of the fifteenth century, now independent and strong, Russia came to encounter hitherto sovereign successor Muslim states to the Golden Horde. Having been a subject of the Muslim Golden Horde, Russia itself now started becoming a suzerain of Muslims. The first such vassal Muslim entity of Russia was the Kasimov khanate on the Oka river, which after splitting from the Golden Horde in the middle of the fifteenth century (1446) threw in its lot with Moscow, this way becoming 'the first Islamic enclave within the Rus Orthodox mainland' (Yemelianova 2002: 22–3).

Towards the end of the fifteenth century, Russia managed to establish 'a Russian protectorate' over the Kazan khanate that lasted between 1487 and 1506 (Yemelianova 2002: 29). After being pushed out Russia made several other attempts, among them the unsuccessful 1545 and 1547 campaigns (Yemelianova 2002: 30), before, finally, in 1552 Kazan was conquered by Russia and the Kazan khanate ceased to exist as a sovereign state. The Astrakhan khanate fell to Russia not long after Kazan; in 1556, the same czar, Ivan IV, who several years earlier had annexed Kazan did the same to this other successor state of the Golden Horde. This had repercussions for Russia itself as '[a]fter 1552, Russia became a multi-ethnic and poly-confessional state and the Russian rulers were faced with the difficult task of redefining its state and national policy'

(Yemelianova 2002: 30). But what is most important, as Yemelianova argues, is that 'the Genghizid and Islamicized eastern influences remained a powerful factor in the Russian state and society until the westernizing reforms of Peter the Great in the early eighteenth century' (Yemelianova 2002: 35).

Having conquered the khanates of Kazan, Astrakhan and other successor states of the Golden Horde in Eurasia, the Russian expansionist gaze later turned southwards – towards Crimea and the Caucasus. The Crimean khanate was the sole surviving successor state of the Golden Horde but, by the eighteenth century, it had been reduced to the state of a vassal of the Ottoman Empire. So, technically, it was not a subject of international relations anymore and Russia's pursuit to occupy it meant going into direct conflict with the Ottoman state – which it did. In 1771, Russian troops occupied the Crimean Peninsula within the framework of the ongoing Russo-Ottoman war of 1768–74. With the Kuchuk-Kaynardji Treaty of 1774, which terminated the war between the two empires, the Ottomans formally gave up their claims to this Muslim-majority land. In 1783, Russia annexed the peninsula despite protests from the Ottomans who eventually, in 1792, 'recognized Russia's suzerainty over Crimea, Kuban and the territories between the rivers Bug and Dniester' (Yemelianova 2002: 41).

At around the same time, Russia also turned westwards and, after having occupied what today are Finland, Estonia and Latvia in the mid-eighteenth century, in the last quarter of the eighteenth century it divided the spoils of the collapsed Polish–Lithuanian Commonwealth (*Rzeczpospolita*) annexing in 1795 the entire territories of today's Lithuania and Belarus and major parts of Poland and Ukraine. With the final partition of the *Rzeczpospolita*, most Muslims of the defunct state found themselves subjects of the Russian Empire. Moreover, in the nineteenth century, the newly incorporated north-western provinces witnessed the arrival and settlement of Muslims from Central Russia. The previously virtually Muslim-free Latvia, Estonia and Finland received their first Muslim settlers in the second part of that century (especially after abolition of serfdom in 1863); Muslims (mainly Tatars) decommissioned from the Russian czarist army and tradesmen started arriving and settling in the north-westernmost corner of the Russian Empire (mainly in the Baltic port cities, especially in the territory of present-day Latvia, though Estonia and Finland received their share also). In Warsaw, a Muslim military cemetery was opened in the second part of the nineteenth century.

Finally, emboldened by Russia's success in Crimea and on other fronts, Empress Catherine the Great in the 1780s 'launched a full-scale military campaign aimed at the annexation of the North Caucasus' (Yemelianova 2002: 48). As pointed out above, Islam arrived in the North Caucasus within decades of its inception, but the process of Islamisation of the region, particularly its mountainous areas, took more than a millennium, with some of the ethnic groups, like

Adyghs, Karachays, Balkars, Chechens and Ingushes becoming Muslim as late as the turn of the seventeenth and eighteenth centuries (Yemelianova 2002: 47). However,

> [c]ompared to Kabarda and northern Dagestan, where the Russian presence met relatively passive resistance, in Chechnya and the mountainous areas of the North Caucasus the Russians faced the ferocious resistance of the local Muslim population ... Having met severe resistance, St Petersburg turned from individual military campaigns to continuous warfare. (Yemelianova 2002: 48)

Between the 1830s and the 1850s, the Russian authorities were faced with particularly robust resistance by North Caucasians, led by a charismatic leader Imam Shamil (1797–1871), who not only successfully withstood the Russian advance but also managed to found a theocratic state – imamate – covering the territories of Daghestan, Chechnya and Ingushetia, which he led for a quarter of a century (1834–59) (Yemelianova 2002: 50).

With the continuous expansion in the latter part of the nineteenth century into the Central Asian lands populated exclusively by Muslims, the Russian Empire, in absolute numbers and also percentage-wise, became a major Muslim population-holding state: '[b]y the early twentieth century, the empire was home to some twenty million Muslims (15 percent of the total population), forming the largest non-Orthodox group' (Crews 2006: 1) and at that time 'the Muslim population of the Romanov empire was larger than that under the Ottoman sultan' (Crews 2006: 4), with '[m]ore than three and a half million Muslims liv[ing] in the provinces designated as "European Russia"' (Crews 2006: 13). The presence of such an imposing number of Muslim subjects required a comprehensive approach to them by the state, which had to legislate on its relations with them and also on the inner developments of the Muslim communities. This, inter alia, required the state to determine what it deemed as acceptable and therefore tolerated forms of Islam and which ones it saw as deviant and thus dangerous to both itself and its Muslim commonwealth.

The history of governance of Islam in tsarist Russia is almost uniformly seen by historians to fall into two distinctive periods: between the sixteenth century, when the conquests of Muslim-majority lands started, and the second part of the eighteenth century; and from when Empress Catherine the Great (also known as Yekaterina; ruled 1762–96) introduced far-reaching legislative changes regarding governance of Islam, to the end of the empire itself in 1917. The first period is universally seen as having been very difficult for Russia's Muslims who had been discriminated against and Islam, though never formally banned, had been regarded with contempt by both the state and the powerful Orthodox Church. Since the very beginning of the annexations of Muslim-majority lands, attempts at marginalisation or even eradication of Islam were made through, at times even forced, conversion to Orthodox Christianity and extremely restrictive laws.

Mosques in particular were targeted for destruction. Well into the eighteenth century, mosque destruction persisted unabated, either directly supported by the top authorities or at least tolerated by them. So, it is claimed that, for instance, '[i]n 1743 alone, state officials and churchmen may have destroyed 418 of the 536 mosques in the town and district of Kazan' (Crews 2006: 38). Furthermore, the then Empress Elizabeth (ruled 1741–61) is reported to have forbidden 'the building of mosques in villages with Orthodox Christian inhabitants and set a minimum population requirement of two hundred males for the existence of a mosque' (Crews 2006: 38). However, though scores of Kazan Muslims had been converted to Orthodox Christianity (and are known in the historiography as *kreshchenny* – christened), many of them led a double life, retaining their allegiance to Islam and sometimes even openly reverting to it. Even so, as Yemelianova (2002: 40) argues,

> almost two centuries of ruthless state suppression dealt a severe blow to Russia's Islam and Islamic elite, in particular. It led to their dramatic quantitative and qualitative reduction and the break-up of the traditions of high intellectual Islam. Islam survived predominantly in its unsophisticated popular form.

Incorporation into the empire during the eighteen century of more lands inhabited by Muslims might have encouraged Empress Catherine to consider legislative changes that would enable the state to control Muslim subjects in less oppressive ways and potentially make them more loyal to the Crown. This was made even more urgent as the Sublime Porte had been constantly claiming spiritual patronage over Russia's Muslims, something that, in view of several Russo-Ottoman wars in the eighteenth century, could have potentially led to negative political repercussions for Russia. By the beginning of the eighteenth century, Muslims themselves are reported to have sought an entente with the state: '[i]nitiated by Bashkir religious scholars in the 1730s, Muslim overtures to the state had sought official recognition for their shari'a courts and special recognition for esteemed Muslim jurists (*ākhūns* or *akhunds*)' (Crews 2006: 51).

So, with the loyalty and governability of the ever-expanding body of Muslim subjects of the empire at stake, the Russian monarchy resorted to unprecedented moves in the state's policies toward its Muslims. Soon after her ascension to the throne, in 1773, Empress Catherine promulgated a ground-breaking law on religious tolerance which curtailed the Russian Orthodox Church's interference in the religious life of the empire's Muslims. Among other things,

> [t]he law enabled the local authorities to take decisions regarding mosques, medresses, caravansarais (trade stations), waqfs and other Islamic institutions. The Government returned some of the previously confiscated waqf property to the local Islamic communities and permitted the building of a new mosque in any area populated by three hundred or more Muslim men. (Yemelianova 2002: 44)

Though this initial move by the monarchy might have alleviated the situation of Muslims in the country, the authorities could not have expected to tame Islam without domesticating it, that is without transferring the centres of spiritual authority (and natural gravity) from outside the empire's borders to within them. To this end, as Crews (2006: 33) argues,

> [t]o domesticate Islam in the empire, and to turn Muslims away from alternative sources of authority in Kabul, Istanbul, and elsewhere, Catherine and her officials opted to introduce a churchlike organization among a population that had previously known no such institutions.

In 1788, she 'invented the institution of muftiate as a medium of state control of her Muslim subjects' (Yemelianova 2003: 139): '[i]n two decrees of September 1788, Catherine called for the establishment in Ufa of an "Ecclesiastical Assembly of the Muhammadan Creed"' (Crews 2006: 52), later to be renamed the Orenburg Muhammadan Ecclesiastical Assembly. However, the significant increase in the following decades in Muslim subjects in the empire living in territories far removed from each other soon required organisational adjustments to allow for better monitoring and controlling of their religious and other social activities. To this end, the state founded two other muftiates – one in Crimea (Bakhchesaray) in 1831 (to whose authority Muslims of the Western provinces, among them the Tatars of the former Grand Duchy of Lithuania, were also formally subjected) and another in Baku (for Transcaucasus) in 1872.

With her legislative and executive reforms, Catherine, arguably, 'had not merely established a legal basis for the existence of these institutions in Russia. She had instead transformed the imperial regime into a patron of Islam' (Crews 2006: 32). The founding of official Muslim institutions in the form of spiritual boards paved the way not only for the professionalisation of the *ulama* class but through 'rules restrict[ing] the legal performance of clerical duties to men licensed by the state, effectively creat[ed] an official Muslim clergy where none had existed before' (Crews 2006: 54). Furthermore, '[t]he Muftiis were on the payroll of the Ministry of the Interior and the most co-operative of them received imperial decorations. The Muftiis reported directly to the Interior Minister who sanctioned their appointments and major initiatives' (Yemelianova 2002: 55). Still, control of the minds and bodies of the Muslim subjects was not without obstacles. As Crews (2006: 97) argues,

> [d]espite the bureaucratic strictures of exams, licenses, and parish record-keeping, religious leadership remained highly variable and informal. The opinion of influential members of mosque communities, not a license from the state, defined the moral standing and authority of would-be religious leaders.

Though Islamic education in the form of primary, secondary and even high schooling was widespread in Volga Bulgaria, the Golden Horde and its successor states, it suffered badly for the first few centuries under Russian rule. With the Catherinian reforms, Islamic schooling was revived and continuously strengthened. As such, '*mektebs* and *medresses* were the main reservoirs and transmitters of the national cultural distinctiveness of various Muslim peoples and perpetuated their social and cultural segregation within Russia' (Yemelianova 2002: 74). Until 1874, when they were placed under the jurisdiction of the Ministry of Education with teaching of Russian and in Russian made compulsory, the Islamic institutions of education were under the direct control of the muftiates, which would not only administer their work but also determine the content of the Islam taught and practised. However, by the middle of the nineteenth century, in view of regional (annexation of Central Asia with its strong Sufi traditions) as well as more global (such as the rise of Islamic revivalism) processes, Islamic education had become a sensitive issue – the muftiates proved to be incapable of fully monitoring the institutions of religious education and ultimately controlling the content of Islam practised by their nominal flock, be it non-threatening and therefore tolerable folk Islam or uncontrollable and therefore potentially dangerous mystical Islam of the Sufis or, even worse, actually threatening revivalist Islam in its Wahhabi form.

Folk Islam was equally widespread in the Volga-Urals and Caucasus, where, next to unique local religious traditions and customs, both pre-Islamic and Christian beliefs and practices had also crept into daily lives and religious activities of the local Muslim populations, particularly in remote villages far removed from the seats of normative Islam nurtured by the muftiates. Localised pilgrimages to 'holy' sites – graves of 'saints' but also natural objects like springs, trees, caves and the like – and performance of individual and collective rituals there, supervised by 'holy' men, recourse to sorcery and amulets, use of folk medicine imbued with religious symbols and formulas, all thrived unabated despite state and muftiates' joint efforts at reigning them in or even eradicating them. The official policies and efforts were often thwarted on the local level even by licensed imams who themselves happily served as local 'holy' men with blessing and healing powers or at least tolerated the presence of non-licensed informal spiritual guides and healers in the vicinity (in some cases because they found themselves in the weaker position), who

> thrived in a gray religious underground as itinerant preachers, tutors, reciters of the Qur'an, storytellers, poets, and informal mentors and spiritual guides. Supported by patrons and disciples, they continued to elude the police and operate outside the official Islamic establishment, outliving the tsarist regime itself. (Crews 2006: 97)

The volume of the activities of 'folk clergy' may be implied from the fact that the Russian state had even resorted to criminalisation of religious rituals performed by informal spiritual guides:

[t]he criminal code of 1845 reserved several articles for those claiming to be 'gifted with some kind of supernatural, miraculous power, or holiness', particularly when such a person deceived the folk and spawned 'disquiet, unrest, or despondency' or provoked 'disobedience toward established authorities'. Another section of the criminal code was devoted to 'the false appearance of miracles and other deceptions of this kind' (Crews 2006: 135)

with detailed punishments listed therein.

Another dimension of non-legalist Islam, Islamic mysticism, is thought to have arrived in the form of several Sufi brotherhoods in the territories to be later incorporated into the Russian Empire, well before their annexation by the latter. As Yemelianova maintains,

> Sufism, which presented a rural and tribal alternative to the legalistic Islam of the cities, fitted well into the local tribal and clan social structures. The first Sufis turned up in the region in the twelfth century . . . By the seventeenth century a substantial part of the Muslims of the North Caucasus, especially in Dagestan and Chechnya, were Sufis. Sufism became deeply integrated into the system of traditional community, providing its spiritual substance. (Yemelianova 2002: 47–8)

Though Sufism proved to be strongest in the Caucasus, it was also present, albeit to a lesser degree, in the Volga-Urals region where it had to compete (or rather intertwine) with folk Islam.

Sufism was a double challenge: for the formal Muslim administrative authorities and their affiliated *ulama*, and for the lay state authorities charged with supervising religious affairs. Reports abound (Crews 2006) of official *ulama* complaining to the local or even central state authorities about the activities of Sufis, some of whom were in fact also members of the *ulama* class, and some of them even licensed mullahs in local mosques. This shows, apart from the fact of the existence of mystical Islam in imperial Russia, that legalist and mystical Islam at times were intertwined. As is seen from historical material, the supreme Muslim authorities in the form of the spiritual boards would tacitly approve some Sufi practices if they did not deviate significantly from the conventional normative practices and did not challenge the Muslim or state authorities.

The strength (and danger, looking from the perspective of the Russian state) of Sufism in North Caucasus showed itself in prolonged resistance to the Russian occupation. In fact, it was Sufis – their shaykhs and adepts – who were at the forefront of the struggle with the Russian army. The most notorious resistance leader was the previously mentioned imam, Shamil, who hailed from the Naqshbandiyya brotherhood along with the rank and file of his resistance troops. After the final defeat of the rebels in the 1860s, many Sufis (particularly of the Naqshbandiyya brotherhood, which was pivotal in the resistance) were prosecuted – with sentences of incarceration, death or exile; to avoid such consequences, many others chose to flee to the Ottoman realm. Those who survived and remained in the region 'were forced either to move to other *tariqas* which were not associated with the recent *gazawat*, or to hide in the mountains' (Yemelianova 2002: 54–5)

As of the late nineteenth century, various traits of Islamic reformism also made their way into the Russian realm. The most significant of them was Jadidism, propagated by Ismail Gasprinskii (d. 1914), who is reported to have introduced in 1884

> a new method (*al-usul al-jadid*, in Arabic) of teaching in the Tatar *mekteb* in his home village in the Crimea. Subsequently, the proponents of this method were called jadidists, while the advocates of the preservation of the old syllabic method of teaching (*al-usul al-qadim*, in Arabic) were called qadimists. The *al-usul al-jadid* involved the phonetization of reading instead of memorization from Arabic, the translation of the Koran into the Tatar language and the introduction of secular subjects like arithmetic, geography, history and the Russian language into the school curriculum. (Yemelianova 2002: 75)

In the late 1880s, some of the madrasas in the Volga-Urals switched to this *al-usul al-jadid*; however, 'proliferation of the new method was slow because of the strong opposition of qadimists, on the one hand, and the Russian authorities and the Orthodox Church, on the other' (Yemelianova 2002: 77).

It is argued that towards the end of the nineteenth century, '[t]he political activity of various Muslim elites gained new momentum in 1886 when St Petersburg granted Russia's Muslims equal political rights with its other subjects' (Yemelianova 2002: 70). At the same time, Russian authorities eased regulations on both hajj and emigration in consequence of which '[i]n the year 1899 alone 120 000 Kuban Muslims fled Russia' (Yemelianova 2002: 70). Finally, with the 1905 revolution, or rather as its outcome, Russia's Muslims won not only religious recognition but also political rights; in the beginning of 1906, the first Islamic political party – Union of Muslims (Ittifaq-i-Muslimin) – was formed. Other Muslim political parties soon followed: the Islamic Popular Party, the Azeri National Party Musawat ('Equality') and the Kazakh National Party Alash. They took part in all four elections to the Russian parliament, the Duma, and some of them had their Muslim members elected as MPs (Yemelianova 2002: 88).

The fateful events of 1917 (the so-called February and October Revolutions) in Russia brought about not only the end of the 400-year-long rule of the Romanov House and the monarchy itself but, through ushering the Bolsheviks into power – who immediately proceeded with sweeping political, economic and social reforms meant to bring communism to Russia – also profound change in the ideological basis of its political system. This all had a deep effect on the status of Islam and long-lasting consequences for Russia's Muslim communities (and, from the end of 1922, the USSR's, which on the European side also included the Socialist republics of Ukraine, Byelorussia and Transcaucasus). However, the First World War, which began in 1914, caused Russia to lose its westernmost provinces: after the war (in 1918) they became the independent nation states of Poland, Lithuania, Latvia, Estonia and Finland. While in the latter three, Muslim communities throughout the interwar period remained miniscule, in both Lithuania and particularly Poland, the more sizeable Muslim communities now independent of Russian/Soviet muftiates, sought to create their own spiritual-administrative institutions.

Ottoman possessions in South-eastern Europe

Islam not only arrived with force to the Balkans in the second part of the four-teenth century but made its presence permanent, though it first had to compete for the souls of the local populations with the already established Christian churches, both Catholic and Orthodox. While the bulk of today's Balkan Muslims are members of indigenous ethnic groups, both Slavic and Albanian speaking, whose ancestors had converted to Islam in the late Middle Ages/ early Modern Times (that is, between the fifteenth and seventeenth centuries), a significant proportion are of 'colonist' background – descendants of Turkic-speaking and other immigrants from Anatolia and beyond in the Middle East.

The Ottoman state started forming in the second half of the thirteenth century in Asia Minor and by the second half of the fourteenth century had expanded to overflow into South-eastern Europe. The first military expeditions of the Ottomans into this part of Europe started in 1352 in Bulgaria. In 1371, a Serbian-led allied army was defeated allowing the Ottomans to capture much of Macedonia and southern Albania. However, it was the decisive Battle of Kosovo in 1389 that sealed the fate of hitherto independent Balkan (Christian) states and opened the way for not only territorial Ottoman expansion into South-eastern Europe but also its effective Islamisation, both through colonisa-tion and conversion. By 1396, the Ottomans had conquered all the territories of medieval Bulgaria.

The Ottomans first moved their capital to the south-eastern tip of Europe (Edirne/Adrianople) in 1402. After a short interim period, the expansion into Eastern Europe continued in the late 1410s northwards into southern Romanian lands and Wallachia. In 1439, the Ottomans briefly occupied Serbia. After conquering Constantinople and doing away with the Byzantine Empire in 1453, the Ottomans made this sprawling city their permanent capital. From there the conquest and subsequent control of European possessions was made easier. In 1456, Moldavia became an Ottoman tributary and soon thereafter, in 1459, the Ottomans dealt the decisive blow to the fledgling Serbian state. In 1463, they crushed the Bosnian resistance and by 1482 secured their rule in Bosnia. The Crimean khanate, the leftover of the Golden Horde, though never directly conquered by the Ottomans, in 1475 became their vassal. With the capture of Shkodër in 1479 and Durrës in 1501, the entirety of Albania was added to the Ottoman Empire. In 1538, the Ottomans invaded Moldavia.

Though the Ottoman legacy in Eastern Europe is foremost related to South-eastern Europe, throughout the sixteenth and seventeenth centuries the Ottomans sought to conquer lands deep in South (Italy), Central (Austria) and Eastern (Podolia, Moldavia) Europe. The furthest they got was to Nové Zámky (in the territory of today's Slovakia), which they managed to take in the 1663/64 campaign, and the south-western part of today's Ukraine (Podolia), which the Ottomans controlled for a couple of decades in the late seventeenth century. Of all those places, they were relatively successful in Hungary, which they started conquering in 1526 and ruled for a century and a half – until 1683. Hungary was invaded as the precursor of the Ottoman-Austrian war. This war saw Ottomans for the first time advance as far as Vienna, where they laid siege albeit unsuccessfully to the city in 1529. The second attempt by the Ottomans to take Vienna took place in 1683. That also was unsuccessful, as by the end of the seventeenth century the balance of power, and with it fortunes, had changed. The so-called 'Holy League' (established in 1684), comprised of several European Christian states, managed not only to thwart the Ottoman advance but even push them back and out of Hungary, which subsequently was won over by the Habsburg Empire. Austrian troops even briefly (1688–90) occupied Belgrade with parts of Serbia. In the following decades, the Ottomans lost control of Slavonia, Transylvania, Dalmatia and Podolia to different encroaching European powers. Two of them, the Austrian and Russian empires, with their growing appetites for lands including those ruled by the Ottomans, soon became the menace of the weakening Ottoman state.

Though the fortunes of the Ottomans in Central Europe were short-lived, in the Balkans and wider South-east Europe their political, and consequently religious, supremacy lasted for several centuries more, all the way into the nineteenth century and in certain regions even until the beginning of the twentieth. So, *Pax Ottomanica*, and with it Muslim if not Islamic rule, in most parts of South-eastern Europe persevered for 300–400 years and had profound consequences for the development of Balkan societies, including the development of multiple forms of Islam in the peninsula.

Islamisation of the Balkans, and particularly Bosnia and the Albanian lands, is one of the hotly debated topics in the historiography of the region (Zhelyazkova 2002; Merdjanova 2013: 2). Though the Islamisation process was undoubtedly enhanced by the mass immigration of Turkish and other colonists from the Middle East, it remains undecided how (and indeed why) some of the local populations accepted Islam while others remained non-Muslim. The nationalist (particularly Bulgarian and Serbian) historiography in the Balkans often insists on forced conversion of Slavic-speaking Christians, while the majority of Turkish, Albanian and Slavic Muslim historians go out of their way in arguing that the overwhelming majority of those Eastern Europeans who accepted Islam as their faith did this of their own free will, though the motives might have varied. The socio-economic incentives to convert must have weighed heavily as being/becoming Muslim appeared to enhance one's socio-economic status and provide a foot up the social ladder. There is also the explanation that it was those individuals and social groups who had less attachment to their hitherto religious identity (for instance, heterodox Christians, like the Bogumils) who opted to switch their religious affiliation. It is hard to assess to what extent Islam as a faith impressed the local populations who might then have converted out of a conviction that it was the better, if not the best, faith and way of life.

Though precise numbers are hard to come by and even harder to verify, some writers report that in the European part of the still expanding Ottoman Empire 'by the middle of the sixteenth century around a third of the population embraced the new faith' (Koller 2012). In any case, retrospectively, Islamisation appears to have proceeded unevenly:

> [d]uring th[e] first phase, Islamisation was mostly limited to towns and cities, where religious infrastructure like mosques, dervish monasteries and pious foundations developed. From the middle of the sixteenth century onwards Islamisation spread to the more rural areas, reaching its peak in many regions of South-East Europe during the 1640s. Bosnia and Herzegovina were the only regions where the Muslims became the largest group of the population as early as the late sixteenth or early seventeenth century. (Koller 2012)

As a result, while fairly deeply into Europe, in the territory of today's Bosnia, Kosovo, Albania, and to a lesser degree Serbia, Montenegro and Macedonia, Islam did gain a strong foothold through conversions; elsewhere – in the territories of contemporary Romania and Bulgaria – it made its presence visible, if at all, mainly through colonists and immigrants.

The religious map of South-eastern Europe is therefore very patchy. While in some parts (like western and central Bosnia, both Serbian and Montenegrin parts of Sandžak, northern and central Albania, almost all Kosovo, and western Macedonia) Muslims make up the overwhelming majority of the local inhabitants, in other parts (like the remaining part of Serbia, south-western Montenegro, eastern Macedonia, as well as most territories of Romania and Bulgaria) the Muslim presence, both historical – through monuments left behind – and current, may be hardly felt at all.

Unlike in South-eastern Europe, the Ottoman rule in Hungary did not translate into Islamisation of the Hungarian population either through immigration and settling of Muslim colonists from Anatolia or through mass conversion of the indigenous population. As Rozsa (2013: 242) argues, this might have been due to the dangers and unattractiveness of the border province for Turks and the local Christian population's preoccupation with the Reformation/Counter-reformation struggles. Nonetheless, the Ottoman-Turkish heritage in Hungary is attested to by surviving monuments of the era, including several mosques, mausoleums (like that of Gul Baba, a Bektashi dervish who died in 1541), cemeteries, public baths and other smaller symbolic relics, such as a *mihrab* in a side wall of one of Budapest's Catholic churches.

In any case, in Ottoman times, the socio-political system in the Balkan possessions was dictated by Islamic precepts, which meant that the laws were derived from the founding texts of the religion and were applicable to the entire population, not only the Muslims. However, the Ottomans are also known to have developed the so-called '*millet* system', which allowed for and even enabled non-Muslim communities of recognised confessions (primarily meaning various Orthodox and Catholic Christians as well as Jews) to self-govern their daily affairs through their autonomous religious-administrative institutions, as long as this did not involve Muslims. In all cases where Muslim interests were involved, state (Islamic or at least Islam-based) laws would apply.

Since the Hanafi *madhhab* was the preferred Ottoman Islamic legal tradition, in all Ottoman possessions in Europe this branch of legalist Islam prevailed. The administration of (legalist) Islam was executed through administrative judicial institutions presided over by *ulama*, who were subordinate to the higher religio-bureaucratic hierarchy, running all the way to the spiritual head, the Grand Mufti of Istanbul, formally titled *shaykh al-islam*. Naturally, the Grand Mufti himself was subordinate to the Sultan. Justice was dispensed by *qadis* of the Hanafi tradition while the more theoretical level of advice-giving was maintained by muftis. To meet the required standards, all these *ulama* had to go through formal religious (including legal) education. For this purpose, numerous institutions of higher education – madrasas – were established throughout the region.

However, like elsewhere in the world, custodians of normative Islam had to deal with carriers of alternative forms of Islam, comprising Sufism and folk Islam. Sufism came to South-eastern Europe with the Ottoman conquest; itinerant Sufis even accompanied the advancing Ottoman armies. Some of them settled permanently and started their own groups of followers. However, unlike in the Russian Empire, Sufis (or at least those whose beliefs did not deviate significantly from normative Islam) were not seen as a threat by the Ottoman state authorities and some of their *tariqas* were even accepted as a legitimate, integral part of the Ottoman socio-political network. Rather than seeking to curtail or eradicate Sufi activities (as Russia had), the Ottoman state endeavoured to use them for its own benefit. Towards the end of its existence, the Ottoman state even sought to institutionalise Sufism by forming a Council of Shaykhs in 1866, directly subordinate to *shaykh al-islam* (Clayer 2012: 185).

Recognising their organisational skills, discipline and charisma, early on in their conquests the Ottoman state authorities saw Sufi brotherhoods as a means of both mobilising Muslims and potentially attracting converts, something very handy in the newly acquired provinces in South-eastern Europe. And indeed, Sufi appeal in the Balkans was impressive – in several hundred years from the Ottoman conquests, Sufi brotherhoods proliferated widely, with the Khalwatiyya dominating in Albania, Kosovo and Macedonia, and the Naqshbandiyya in Bosnia and Bulgaria (Merdjanova 2013: 6). The volume of Sufi presence in Ottoman Serbia may be sensed by the fact that in the mid-seventeenth century in Belgrade alone Sufis had at least seventeen lodges (tekkes; Vukomanović 2007: 83). Numerous tombs of prominent Sufi masters dotting the Balkan landscape became shrines visited not only by Sufis but also by local practitioners of folk Islam.

Apart from other brotherhoods, the Bektashiyya permeated the Western Balkans to the point that it almost rivaled Hanafism in certain areas, particularly those inhabited by Albanians. However, Bektashi beliefs and practices are at significant variance with not only normative Islam but even other tariqas. For this reason, Bektashis have been and are often seen by many Muslims (particularly outside the region) to be beyond the pale, that is, outside the universal Muslim commonwealth or umma. They themselves also distinguish their community as apart from the rest of Muslims so much as to claim to be followers of, if not a separate religion, then at least a branch of Islam distinct from both Sunnism and Shi'ism. Bektashism gained its largest following among Albanians and is claimed to have been instrumental in their nascent nationalism in the second part of the nineteenth century, directed against (Sunni) Ottomans/Turks.

Finally, folk Islam, like elsewhere in Eastern Europe and beyond, took on divergent local forms, also heavily permeated by both pre-Islamic (Bogumil) and Christian beliefs and practices, but also those brought over by Turks from Asia Minor. Most prominent among them were communal prayers in the open on certain days with the explicit purpose of asking for rain and/or a good harvest, seeking healers' help through use of Islamic formulas and Quranic verses, the wearing of amulets, and so on. As mentioned earlier, visiting the tombs of 'saints', both of Sufi and non-Sufi nature, as well as other 'holy' places, was also widespread.

The waves of Islamic revivalism and reformism in the nineteenth and beginning of the twentieth centuries were present in South-eastern Europe even more so than in tsarist Russia. Wahhabis were a serious headache to the Ottomans, particularly in the Middle East, where the Ottomans even had to engage them in military encounters in order to disband the first Wahhabi state in the territory of Najd at the beginning of the nineteenth century. Islamic reformism, on the other hand, was strengthened by the Ottoman authorities as they sought to modernise their state and society in the second part of the same century. The famous pan-Islamic reformer Jamal al-Deen Afghani (1838–97) is reported to have attempted to persuade the Sultan to follow his programme of rejuvenation of Islam and Muslims of the Ottoman realm, but was turned away.

However, in some cases (foremost among Bosnian Muslims and Albanians), Islamic reformism went hand in hand with the nationalist aspirations of the Balkan populations and as such was not only nationalist but also anti-Ottoman. So, rather than being pan-Islamist and pro-caliphatist, this Balkan Islamic reformism started showing signs of what soon, in the post-Ottoman era of nation states, was to be identified as 'European Islam', as distinct from Middle Eastern (Turkish and Arab) Islam.

Though there were numerous rebellions by local populations in the Balkans throughout the centuries of Ottoman rule, it was in the nineteenth century when, finally, the rebellious Slavs and later Albanians were successful in casting off the Ottoman suzerainty (though admittedly, not without tacit and often very manifest help from such regional powers as Austro-Hungary and Russia). First it was the Serbs who, in 1829, secured political autonomy from the Sublime Porte. They were later followed by Bulgarians who, in the aftermath of the Berlin Conference, also attained autonomy in 1878, while Serbia became totally independent, as did Montenegro and Romania. Also the same year, the Habsburg Empire occupied Bosnia, which it formally annexed in 1908. Finally, with the Balkan War of 1912–13, the Ottomans lost Macedonia and Kosovo to Serbia, while Albania became independent.

As argued by Merdjanova, the emergence of independent Slavic-Orthodox majority states with their 'processes of nation- and state-building triggered the collapse of the established interreligious relations and the microstructure of society and brought about a profound reconfiguration in the region's social and political geography' (Merdjanova 2013: 7). While the hitherto second-class (*dhimmi*) Slavic-speaking Christian Orthodox citizens became the political and social core of the new nations, the formerly politically and socially (though not demographically) dominant Muslims were almost overnight stripped of their status: '[f]rom followers of the dominant faith in the Ottoman Empire who enjoyed a privileged legal and social position, Muslims turned into religious minorities who had to struggle continually to define their place in non-Muslim polities' (Merdjanova 2013: 7).

Furthermore, the secession of former Ottoman provinces in South-eastern Europe was accompanied by profound demographic changes. Though international treaties obliged the nascent Balkan nation states to protect ethno-confessional minorities and guarantee their civil rights, nonetheless, hundreds of thousands (up to 1.5 million; McCarthy 2000: 37) of Muslims (particularly Turks but also Albanians and Slavic-speakers) were forced out or, out of fear for their lives, chose to flee the newly formed nation states, while tens of thousands lost their lives. It is reported that '[f]rom 1876 to 1882, nearly 600,000

Muslims either died or left Europe, mainly for Anatolia' (McCarthy 2000: 34–5).

The First World War was as fateful to the Ottoman Empire as to its Russian counterpart: in the aftermath of the war, the Ottoman monarchy was abolished and the state dismembered allowing for a number of nation states to rise on its former territories in the Middle East, with Turkey in Anatolia becoming a republic. In addition, in 1924 the new Turkish government formally abolished the *khalifa* institute (and with it the office of *shaykh al-islam*), which meant that, even if only symbolic, there was no longer a top Sunni Muslim spiritual authority in the world. With the abolition of the *khalifa* institute, Muslims of South-eastern Europe, as elsewhere, ceased to be formally or even symbolically subordinate to the Constantinople mufti (*shaykh al-islam*) as the top ecclesiastical authority, and all national Muslim religious authorities in South-eastern Europe became autocephalous, though not necessarily independent of the state authorities.

Finally, the First World War led to another major European empire's dismembering: the Austro-Hungarian Empire succumbed under the weight of war exigencies. In its place, several independent nation states emerged in Central Europe and the Western Balkans: Austria, Hungary, Czechoslovakia and Yugoslavia. Though newly arisen Hungary and Czechoslovakia (as well as Austria) had practically no (more) Muslims in their territories, Yugoslavia (until 1929, called the Kingdom of Serbs, Croats and Slovenes), as well as the earlier-formed Romanian, Bulgarian and Albanian states, did have fairly big Muslim communities (in Albania, even the majority). These states, irrespective of the size of the Muslim populations in their territories, had to come up with formal and informal ways of treating Islam and dealing with its adherents, who in practically all cases became citizens of these nation states.

A note on the communist period

The communist period in the history of Europe may be tentatively divided into two sub-periods: the interwar period (1917–39), when it was only Russia/the USSR that was ruled by communists, and the Cold War period (1945–89/90), when besides the expanded USSR, practically all Central and Eastern European countries were under communist control.

The Second World War presented the USSR with the opportunity in 1940 to reclaim some of the territories formerly held by tsarist Russia, namely, the Baltic States, though it also took over a fairly sizeable chunk of the interwar Polish Republic – its eastern part, distributed among the constituent Soviet republics of Lithuania, Byelorussia and Ukraine. In this way, almost the entire Lithuanian Tatar community was once again reunited in a single state – the USSR. In addition, the same year, the USSR occupied and annexed a part of Romania making it the Soviet Republic of Moldavia. After the Second World War, communist USSR not only emerged victorious but almost as large as the

Box 2.1 Nazi intermezzo

Between 1939 and 1944 – during the Second World War – Nazi Germany had either directly occupied or had allied and puppet regimes in all of Eastern Europe. For a brief period, Germans controlled not only Tatar-populated Crimea but also a significant part of the Caucasus, while the Fascist regime of the Independent State of Croatia was in control of the Muslim-inhabited territories of Yugoslavia, with Albanian and Bulgarian Muslims under the rule of Nazi-friendly regimes.

Nazis are reported to have had a generally favourable view of Eastern European Muslims and sought to instrumentalise them in their propaganda war against their enemies, particularly communists, be it the USSR or local communists in South-eastern Europe. The Nazis/Fascists had some luck in this – in some lands (Lithuania, Czechoslovakia, Croatia, Bosnia, North Caucasus and Crimea), local *ulama* and some lay Muslims allied with the Nazis (Motadel 2013, 2014). Crimean Tatars even formed armed units to fight the Soviets alongside the German troops. Many of those Muslims who actively cooperated with the Germans (like the muftis of Ostland and Crimea), particularly in the territories formerly under Soviet control, migrated with the retreating German troops and after the war found refuge in the West. Support and cooperation with the occupational German administration earned the local Eastern European Muslims the damning label of 'collaborators' and, under the subsequent (returning) communist governments, led to their persecution and prosecution in the aftermath of the war. In some cases, for example, the Chechen and Crimean Tatars in 1944, entire populations were punished by deportation to Central Asia and Siberia from which they were allowed to return only towards the very end of USSR power, in the 1980s.

former Russian Empire; it held on to the territories annexed in 1940 and also gained new ones in East Prussia.

After the Second World War, all of South-eastern and Central Europe (with the notable exceptions of Greece and Austria) also came under communist rule, in most cases closely watched over by 'Big Brother' – the USSR. The symbolic border between the western (capitalist) and eastern (communist) parts of the Old Continent was labelled 'the Iron Curtain' because movement of people (and even ideas) from behind this border was severely restricted, and in fact, was also restricted among the states on the communist side of it. However, socialist Yugoslavia, though still firmly under communist rule, parted with the USSR in 1948 and broke out of the camp supervised by it to become a founding member of the bloc of 'non-aligned' states.

Speaking generally, the situations of Muslim communities in all the communist-ruled Eastern European countries were similar. All over the 'Eastern bloc', the practice of Islam had been made difficult by menacing and harassing state policies that placed numerous restrictions on these communities. The most severe case was, without doubt, that of Albania, where between 1967 and 1990 no religion was allowed to be practised in any form. Bulgaria's Muslims, though not as severely affected, also had to bear the brunt of the state's double-natured atheist-cum-nationalist policies, when Turks, who made up the bulk of Bulgaria's Muslims, were denied their ethnic identity and culture (including religious practice). The Yugoslav parting from the USSR, inter alia, had tentatively positive consequences for the state and development of Yugoslavian Muslim communities – their fate may be regarded to have been more favourable, not only when compared with Albania or Bulgaria but also the USSR, where the practice of Islam, though never officially outlawed, was nonetheless severely restricted and its followers persecuted.

Therefore, when talking about the trials and tribulations of Eastern European Muslims under the communist yoke, one may subdivide this part of the continent into three geographic/political regions: the USSR, the SFRY and the rest (namely, Poland, Hungary, Czechoslavakia, Romania, Bulgaria and Albania – though the latter, due to both its strained relations with the USSR and an extreme case of religious governance, may be treated separately). In the subsequent chapters (3–6), the fate of Muslim communities in the identified subregions under communist rule are dealt with in more detail.

CHAPTER 3

North-eastern Europe

The Union of the Soviet Socialist Republics and its legacy

The borders of the Union of the Soviet Socialist Republics (USSR) – which lasted between 1922 and 1991 and comprised fifteen states in both Eastern Europe and Central Asia – almost matched those of the tsarist Russian Empire, particularly after the annexation of the Baltic States in 1940. The USSR could be seen as having continued the state policies of the former empire vis-à-vis its Muslim populations, particularly in regards to the governance of religion – oscillating between attempts at suppression, if not eradication, of Islam and endeavours to control its Muslim citizens through state-recognised (and practically directly controlled) institutions. Though the USSR is popularly perceived to have been an atheist state, unlike truly atheist Albania of that period, its stance toward religion was generally more laicist – with the lay state authorities in control of religious establishments.

The Bolshevik state authorities of Russia initially appeared to have even been rather tolerant of local Muslims. As argued by Yemelianova, 'the initial Bolshevik policy towards Islam and Muslims was characterized by considerable flexibility, tolerance and tactfulness' (Yemelianova 2002: 103). They tacitly supported the Muslim anti-tsarist sentiment which they sought to turn into an anti-capitalist (anti-imperialist) and ultimately pro-proletariat communist ideological stance. The top Bolshevik figures, including Stalin and Kirov, are reported to have spoken 'favourably about Islam and Shariat. In particular, they stressed that there was no conflict between the Soviet system and Islam and promised the preservation of the Shariat courts in the Islamic regions of Russia' (Yemelianova 2002: 103). The Soviet government even

> permitted the reestablishment of an official Islamic hierarchy in Ufa in 1923 . . . Renamed the Ecclesiastical Administration for the Muslims of Russia and Siberia, it revived many of the functions of its predecessor but assumed an even more important role in representing the Soviet state before foreign Muslims. Elsewhere, Islamic law courts and schools persisted – and in some locales, even thrived. (Crews 2006: 365)

This, however, does not appear to have been a successful approach and, after suppressing the Christian churches (first of all, the Russian Orthodox Church), the communists soon turned against Islam. Like several centuries earlier when under tsarist rule, the mosques were targeted by communists with particular virulence: it is claimed that by 1930, more than 70 per cent of all mosques in the Soviet Union had been closed (Kubanova 2008: 3) with only 980 out of over 2,220 mosques remaining open in Tatarstan, while in Kabardino Balkaria and Adyghea reportedly 'not a single mosque was left' (Yemelianova 2002: 114).

By the late 1920s, hundreds even of the so-called 'red mullahs' (who had sided with the Bolsheviks), along with thousands of other Muslims, had been targeted by the Soviet authorities – some simply removed from their positions but many tried and convicted of counter-revolutionary activities and subsequently executed or sent off to concentration camps or exile. With the closure of mosques, reportedly 90 per cent of mullahs were deprived of the ability to perform their duties (Kubanova 2008: 3). Not only religious but intellectual activities were severely affected by purges – educational establishments shut down, publishing houses and media closed, publications banned. All of the establishments of Islamic religious education on the European side of the USSR were closed and only two in Central Asia were allowed to remain open, one in Bukhara and the other one in Tashkent. Finally, the Soviet authorities went as far as changing the alphabet used by Muslims of territories under Soviet rule: they changed the Arabic alphabet used for centuries first to Latin (in 1929–31) and ultimately, in 1939, to Cyrillic, that arguably 'dealt yet another severe blow to Islamic scholarship in the USSR. This double change cut Soviet Muslims off both from their religious and cultural heritage, and from their co-religionists outside the USSR' (Yemelianova 2002: 115).

All these state policies arguably led to the destruction of the Islamic infrastructure and, as Yemelianova argues, '"high", intellectual Islam, which developed from the late eighteenth century and persisted until 1917, was virtually destroyed' (Yemelianova 2002: 115). Moreover,

> [t]he Islamic infrastructure was considerably undermined by the 1929 Law of Religious Associations, which imposed strict controls over religious practices, charitable community actions, financial assistance, medical aid and any other religious network of community support. The purges of the 1930s, followed by further anti-religious laws, or a pure lack of attention to Muslim issues, drove Islam underground and reduced it to a set of cultural rituals and non-threatening relics of the past. (Braginskaia 2012: 603)

However, during the Second World War, maybe in part as a reaction to the 'pro-Muslim' stance of the Nazis, Soviet authorities eased restrictions on Islamic organisations and practices – four muftiates (in Ufa, Tashkent, Baku and Buynaksk) were (re)established, and *ulama* allowed to speak and write more openly, especially, when in support of the Soviet struggle against Nazi Germany. After the Second World War, the muftiate based in the Uzbek capital Tashkent was recognised by the Soviet authorities as the leading Islamic administration in the country, with other muftiates becoming its subordinates. The Tashkent muftiate was charged with supervising Muslims living in the Central Asian republics (namely, Turkmenistan, Uzbekistan, Kazakhstan, Kirgizstan and Tajikistan), where incidentally, they made up the majority of the local populations; the ones in Baku and Buynaksk were tasked with the supervision of the Caucasian Muslims; and Ufan with supervising the affairs of not only Muslims of the European part of Russia but also of the Southern Caucasus republics as well as the rest of the European part of the USSR. However, as in Estonia, Latvia and Moldova there were practically no functioning Muslim congregations, the authority of the Ufan muftiate extended only to the Lithuanian, Byelorussian and Ukrainian communities.

The status quo continued for a while before being swept away by new anti-religious measures aimed at the atheisation of Soviet society. In 1954, the government once again

> introduced tough restrictions on the social, educational and cultural activities of religious institutions and societies. Thus, Muslims were prohibited from opening new mosques, medresses and mektebs. Moreover, the Soviet authorities, like their Tsarist predecessors, encouraged the incorporation of pre-Islamic customs into 'socialist national cultures' and their cleansing from the Islamic components. (Yemelianova 2002: 125–6)

Nonetheless, devout Muslims of the USSR managed to hold onto their religious practices – for instance, in Tatarstan, they successfully circumvented the ban on fasting during Ramadan by finding ways to sabotage the official working hours, for example, closing shops or cafeterias for renovation during the period of Ramadan (Korolev 2007: 83).

A decade later, in view of persistent Islamic religious practices, particularly those related to family occasions like marriage and birth, in 1962 the authorities came up with a plan to introduce lay alternatives; for example, wedding and name-giving ceremonies performed at a civil registry office without a religious note. However, as noted by Korolev (2007: 86–7), the new socialist rituals did not squeeze out the religious ones but instead supplemented them. In the early 1980s, the government called for renewed efforts to suppress Islamic activism through 'reinforce[ing] atheistic propaganda vis-à-vis the Islamic community and . . . buttress[ing] efforts against violation of the legislation on religion by either government officials or clerics' (Yemelianova 2002: 132). Faced with anti-religious state propaganda enhanced by repressive policies, official *ulama* found themselves between a rock and a hard place. The official leadership then opted for a 'Saliamonic' decision to marry Islam and the communist ideology. To this end, '[t]he official ulama were endeavouring to reconcile Islam with science and progress' (Erşahin 2005: 1).

With the institutions of legalist Islam incapacitated and under tight state control, 'the religious life of ordinary Muslims was channelled within parallel Islam, dominated by traditionalism and Sufism' (Yemelianova 2002: 115). Though also negatively affected by repression of spiritual leaders and closure of sanctuaries and other places of pilgrimage, these forms had managed to survive as they had been operating outside the institutions of legalist Islam and therefore almost out of control by either the muftiates or the state. Though taken as ideal types, Sufism and folk Islam are rather distinct dimensions of Islam, in the Soviet context they started getting closer, all the way to the point where one was hardly separable from another.

This 'parallel' Islam was nurtured by spiritual guides of a double nature – Sufis (mainly in North Caucasus, where Sufism survived less scathed by the repressions of the Stalinist period) and 'wandering mullahs' (mainly in the Volga-Urals region). Though sometimes Sufis themselves became wandering mullahs, many of the wandering mullahs were not Sufis, as many Sufis never took on the duties of wandering mullahs. It is claimed (Guseva 2013: 39) that by the beginning of the 1980s, there might have been as many as 5,000 wandering mullahs, six times the number of official mullahs. These spiritual guides served communities in

> Sufi shrines and underground mosques which were disguised as clubs, *chaikhanas* (tea-rooms), bakeries or some other non-religious public places. However, inside they had a disguised *qibla* (the orientation towards Mecca) and a *mihrab* (a niche in the wall directed towards Mecca). (Yemelianova 2002: 127)

Unlike most official *ulama*, the unofficial spiritual guides of the Soviet Muslims

> were venerated for their allegedly virtuous life and the ability to conduct essential Islamic rituals and to solve disputes . . . Most of these unofficial Islamic authorities were self-educated and often knew only the basics of Islam. Nevertheless, they frequently commanded higher moral authority than the various representatives of official Islam. (Yemelianova 2002: 127)

Some wandering mullahs also engaged in healing practices (Guseva 2013: 40). The custodians of parallel Islam were naturally detested by the Soviet authorities and even seen as dangerous. Therefore, '[i]n order to discredit itinerant Sufis, Soviet officials vilified them as opportunistic seekers of riches who used religion to accumulate wealth' (Yemelianova 2002: 128).

But even with the supervision of Islamic activities by informal religious authorities such as Sufis and wandering mullahs,

> the official suppression, as well as the lengthy isolation of Soviet Muslims from their co-religionists abroad, exaggerated the specific characteristics of Soviet Islam, which was overloaded with pre-Islamic and *adat* beliefs and norms. This related to the prominence in some Muslim-populated regions of the USSR of

the pantheon of spirits, sprites, goblins, animals, heroes, princes and princesses as well as old 'sages' and poet-lyrical singers. Their tombs were places of great veneration and miracles, destinations for pilgrimage and seasonal reunions. (Yemelianova 2002: 127)

On the other hand, Islamic revivalist tendencies had managed to creep into the Soviet realm, arguably through Afghanistan, which was under a virtual Soviet occupation for practically all the 1980s and where the Soviets and the puppet regime in Kabul were bogged down in fighting a religiously inspired opposition. As many of the Soviet conscript soldiers hailed from Central Asia, the languages of which (like Uzbek, Turkmen and particularly Tajik) are also spoken in Afghanistan, these returning Muslim soldiers are credited with having brought home to the Soviet Union some of the revivalist ideas and literature, which were disseminated first in Soviet Central Asia, and then further afield. By the late 1980s, Islamic revivalism had already gained a firm foothold in Muslim-populated areas of the USSR.

In 1990, the parliament of the already crumbling USSR (the Baltic States by then had declared their secession from the Soviet empire) adopted a new, arguably significantly more liberal law on religion, which not only reaffirmed the freedom of conscience but effectively opened a way for more diversity in the forms of religious activities. One of the main features of the new law was that it prohibited persecution on religious grounds, something that had been the basis of Soviet governance of religion. The law opened the way for the re-emergence of Islam in public, and Muslims immediately proceeded to publicly observe religious duties and celebrate religious feasts. Mosques reopened and the construction of new ones was initiated in Muslim-populated areas so that '[b]y 1990 there were already 1330 registered mosques in the USSR and 94 mosques in Russia. The number of medresse students rose to several hundreds' (Yemelianova 2002: 133).

The events of 1991, culminating in a die-hard communist-led last ditch attempt, known as the '*putch*', to salvage the Soviet empire left no choice for the last leader of the USSR Mikhail Gorbachev but to officially dissolve it. With the Baltic States already firmly on course to re-establish their sovereignty, a dozen first-time, brand new post-Soviet states emerged in 1991 and 1992. On the European side of the former USSR, alongside the Russian Federation, Belarus, Ukraine, Moldova and three south Caucasian states – Armenia, Georgia and (nominally Muslim-majority) Azerbaijan – emerged. All these by now independent states had to come to grips with a double nation- and state-building process, where, among other things, the place of religion in both state and society had to be taken into account.

The development of current Muslim communities in the north-eastern part of the Old Continent is tightly connected to the legacy of Soviet times, which they all share, though they have designed different ways to deal with it. The first shared feature is that practically all European former constituent republics of the USSR had experienced internal immigration from Muslim-majority regions in Russia as well as Caucasian and Central Asian republics, with tens of thousands of 'colonists' of Muslim cultural background settling in the territories of the Baltic States and Ukraine, and even in Moldova and Belarus. So, by the late 1980s, the numbers of Muslims (or at least of people of Muslim cultural background) in the Soviet Ukraine was around 100,000, in each of Lithuania, Latvia, Estonia and Belarus it hovered around or even exceeded 10,000, and in Moldavia was over 5,000. Russia's own significant historical autochthonous Muslim population had also been supplemented with the steady arrival of people of Muslim cultural background from the Soviet republics in the Caucasus and Central Asia.

In addition to 'colonists', some of the Soviet republics welcomed students from 'friendly' Muslim-majority countries in Africa and Asia. So, the universities in Soviet Russia, Ukraine and Moldavia (and to a lesser extent in Byelorussia), from the 1970s, hosted thousands of Arab and other Muslim students majoring mainly in technical and medical sciences. Although many, particularly those of communist or more general left- or liberal-leaning background were non-religious, some were or later became devout believers. Though the overwhelming majority of graduates were repatriated, scores stayed forming the nucleus of (re)emerging Muslim communities in the late years of the USSR, particularly in Ukraine and Moldavia, and in the early 1990s played a prominent role in missionary activities on behalf of the Muslim Brotherhood, Salafi, Sufi and other movements.

The break-up of the USSR in 1991 had consequences for the size and demographic make-up of Muslim communities in the post-Soviet European states. Independent Ukraine, having had practically no indigenous Muslims during the Soviet period, saw a dramatic increase in its Muslim population through the mass return of Crimean Tatars to their ancestral homeland. The three Baltic States – Estonia, Latvia and Lithuania – to the contrary, witnessed a solid though brief episode of repatriation of many of the Soviet-time colonists (among them numerous individuals of Muslim cultural background) from the now reconstituted states to either the Russian Federation or other parts of the Commonwealth of Independent States (CIS). This exodus drastically diminished the number of (nominal) Muslims in the Baltic States with the overwhelming majority of those remaining in Estonia and Latvia becoming legal aliens in their adopted homelands, while the autochthonous Lithuanian Tatars re-emerged as the leading component in the local Lithuanian Muslim community. Birth of an independent Belarusian (renamed after gaining independence) state facilitated the emergence of an autonomous Belarusian Tatar community (historically having been part of the same Lithuanian Tatar commonwealth). For its part,

Russia continued to attract Muslim citizens of former Soviet republics, particularly from Azerbaijan, who by the turn of the century far outnumbered most of Russia's indigenous ethnic groups of Muslim background. Moldova (also renamed after independence), on the other hand, appears not to have experienced any significant migratory trends involving people of Muslim background.

The other shared feature is the governance of religion, including Islam. The Soviet system was centralised, so all constituent republics had practically identical legislation pertaining to religion. But the religious make-up (speaking both demographically and in respect to religiosity of local populations) of the republics was very different and the presence (and status) of Muslims also varied greatly. Partly because of the ethnic composition and the origins of their Muslim minorities but also because of their internal political dynamics (including approaches to the governance of religion) and international gravitations (like Euro-Atlantic integration), independent states of the European part of the former USSR chose rather different ways to treat their Muslim populations. In some of them (like Lithuania, Russia and Belarus), Islam was officially recognised as a historical faith of the land; in others it did not fall into this category, though other faiths did (like in Latvia, Moldova and Ukraine); or no faiths were recognised as being 'traditional' to the country (like in Estonia).

Russia

As soon became clear, Islam, though bruised, survived the atheist onslaught of the communist regime in Russia. In absolute numbers, the post-Soviet Russian state has the biggest Muslim community among not only Eastern European countries but in the whole of Europe – in fact, with its up to 20 million Muslims,[1] Russia hosts as many Muslims as all other European countries put together. The survival, re-emergence and growth of Islam in Russia may be symbolically recognised in Russia's joining of the Organization of the Islamic Conference in the 2000s (renamed in 2011 as the Organization of Islamic Cooperation) with observer status. The only other European state that has such a status is Bosnia and Herzegovina (since 1994), while Albania has been a full member-state since 1992.

In seven constituent territories of the Russian Federation, Muslims make up the majority of the population. In the North Caucasus (home to some 7 million Muslims), in Ingushetia, Chechnya and Daghestan, Muslims comprise more than 90 per cent of the inhabitants, while in Kabardino Balkaria and Karachaevo Cherkessia they make up two thirds; in the Volga-Urals region, in both Bashkortostan and Tatarstan, Muslims constitute just over half of the population. Though part of the Muslim population is of recent immigrant background, the bulk hail from almost forty indigenous ethnic minorities, mainly of Turkic origin, who have been living in the territory of today's Russian

Map 3.1 Ethno-confessional composition of the Caucasus
Compiled by Davide Calzoni

Federation since the Middle Ages. The biggest ethnic group of Muslim background are Tatars (5.5 million), followed by Bashkirs (1.6 million) and Chechens (1.3 million). Expatriates from Azerbaijan, estimated at more than 1.5 million, are suggested (Malashenko 2009: 322) to be the biggest Muslim group of foreign origin. The majority of Azeris, at least nominally, are Twelver Shi'is.

Though intimated by some Russian researchers that '[r]ather than one united Muslim community in Russia, there are two relatively weakly connected communities' (Malashenko 2009: 323), the situation on the ground is much more complex and one could dissect the body of the Muslim population of Russia not only on ethno-linguistic and ethno-cultural grounds (as Malashenko suggests), but also according to the ideological preferences of believers, which in the Russian case cover the entire spectrum of the forms of religiosity discussed in Chapter 1. Thus, in the form of Russia's Muslims, all three classical dimensions of Islam – the legalist, mystical and folk – as well as the widest possible range of representatives of revivalist Islam may be found throughout the territory of the Russian Federation. However, research findings suggest that many of the North Caucasian Muslims (and this probably can be safely extended to Muslims in other regions of Russia), rather than identifying with a particular trait of Islam, 'consider themselves Muslims in "general"' (Malashenko 2009: 325).

In any case, one may even talk of a sort of Islamic renaissance after the collapse of the USSR. This revival of Islam in post-communist Russia manifests itself in the mushrooming of Muslim religious communities and places of worship: by 2004, there were 3,537 registered Muslim communities and over 7,000 mosques had been opened throughout the country, with Daghestan alone hosting 1,585 registered mosques, Tatarstan another 1,300 and Chechnya and Ingushetia 500 and 300 each (Malashenko 2009: 326). One may be reminded that back in the 1980s, there were only 179 registered mosques in the European part of the USSR (Yemelianova 2002: 137). The opening of the mosques required staffing them with mullahs so,

> in Tatarstan, where there were only thirty Muslim religious figures in the late 1980s, a decade later there were about 5000 Muslim clerics of various ranks. Similarly, in the 1980s in Russia, there was only one medresse at the level of secondary Islamic education in Ufa and no higher Islamic schools at all ... In 1998, there were 106 religious schools and 51 registered religious centres and societies which provided basic Islamic education. In Dagestan alone nine Islamic institutes, including three Islamic universities, 25 medresses, 670 mektebs and 11 Islamic cultural and charity centres were opened. (Yemelianova 2002: 138)

Mosques and other religious institutions are places and tools of what might be called the re-Islamisation of Russia's Muslims. However, in the opinion of some Russian researchers (Yarlykapov 2010: 112; also, Malashenko 2009: 347), 'what has happened in practice is not a revival, but rather a recreation of Islam, that is, a re-Islamization. The form that this recreation took often did not depend on the former traditions that had already been lost.' Therefore, there is a fine, yet very seminal, line between what may be regarded as 'revival' of Islam in Russia and what is seen instead as 're-Islamisation' of its Muslim populations. As suggested by both Malashenko and Yarlykapov, re-Islamisation does not necessarily bring back the old ('traditional') forms of Islamic religiosity. And even if some of the rituals are indeed revived, their contents and functions are often misplaced so that they become exponents of 'new' folk Islam (Yarlykapov 2010).

On the other hand, the number of mosques, restored or newly built, does not always translate into high religiosity, that is, high rates of attendance. Research findings (Nurullina 2014, 2015; Yarlykapov 2010) reveal that, in both the Volga-Urals and North Caucasus regions, local Muslims are indeed very secularised with few attending prayers at mosques and even those attending having very limited religious knowledge because many of the imams themselves lack a proper religious education. This seems to be particularly true of the Volga-Urals region, where, as argued by Braginskaia, '[ex]posed to political integration through forced Christianisation and Sovietisation in the nineteenth and twentieth centuries ... the Tatar Muslims represent arguably the most culturally assimilated Islamic community within Russia's borders' (Braginskaia 2012: 600). Therefore, the leadership of re-emergent Muslim communities, rather than fending off attacks by state authorities as in the communist period, now have to focus on bringing back the part of their nominal flock that has been secularised to a point verging on apostasy.

As Russia is a federal state, governance of religion, including Islam, works on two levels – the federal, applicable throughout the country, and the constituent entities' level, that is applicable within the borders of the autonomous republic. Therefore, at times, governance of religion (Islam) may differ somewhat in different federal republics. For instance, what may be proscribed in one republic may not be illegal in the other. A good example is Chechnya, where the local administration has issued a range of decrees with religious overtones related to gender relations and dress codes, which are not heard of elsewhere. On issues related to religion, lay authorities in constituent republics with Muslim majorities or at least significant minorities cooperate primarily with the official local religious institutions – the muftiates.

As shown in the section on the historical development of Muslim communities in Russia in Chapter 2, upto the late eighteenth century, the state authorities sought to control and directly influence their development through rather oppressive and prohibiting measures and later, through state-founded and tightly controlled formal institutions – 'spiritual directorates'. As a top-down project, these invented institutions were hardly representative of Muslims and had little to do with their spiritual guidance. They were mainly bureaucratic apparatuses and as such certainly a powerful tool in the hands of the state in its governance of Islam; ultimately, it has always been the state that has decided what forms of Islamic piety and behaviour are 'correct'. Throughout tsarist times and the Soviet period, these spiritual directorates served as proxies through which the state sought to ensure that Islamic practices were in compliance with its ideology and interests. This was all supposed to come to an end with the disintegration of the Soviet Union in 1991, followed in 1992–4 by the demise of the Spiritual Administration of Muslims in the European part of Russia and Siberia (SAMES), which in 1994 was renamed the Central Spiritual Board of Muslims of Russia and the CIS. This rejuvenated muftiate initially claimed authority not only over Russia's Muslims but also those in the Baltic States, Belarus and Ukraine. However, with the emergence of local independent muftis in all these countries (with the exception of Latvia), such aspirations were naturally swiped away.

Indeed, even before the collapse of the USSR, in the wake of 'perestroika' its Muslims started creating independent (both of the Soviet-era official spiritual directorates and of the political authorities) Muslim religious organisations and institutions. With the collapse of the USSR, Muslim spiritual administration underwent profound transformations. First of all, in the very last years of the

Soviet empire, alternative muftiates sprang up all around the country wherever a sizeable Muslim population lived and, by the mid-1990s, there were some forty Muslim religious administrations headed by self-proclaimed muftis in what had become a sovereign Russian Federation.

This phenomenon of '[t]he parallel existence of various Islamic administrations has contributed to confusion and double-registration at the level of local Islamic communities. As a result, in some places several parallel Spiritual Boards and *muhtasibats* have emerged' (Yemelianova 2002: 162). This proliferation of Islamic administrations has been referred to as the 'mufti boom' (Yemelianova 2002: 158), which, however, is not necessarily viewed as a positive development. Yemelianova provides a scathing critique of the novo-muftis:

> most new Muftiis have been corrupt and theologically incompetent figures who were dependent on local semi-criminal structures, and on material and doctrinal 'assistance' from foreign Islamic institutions. Their policies and behaviour have often been motivated by internal rivalry, personal ambitions and greed. (Yemelianova 2002: 164)

Secondly, some of these new muftiates soon aspired to take the place of the Soviet-era muftiates as the leading Islamic spiritual-administrative institutions if not state-wide then at least on the regional level, and started competing among themselves. In their drive for power (spiritual and economic but also political), the aspiring muftis soon realised that joining forces could be more beneficial than continuing fighting on their own. Therefore, they soon proceeded to centralise their institutions to increase their bargaining power vis-à-vis not only the fledgling central and regional authorities of Yeltsin-era Russia but also other Muslim umbrella organisations, especially those headed by Soviet-era *ulama*. In 1996, the Council of Russian Muftis, comprising sixteen spiritual directorates, was formed. However, as argued by Yemelianova, '[a]lthough the SMR [the Russian acronym of the Council of Muftis of Russia] claims to be an all-Russian Islamic forum it represents *de facto* the interests of the narrow Moscow-based Tatar Islamic elite under the leadership of Muftii Gaynutdinov' (Yemelianova 2002: 159). Furthermore, there are allegations that

> the SMR is less concerned with representing Muslim interests to the state and more with communicating the state's objectives to the Muslim communities. This leaves the council vulnerable to accusations from some unofficial Muslim organisations that rather than promoting Islam in Russia, it 'domesticates it' and thus isolates Russian Muslims from the rest of the Muslim world. (Braginskaia 2012: 615)

There are also charges that 'excessive institutionalisation results in "over-bureaucratisation" of official Muslim figures which undermines their credentials as spiritual leaders' (Braginskaia 2012: 615).

Moreover, as virtually all muftiates and their muftis are based in the cities, they are reportedly accused by provincial mullahs, who make up the majority of Russia's *ulama*, of failing to provide adequate 'attention and practical assistance, as well as the absence of spiritual leadership . . . Muftiis have often been viewed from below as self-obsessed, over-materialistic, corrupt and theologically incompetent' (Yemelianova 2002: 164). The level of education of provincial muftis and their own capacity to provide spiritual guidance to the believers is also often questioned (Malashenko 2009; Nurullina 2015). As a result, the bulk of the population of various Islamic regions of Russia have not regarded 'career Imams and Islamic politicians as genuine agents of the Islamic revival and have preferred Sufis, elders and other unofficial Islamic authorities to them' (Yemelianova 2002: 164).

As shown in Chapter 2, Sufism has been fairly widespread among Russia's Muslims since before Russia annexed the Muslim-inhabited territories. Moreover, it was perceived by the tsarist authorities to be a potential danger because Sufi authorities were outside the official muftiates' control. Sufism, particularly in North Caucasus, is credited to have been not only a uniting and mobilising factor but actually the life-line for survival of ethno-confessional identity. It is argued that, for instance, during their exile in Central Asia in the communist period, Chechens 'managed to preserve their customs and spiritual values thanks to the activity of the wird [Sufi] brotherhoods' (Akaev 2015: 49), which were also handy in reviving their culture once they returned from exile to post-Soviet Russia.

There are reports that in the last five years of existence of the USSR, during the so-called perestroika period (between 1986 and 1991),

> Sufis emerged from underground and championed grassroots Islamic activities. A characteristic symbol of the Sufi dimension of the latter was the restoration of the traditions of *ziyarat* to over 1000 *mazars*. They strengthened their influence on decision-making at a local level through the promotion of their representatives in village administrations. This enabled the renewal of public Islamic festivals, as well as the reintroduction of some elements of Islamic food norms and dress codes which existed in pre-Soviet times. (Yemelianova 2002: 150)

A recent survey found that 19 per cent of the surveyed Russian Muslims identify as belonging to a Sufi brotherhood (Pew 2012: 31), 82 per cent regard the visiting of shrines acceptable (Pew 2012: 96) and 18 per cent think that making 'offerings to Jinn under Islam' is acceptable (Pew 2012: 102).

So, alongside the revival and thriving of structures of normative Islam, Sufism also made a public comeback, particularly in the North Caucasus: 'Sufi Islam and local Kadiri, Shazali, and Nakshbandi sects have strengthened their positions in the eastern part of the North Caucasus – Chechnya, Dagestan, and to a lesser extent Ingushetia' (Malashenko 2009: 345). Akaev even asserts that wirds encompass about 80 percent of all believers in Chechnya: of these, 60 percent belong to Qadiriyya wirds . . ., while 20 percent are followers of various Naqshbandiyya wirds . . . The wirds play a palpable role in Chechens' social and political mobilization. Moreover, the descendants of the sheikhs and some wird authorities not infrequently have a greater influence on Chechen society than the leaders of the 'prestigious' teips. Political figures are often forced to turn to them during political campaigns or elections with a request to mobilize their 'flock' for support. Besides this, the wird authorities play a key role in reconciling hostile parties, especially concerning 'blood-feuds'. (Akaev 2015: 54; also Yemelianova 2002: 148)

Even more interestingly,

[i]n Dagestan and Chechnya, Sufis hold key positions in all religious offices. Members of the brotherhoods have managed to press and in some instances oust mazhab Islam. Sheikhs have won the 'competition' with mosque imams, and Shafi clergymen have to enlist in the tariqats. (Malashenko 2009: 345; also Yemelianova 2002: 147–8)

Getting involved with the Islamic administrations and, in some cases, taking them over, effectively pushed Sufis onto the political scene, where they encountered encroaching revivalists who were also after both the hearts and souls – and the power – of Russia's Muslim communities.

As mentioned in Chapter 2, revivalist Islam in its various disguises – Wahhabism, Salafism, Islamism, and so on – had been present in Russia since the nineteenth century. The Soviet period may be seen as an intermezzo when, along with other forms of Islamic religiosity, revivalism was suppressed and persecuted. However, it had already made a comeback by the last decade of the USSR, particularly through Afghanistan, where Soviet troops and specialists were stationed for most of the 1980s, many of them of Muslim background from ethnically and culturally related republics in Central Asia. Usually indirectly but sometimes also directly, Soviet citizens came into contact with revivalist ideas espoused by the Afghan and foreign mujahidin fighting the puppet regime of Kabul and its overlord, the USSR. Some of the Soviet Muslims, especially those from Soviet Central Asia, fell for these ideas and started nurturing revivalist aspirations themselves, later to give rise to revivalist movements in Uzbekistan, Tajikistan and elsewhere.

With the easing of restrictions on the movement of people across borders and greater freedom of expression in the final years of the USSR, more and more Soviet (and soon post-Soviet) Muslims had the opportunity to perform hajj or to simply visit Muslim-majority countries. However, in their sojourns, they were exposed to a broad spectrum of interpretations of what the 'correct' content of Islam is and what it is to be a 'true' Muslim, including a plethora of revivalist ones that were often at stark variance with the Islam known and practised by

Russia's Muslims. As a result, '[t]he first Wahhabis turned up in Dagestan in the mid-1980s' (Yemelianova 2002: 152) and '[t]he proliferation of Wahhabism in Chechnya began in 1995–96, which is much later than in Dagestan. Its main agents were foreign Islamists who fought on the Chechen side during the war' (Yemelianova 2002: 183).

The numbers of people espousing Wahhabi ideas and their activities in the North Caucasus in the 1990s increased so much that they started frightening both the local Islamic administrations and the political elite. To a great extent, this was due to the negative attitudes of the Wahhabis toward 'traditional' Islam, first, in the guise of Sufis. The Wahhabis subjected them to targeted criticism, assessing 'the religious activity of the wird brotherhoods as anti-Islamic', something that eventually gave 'rise to intra-religious conflicts, which often escalated into bloody clashes' (Akaev 2015: 50).

In 1997, purportedly under pressure from the local muftiate (controlled by Sufis), the Daghestani parliament resorted to measures to curb the spread of not only militant but also 'intellectual' Wahhabism. It banned Wahhabis, 'who were defined as religious extremists' (Yemelianova 2002: 152); from then on, security agencies proceeded to harass Wahhabis by arresting them, closing down the offices of their organisations and shutting down their publishing activities. However, this purportedly 'had a radicalizing impact on its devotees and pushed them into alliance with Chechen radical nationalists' (Yemelianova 2002: 152), at that time engaged in a deadly encounter with the Russian state over their aspiration to create an independent nation state of Ichkeriya (see Box 3.1). Joining the Daghestani ranks had a side effect on the Chechens themselves, who rapidly started gravitating toward militant Islamic revivalism, epitomised in the declaration of the creation of an Islamic Caucasus Emirate, naturally, at the expense of the earlier-envisioned secular nation state. The realised threat stemming from the militant wing of Wahhabism to the stability of North Caucasian territories soon prompted the issuing of bans on Wahhabis across the region, with Ingushetia, Kabardino Balkaria, Karachaevo-Cherkessia and Chechnya in one form or another seeking to curb or even eliminate them from their territories (Malashenko 2009: 342).

On the other hand, moderate forms of Islamic revivalism were allowed to have a stake in national politics, at least throughout the first post-Soviet decade. The first political party with a religious bent, the Islamic Revival Party, in fact was founded in the time of the USSR, in 1990, in Astrakhan (Malashenko 2009: 333). The emergence of this party may be directly connected to Gorbachevian perestroika, which among other things opened up the Soviet political space. Yemelianova argues that

[i]n terms of its impact, the effect of perestroika on Russia's umma could be compared to the political liberalization at the beginning of the twentieth century.

Both gave a revitalizing impetus to Russia's umma and stimulated the political activity of its members. Gorbachevian Russia witnessed the emergence of a number of political parties and organizations which placed Islam at the centre of their identity. (Yemelianova 2002: 166)

True to its name, the Islamic Revival Party was a revivalist organisation. As argued by Yemelianova, '[t]he doctrinal foundation of the party was Salafi Islam and its declared goal was the re-Islamicization of society and polity in Muslim-populated regions of the USSR' (Yemelianova 2002: 167). Though the Islamic Revival Party did not last long (it fell apart in 1992), a number of other political organisations of Russia's Muslims followed. Some of them had aspirations to be national groups; others, particularly those founded in Tatarstan and Chechnya, were content with a regional status. One of those projecting itself as representative of all Russia's Muslims (with registration in over 70 regions), the Nur Party, formed in 1995 just before the general elections of that year; although it performed very poorly on a nationwide level (it gained only 0.58 per cent of votes), it managed to attract 5 per cent of votes in Tatarstan and even more in Chechnya and Ingushetia. However, its failure sealed its fate. The Refah Party, another political project of aspiring Muslim politicians paid off for its leaders – at the turn of the century, they were elected to the Russian parliament. However, a 2001 law banned parties founded on a religious basis and this closed the chapter of Russia's Muslims experimenting with explicitly Muslim, if not Islamic, political organisations and legal ways of promoting political Islam in Russia.

The interest of Russia's Muslim institutions in Crimean Muslims from 2014 requires a separate note. With the formal annexation of the Crimean Peninsula in 2014, Russia's Muslim population instantly increased by some 250,000 of Crimean Tatars. Though tens of thousands of them chose not only to retain their Ukrainian citizenship but also to evacuate to the Ukrainian mainland, the majority – in the range of 200,000 – stayed put and took on additional Russian citizenship.

The Ukrainian Muslim organisations in Crimea, like all others, lost their legal status and had to re-register as Russian. Consequently, the Spiritual Administration of Muslims of Crimea re-registered as the Spiritual Administration of Muslims of Crimea and Sevastopol, while its rival, the Spiritual Centre of Muslims of Crimea, re-registered as the Tavrian Muftiate. The two organisations received endorsement and support from two rival Russian Muslim spiritual administrations and were even made into proxies in their fight for supremacy over Russia's Muslims. In the end, the Spiritual Administration of Muslims of Crimea and Sevastopol emerged victorious with the Tavrian Muftiate reduced to a marginal status. The mufti of the Spiritual Administration of Muslims of Crimea and Sevastopol became a member of the Russian Council of Muftis.

Box 3.1 The Chechnya case

The case of Chechnya, in terms of the development of Islam (revival or re-Islamisation) in post-Soviet Russia, is exceptional. As indicated in Chapter 2, the Northern Caucasus was finally conquered by Russia in the nineteenth century only after numerous military campaigns that spanned almost a century, with the Chechens having been among those who resisted the occupation most. For this, they were severely punished by the tsarist Russian authorities. The end of the Second World War brought another calamity on the Chechens: in 1944, practically the entire ethnic group was deported by the Soviets to Central Asia and Siberia. After their return from exile, Chechens sought to recreate their national home, first within the crumbling USSR and then as an independent nation state.

In the initial phase of nation- and state-building, between 1990 and 1994, Chechen nationalism and statehood had only a vague relation to Islam. However, with the war against Russia unravelling, from 1994 Islam emerged alongside other mobilising and unifying factors in the Chechen fight for independence from Russia. The process of Islamisation of the Chechen cause and polity accelerated in 1996, when Wahhabism – purportedly promoted by foreign fighters who joined the Chechens in their fight against Russia (Yemelianova 2002: 183), but also as a spillover effect from neighbouring Daghestan – was adopted by part of the Chechen leadership as their ideology. From then on they upgraded their fight to aim for an Islamic Emirate of Caucasus rather than a mere nation state of Ichkeriya.

This caused a split in the Chechen political and military leadership along ideological lines, with the official lay and religious leadership remaining loyal to 'traditionalist' Islam and the nation-state cause, but being increasingly marginalised by field commanders who had opted for hard-line Wahhabi/Salafi-inspired visions (Yemelianova 2002: 181–2). The split resulted not only in the fragmentation of the Chechen political (and military) elite but also in the eventual turn of the entire Chechen fight toward an avatar of the emerging global jihadism, the main feature of which became terrorism. To appease the hard-liners, the official leadership itself turned to Islam and 'abolished the secular courts of justice and created the Supreme Shariat Court with its regional branches. The new Constitution of Chechnya proclaimed Islam as the state religion and the legal basis for the Chechen legislature' (Yemelianova 2002: 181). This, however, proved to be not enough for the hard-liners who continued with their fight for the envisioned Emirate. Fortune changed sides when, in the early 2000s, Vladimir Putin became Russia's president and proceeded with a merciless campaign to crush the rebellion against Russian rule in the North Caucasus. By the mid-2000s, Chechnya had been brought back under Russian control. On the other hand, Russia allowed the newly installed loyal Chechen leadership to amuse itself with introducing and upholding certain Islamic rules and regulations in the lives of the inhabitants of Chechnya.

The situation of other formerly Ukrainian Muslim organisations in Crimea, however, remained precarious.

Ukraine

Though Muslims first settled in the territory of today's Ukraine – chiefly, its eastern part – more than a millennium ago (Brylov 2016: 194–6), it still might be valid to consider the presence of Islam a recent phenomenon in the Ukrainian state. And not least because Ukraine as a sovereign state is a young country (1991), but because until gaining its independence in the early 1990s Ukraine barely had a self-conscious Muslim community, though there certainly were people of Muslim background living in its territory throughout the Soviet period. Most of them were settlers from the Russian Federation, the bulk (some 87,000 in 1989) of whom were Volga-Ural Tatars (as opposed to other Tatar groups, namely, the Crimean Tatars and Tatars of the Grand Duchy of Lithuania), though there were also students-turned-immigrants from the Middle East and other Muslim-majority regions.

Just before the disintegration of the USSR, in the wake of the Gorbachev-initiated reforms known as 'glasnost' and 'perestroika', Soviet Ukraine started seeing a dramatic increase in the number of Muslims in its territory, caused by mass repatriation of Crimean Tatars (the overwhelming majority of whom have historically been of Muslim cultural background) from their exile in Siberia and Central Asia. They had been deported in 1944 by the Soviet regime after having been accused of collaboration with the occupying Nazis during their control of the Crimean Peninsula between 1941 and 1944. It should be mentioned that since the creation of the USSR, Crimea was part of the Russian Federation, so technically, in 1944 when the Soviets liberated the peninsula from the Germans, Crimean Tatars were inhabitants of Russia, not Ukraine. However, since Crimea was given to Ukraine by the Soviet authorities in the 1950s, home-coming Tatars in the 1980s and 1990s were 'returning' to a different country from the one they (or rather their parents and grandparents) had been deported from, namely, Ukraine instead of Russia. Though the overwhelming majority of Crimean Tatars upon their return to (Ukrainian) Crimea became loyal citizens of Ukraine with no sentiments towards Russia, some entertained the idea of an independent Crimea (Kouts and Muratova 2014: 51–63), though it never gained any momentum in Crimean local, let alone Ukrainian national, politics.

With a steady flow of Tatars returning to their ancestral land of Crimea, their number in the post-Soviet independent Ukraine eventually reached more than 300,000, with some estimates giving an even higher figure. As Crimean Tatars are generally perceived to be Muslim, the number (at least nominally) of Muslims in Ukraine sky-rocketed from an estimated 100,000 or less in the last years of the USSR to close to half a million by the beginning of the second decade of the twenty-first century. Unfortunately, currently there is no reliable data on the numbers, demographic composition or distribution of Ukraine's Muslims, as the last official census was conducted in 2007. Moreover, the question on religion was not even asked directly and therefore any figures in circulation are extrapolations based on answers to other questions – first of all, those related to ethnicity and country of birth/origin. In any case, the largest concentration of Ukrainian Muslims is in Crimea (up to 300,000), followed by Eastern Ukraine, where it is estimated the number of Muslims may be around 100,000. The rest of Ukraine (the central and western parts, including the capital Kiev) may host another 100,000 Muslims of various ethnic backgrounds, as well as Tatars including not only immigrants from the Middle East (particularly Palestine and Jordan; Bogomolov *et al.* 2006: 22) and other Muslim-majority regions but also local Slav converts. On the other hand, some regions in the north and west of the country are virtually 'Muslim-free' (Bogomolov *et al.* 2006: 24).

Nonetheless, even with such a shaky numerical foundation, one can distinguish among the different groups of Ukraine's Muslims based on their origins, something that (as will be shown below) translates into different organisational structures/religious institutions led by competing (and even rival) spiritual leaderships. To begin, the largest group comprising up to two thirds of people of Muslim background in Ukraine are Crimean Tatars. The overwhelming majority of them are concentrated in Crimea with some living in adjacent regions and the capital city Kiev. The second largest ethnic group are the already mentioned Volga-Ural Tatars (some 73,000 in 2001), the overwhelming majority of whom live in Eastern Ukraine, in particular the Donetsk and Lugansk regions, and Crimea. Azerbaijanis (over 45,000 in 2001) are estimated to be the third largest group of people of Muslim background.

However, in 2014, when Russia annexed the Crimean Peninsula and separatist forces established self-proclaimed Donetsk and Lugansk 'people's republics', some 80 per cent of Ukraine's Muslims found themselves in territories not controlled by the Ukrainian government. This radical shift in their status forced Muslims of those territories to reconsider their national identity and belonging. Though an estimated 20,000 to 35,000 Crimean Tatars left the annexed peninsula and settled in central and western Ukraine – followed by a similar or lower number of Muslims from Eastern Ukraine – the bulk stayed, though they retained Ukrainian citizenship alongside their newly acquired Russian one. Those who remained were obliged to reconstitute their religious organisations: first, to sever their relations with the Ukrainian (Kiev-based or at least pro-Ukrainian) former mother organisations and then align with the pan-Russian ones. The interest from Russian Muslim organisations in taking the Muslim communities of Crimea into their fold has already been noted in the section on Russia. Suffice it to say here that some among the Crimean Muslim leadership appear to have successfully made the shift in their political and also spiritual allegiance.

Though with the events of 2014 and subsequent developments Ukraine was left with a severely diminished number of people of Muslim cultural background under its direct control, the spectrum of ethnically and/or ideologically based Muslim organisations not only did not decrease but actually increased somewhat. This happened first of all because of the flight of revivalist-inclined Muslim groups from Russian-controlled territories; Hizb at-Tahrir, Salafi and Islamist-leaning individual Muslims and their hitherto legally operating organisations, particularly from Crimea, found themselves beyond the pale with regards the Russian authorities' sanctioned Islamic beliefs and practices and had simply to leave (or cease/conceal practising their version of Islam). The resettling of Muslims from Crimea and eastern Ukraine resulted not only in the founding of new Muslim communities/organisations (such as a Salafi Association of Ukrainian Muslims) in central and western parts of Ukraine, where the Muslim presence had hitherto been minimal, but also in the establishment of new/alternative Crimean Tatar organisations, like the Spiritual Administration of Muslims of Crimea. The latter was founded by fourteen Crimean Tatar communities based in mainland Ukraine to replace an organisation of the same name that had switched sides after the annexation of Crimea by Russia in 2014. This new-old organisation has a Council of Ulama, which includes, among others, Salafi imams.

But even before the annexation of Crimea by Russia and the beginning of the armed conflict in the Donbass region, Ukraine has hosted a rather wide spectrum of Muslim religious organisations, a number of which aspire to the status of muftiates. Two of them (the Spiritual Administration of Ukrainian Muslims (SAUM) and the Spiritual Administration of Ukrainian Muslims – Ummah) claim to be Ukraine-wide organisations, with others making a stake for themselves as (representative) regional organisations, among which the Spiritual Administration of Muslims of Crimea (SAMC), the Spiritual Centre of Muslims of Crimea (SCMC) and the Spiritual Administration of Muslims of Donbass (SAMD) are the most prominent. There is also a Kiev muftiate. All of these organisations are Sunni. Ukraine's fledgling Shi'i community has its informal organisation in Kiev. In addition, since early on, Ukraine has had a chapter of the global Hizb at-Tahrir movement as well as informal Salafi groups (Bulatov 2014).

Of all these organisations, SAUM appears to have succeeded not only in gaining the allegiance of the largest number of local Muslim congregations but also tacit recognition by the Ukrainian political establishment of its status as the representative Muslim organisation both inside and outside the country. Since its inception, SAUM has been headed by a Lebanese who came to Soviet Ukraine in the 1970s to pursue technical studies but since has become one of the *ulama* and the mufti to his followers. SAUM began as a student organisation, gathering together Muslim students who had come to study in Ukraine and those graduates who stayed on after completion of their studies. By the mid-2010s, SAUM had become not only a well-established organisation but a very visible one; set on a hill top in central Kiev, its imposing headquarters are impressive and reveal the relative wealth and power of the organisation – housing, besides a spacious mosque with a tall minaret, offices, a shop and lecture rooms for an Islamic university.

In the mid-1990s an alternative, initially non-governmental organisation (NGO) ar-Raid was formed, also by and for foreign Muslim students. Subsequently, ar-Raid formed a rival Spiritual Administration of Ukrainian Muslims – Ummah, headed by a mufti of its own. Ummah also has rather impressive buildings, where besides a prayer space and offices, there is an educational establishment for children. It was instrumental in setting up the ill-fated Council of Representatives of Muslim Spiritual Administrations and Centres of Ukraine (2009–11) to balance the disproportionate power (particularly in distributing hajj quotas) of SAUM.

Besides these two, arguably, most powerful and visible Islamic administrations, Kiev hosts a plethora of other Muslim organisations, among them the already mentioned Kiev muftiate, at least one Salafi organisation of Crimean Tatars, a Shi'i group, and others. In this regard, Kiev is the centre of Muslim power and life in continental Ukraine, with other cities, particularly in western and central parts, having had rather small and inactive Muslim communities up until 2014.

Nonetheless, at least before its annexation by Russia, the most vibrant religious life was observable in Crimea (Kouts and Muratova 2014). After having returned to their motherland from exile, the Crimean Tatars proceeded to restore both their material and spiritual heritage – in a matter of a decade they restored to use several hundred historic mosques and built a dozen new ones, reopened several madrasas, and started publishing religious literature. As the returning Tatars had no financial capabilities to carry out these projects and the Ukrainian state did not make them available either, it fell on the shoulders of foreign-based and foreign-sponsored Ukrainian Muslim organisations to provide the funding. Next to SAUM and ar-Raid (lately, SAUM-Ummah), Arab and particularly Turkish governmental agencies and NGOs provided generous financial support accompanied by ideological underpinnings. So, for instance, Fethullah Gülen's movement built numerous educational institutions around Crimea and sent movement-affiliated Turkish teachers (Bogomolov et al. 2006: 90-91), with the Turkish Directorate for Religious Affairs (Diyanet) supplying Islamic literature and Turkish imams and also providing scholarships to Tatars seeking higher religious education at Turkish Islamic seminaries.

Next to strictly religious authorities like SAMC and SCMC, Crimean Tatars founded a lay political body – the Majlis of the Crimean Tatars – a surrogate parliament to steer their socio-economic life. Though, strictly speaking, not a religious institution, being composed of (Muslim) Tatar representatives the Majlis was widely regarded as a 'Muslim' organisation, albeit of an ethnic, that is, Crimean Tatar, nature. A close relationship between the Majlis and the SAMC (the Majlis had a representative on the SAMC board) made some regard them as a two-headed single structure (Kouts and Muratova 2014: 37–45). Consequently, those Crimean Muslims, both Tatar and Slav, who could not or did not want to be part of or follow the Majlis-SAMC line, founded and joined a number of alternative religious organisations, chiefly Hizb at-Tahrir and Salafis.

The rather wide spectrum of Muslim religious organisations was made possible by Ukraine's liberal (some would say indifferent) position in regards to the governance of religion (or at least Islam) in the country – there is neither a state religion nor a legal hierarchy of religions by, for instance, distinguishing them as 'historical', 'indigenous', 'foreign' or otherwise. Consequently, there is no formally (or even informally) recognised version of Islam as 'historical'/'traditional' to the country.

The liberal legal framework that allows unhindered formation of Muslim religious organisations first of all irritates Crimean Tatars affiliated with Majlis-SAMC, who see the Tatar community being torn apart by encroaching local and foreign ideologically based groupings. In this, one may see a cleavage between what most of the Tatars themselves consider 'traditional' Crimean (and by extension 'Ukrainian') Islam and what they regard as alien (read, unacceptable) forms of Islam, some of which are even seen as dangerous. In the end, the split in Crimea among religious Tatars is along 'traditional'/'non-traditional' Islam lines (Bogomolov *et al.* 2006: 108–110; Muratova 2015: 31).

However, this division is not the only one. With the two SAUMs representing alternative Islams, the Crimean Tatars also find themselves at different ends of the Islamic beliefs and practices' spectrum – while SAUM is seen by outsiders to be a crypto-Sufi organisation (closely affiliated if not directly controlled by the Habashi movement), SAUM-Ummah is accused by outsiders of being a representative organisation of the Muslim Brotherhood. To make things more complicated, SAUM itself labels SAUM-Ummah as Wahhabis while SAUM-Ummah in return labels SAUM followers Habashis.

Despite the numerical volume of Muslim religious organisations in Ukraine and the wide spectrum of Islamic beliefs and practices that they represent and propagate, the overall religiosity of the country's Muslim population may not always be that high. The available research results suggest, for instance, that only 18 per cent of Crimean Tatars consider themselves deeply religious (Muratova 2009: 11) and performance of the required basic duties like ritual prayer, fasting and paying of religious tax is also very low (Muratova 2009: 12–21). Thus, like in Russia, the restoration of historic mosques and building of new did not translate into a high demand for normative Islam offered in and through mosques. It may be inferred that converts constitute the most religious component among Ukraine's Muslims, with the bulk of them belonging to SAUM-Ummah or fringe groups like Hizb at-Tahrir and Salafis, though none of these groups are yet controlled by converts.

Most Tatars (80 per cent) perceive Islam as their historical-cultural tradition (Muratova 2009: 11) but are found to be unable to 'differentiate between customs and religious rituals' (Muratova 2015: 32). The arguably low levels of practice of normative Islam are somewhat compensated by practice of folk Islam, particularly among the Crimean Tatars, who, after returning to Crimea from exile, 'rediscovered' and recovered some of the 'sacred sites' – places of local pilgrimage and worship. On the other hand, Sufi Islam appears to be hardly practised in Crimea, though some Turkey-related Sufi organisations appeared on the peninsula as early as the beginning of the 1990s (Bogomolov *et al.* 2006: 101–2).

Civil and political participation of Muslims in Ukraine's public life, individually and through their organisations, is another aspect to consider. In the 1990s, there was even a Muslim party (founded in 1997). After having performed miserably in elections, it merged in 2006 with the Viktor Yanukovich (Prime Minister 2002–5, 2006–7, President 2010–14) bloc. During the 2014 events in Kiev, known as the Maidan Revolution, which dethroned Yanukovich, some of the Crimean Tatars took part in the sit-ins and subsequent clashes with police and armed forces loyal to the ill-fated President. Likewise, some of the Tatars took to the streets of Crimean cities to protest the imminent annexation of Crimea by Russia. In post-Maidan Ukraine, Mustafa Dzhamilev, the long-term Chairman of Majlis, was elected to parliament on the Ukrainian President's electoral list, along with his former deputy and successor in the post of the Chairman of Majlis, Refat Chubarov. Said Ismagilov, the leader (seen by his followers as the mufti) of SAUM-Ummah, attempted to get into parliament during the same elections but failed.

At the same time that Russia took over Crimea, Ukraine lost control to pro-Russian armed groups of parts of two eastern provinces – Donetsk and Lugansk (popularly known as 'Donbass' – the basin of Don river), where an estimated 100,000 Muslims had been living in 2014. And like in the Crimean case, though a certain percentage of the Donbass Muslims chose to remain loyal to Ukraine and flee the rebellious region, the bulk of the region's Muslims, chiefly comprised of Volga-Ural Tatars, stayed in the separatist-controlled areas, though their organisations (particularly pro- and pan-Ukrainian) scaled down their activities.

The Baltic States

As discussed in Chapter 2, Muslims have been living in the Eastern Baltic rim (chiefly in Lithuania) for several hundred years as citizens of the Grand Duchy of

Lithuania and, later, the Commonwealth of the Two Nations. Incorporation of the Estonian, Latvian and Lithuanian territories into the tsarist Russian Empire opened the ways, inter alia, for settlement of Muslims from other parts of Russia in these territories as itinerant tradesmen, state employees and military personnel. Though in Lithuania their influx did not alter the composition or practices of the local Muslim (Tatar) communities in any visible way, in both Latvia and Estonia it led to the emergence of the first ever Muslim religious communities in this part of Eastern Europe.

In Latvia, the first Muslim congregation in the future capital of Latvia, Riga, was established in 1902. It soon opened its prayer hall. By the beginning of the First World War, the Muslim population in the territory of present-day Latvia had grown to around 1,000. However, following the war, the Muslim population in newly independent Latvia shrank significantly to negligible numbers: by 1920 the Latvian Muslim community was estimated to be merely 150 and further declined to less than 70 by 1935.

As for Estonia, though according to the 1897 census only 109 Tatars (presumed to be Muslim) lived in the territory of today's Estonia, it is believed (Abiline 2008: 66–8) that the Muslim population at the turn of the twentieth century should have been well over 1,000. However, very much like in Latvia, the Muslim population of Estonia also declined and according to the 1934 census was only around 170 strong. The first Estonian Muslim congregation officially registered in 1928 in the eastern town of Narva to be followed by one in the capital Tallinn, registered in 1940.

Interwar Lithuania maintained a 1,000-strong Muslim community, chiefly comprised of autochthonous Lithuanian Tatars, mainly living compactly in the southern part of the country. Though by the beginning of the twentieth century a dozen historic Tatar mosques still remained in the territory of the former Grand Duchy of Lithuania, only two of them were situated in the territory of interwar Lithuania, with the rest in Poland and Soviet Byelorussia. In the interim capital Kaunas, a new brick mosque (the only one of its sort to this day in Lithuania) was built on the spot of a former makeshift mosque and opened its doors to worshippers in 1932. Muslims based in the capital attempted several times to unite the dispersed congregations into a Lithuania-wide Muslim umbrella organisation modelled after the one in Poland but failed to obtain consent from the provincial communities.

The Constitution of interwar Lithuania assured general religious freedom. However, no further legal regulations between the Lithuanian state and its Muslims were promulgated and the practical relations between them appear to have been based more on moral commitment and goodwill from the state's side rather than formal obligation. Loyalty to the state routinely openly professed by Lithuanian Tatars was generously rewarded by the government – it provided not only for salaries of imams but also the bulk of the funding for a new brick mosque in Kaunas. Though initiated by the Kaunas Tatars in 1930, the financial burden of bringing the mosque to completion from inception was seen by the Tatars to be the state's responsibility. Local Tatars (200 souls in the entire Kaunas region with just 70 in Kaunas city itself) could have never expected to collect the amount needed, thus they immediately proceeded with lobbying the government to make the funds available. The Kaunas mayor and other relevant authorities approved the construction.

At the dawn of the Second World War, after establising control over the lands formerly held by Poland in late 1939, Lithuania increased its Muslim community threefold. However, the Lithuanian authorities outlawed all former Polish-registered organisations, and among them, the Vilnius-based muftiate; its premises were locked and sealed, bringing to an end the Muslim institutions of interwar Poland.

Soon, however, in mid-1940, all three Baltic States were swallowed by the Soviet empire within the jurisdiction of which they remained for the following half a century, save for a brief period of Nazi occupation between 1941 and 1944. Islamic practices in the Baltic republics during the Soviet period were treated identically by local communist authorities as elsewhere in the USSR and the survival of the Muslim communities (chiefly in Lithuania) pretty much depended on kin relations, while the forms of Islam practised encompassed the basics and features of folk Islam. Of all the Baltic republics, only Lithuania had had mosques and of them only a single mosque in a remote southern village was left open to worshippers, attended mainly by local Lithuanian Tatars; other mosques were turned into warehouses or even demolished – like the one in the capital Vilnius.

The Baltic republics were flooded with colonists from other parts of the USSR. Since among the hundreds of thousands there was a rather significant share of those of Muslim cultural background (some 10,000 in each), one might expect that there must have also been devout Muslims among them. However, there is practically no ethnographic research on the religious practices of colonists of Muslim background in the Baltic republics. It might also be noted that unlike most of other communist-ruled countries and the Soviet republics, the Baltic republics did not host any foreign students from 'friendly' Asian or African countries, so when they re-emerged as independent countries, they – unlike Ukraine or Moldova, not to mention some Central European or Balkan states – had no presence in their territories of Muslims of student-turned-immigrant background.

With the re-emergence of the nationalistically minded independent Baltic States, scores of colonists (among them those of Muslim background) repatriated to Russia and other parts of the former USSR. Nonetheless, most Latvian, Estonian and a significant portion of Lithuanian Muslims in post-Soviet Baltic States to this day are settlers and descendants of settlers from the Soviet period, with Volga-Ural Tatars being the biggest ethnic group of Muslim background in both Latvia and Estonia (in Lithuania, it is Lithuanian Tatars), followed by Azerbaijanis in all three countries.

As the official censuses in Latvia do not include a question on religious identity, no official number for the size of the Muslim community in Latvia is available. However, there are figures for the ethnic composition of the Latvian population. The results of the 2011 census show that there were some 2,164 Tatars, 1,657 Azerbaijanis, 339 Uzbeks and 241 Kazakhs living in Latvia at that time. The 2011 census results showed that in Estonia, 1,508 persons aged fifteen and older identified themselves as Muslim. Of them, 40 per cent were Tatars and almost 20 per cent Azerbaijanis, with Estonians (almost 10 per cent) in third place. In Lithuania, the total number of Sunni Muslims (the number for Shi'is is unknown as the census questionnaire only included a question on Sunnis) that year was 2,727 of whom almost 53 per cent were Tatars and almost 14 per cent Lithuanians. It may be pointed out that, according to the 2011 census figures, almost half of the Lithuanian Tatars and two thirds of Estonia's Tatars did not identify with Islam.

The legal status of ethnic (and by extension religious) minorities in the three Baltic States falls into two distinctly different categories. Upon regaining independence, Lithuania decided on a 'zero option' approach: that is, awarding citizenship to practically all residents of the country at the time, irrespective of their ethnicity or religion. This naturally included those of Muslim background, both of autochthonous (like Lithuanian Tatars) and of immigrant (Volga-Ural Tatars, Azerbaijanis, Uzbeks, Tajiks, and the like) background. On the other hand, both Latvia and Estonia opted for a basically titular ethnicity-based granting of citizenship and the two countries ended up with a huge share of their population becoming aliens and in due course even stateless persons, as significant numbers of them decided against taking up any other citizenship, while others became Russian citizens.

If the three countries differ in the ethnic composition and citizenship status of their populations (and especially their Muslim component), they are also dissimilar with regard to the system of governance of religion. Registration of religious organisations with the state means their recognition by it. However, the level of recognition might differ, depending on the classification of religious communities in a given country. So, for instance, according to the law on religious communities, '[t]he state recognizes nine traditional religious communities and associations existing in Lithuania, which comprise a part of the historical, spiritual and social heritage of Lithuania' and Sunni Muslims are one of them. Latvia in practice also makes a distinction between 'traditional' and 'non-traditional' religious communities, with several Christian denominations and Judaists, but not Muslims, falling into the former category (Balodis 2010: 478). In Estonia, there is no such legal concept as 'traditional/non-traditional' religious communities.

In this respect, Sunni Muslims in Lithuania find themselves in an advantageous situation not only vis-à-vis Shi'is in the country but Muslims in both Latvia and Estonia, and indeed in much of Europe. The legal regulation in Lithuania has facilitated the formation and preservation of a unitary Muslim community, headed by an umbrella organisation (the Spiritual Centre of the Lithuanian Sunni Muslims-Muftiate), dominated since its establishment in 1998 by Lithuanian Tatars and recognised by the state as the sole representative body of all Sunni Muslims in the country. The chairman of the muftiate, the mufti, is recognised by the state as the ecclesiastical head of the entire Sunni Muslim community. All other Islamic organisations in Lithuania – mostly village and small-town communities (also dominated by Lithuanian Tatars) – are subordinate to the muftiate, since either their members serve on the muftiate's board or the muftiate approved of their formation. Unlike in Latvia and Estonia, where the state is prohibited from financing religious organisations and institutions, 'traditional' faith communities in Lithuania receive annual pay-outs from the state. As a result, through its official representative, the muftiate, Lithuania's Sunni Muslim community, as one of the 'traditional' faith communities, has been annually receiving modest amounts to be spent at its discretion.

The legal status of being a 'traditional' religious community, inter alia, allows Lithuanian Muslims to practise their religion outside of mosques. Not only can they found religious organisations and establish congregations unhindered but Sunni Muslim parents may request religious instruction in state schools; Muslim inmates in prisons, the sick in hospitals and military personnel may request halal meals and spiritual services in these state institutions and facilities; Muslims are allowed to slaughter their animals according to the Islamic requirements (by slitting the throat of the animal without prior stunning); wear 'Islamic' clothing in public and on official photos; perform *nikah* wedding ceremonies which are then duly recognised by the state; and so forth. Most of these privileges are not available to Muslims in Latvia and Estonia.

The institutional make-up of the Muslim communities in Latvia and Estonia significantly differ from that in Lithuania, but they are similar to each other – in both, the Muslim communities have split into several parallel, if not rival, congregations, some of which aspire to become representative of the whole country's Muslims. In neither, however, this has been achieved by any Muslim organisation, though some have gained a degree of recognition from the state of their status as more important and relevant. In Estonia, it is the Estonian Islamic Congregation, officially registered in 1994. In 2008, the Congregation established the Islamic Cultural Centre 'Turath', in whose activities (educational, public relations, publishing and missionary) Estonian converts to Islam play a prominent role. In 1995, a small splinter organisation, the Estonian Muslim Sunni Congregation, also based in Tallinn, was formed. Next to these two registered and Tallinn-based organisations, there are other informal groupings of Estonia's Muslims: the Azeri-dominated Nur Centre of Islamic Religion and Culture in Maardu (established in 2001) and the Islamic Crescent in Estonia (established in 2000).

The Latvian Islamic Community (including the Islamic Cultural Centre) in Riga, established in 1993, is arguably the main Islamic organisation in the country and is dominated by Volga-Ural Tatars and Bashkirs. The Community has several affiliate congregations all over the country, established with the express purpose of forming a union of Muslim congregations to increase their bargaining power vis-à-vis the state and to more successfully lobby for Muslims' rights in the country. However, the number of registered friendly congregations is so far not sufficient to attain the desired goal of a union. Moreover, in October 2009, after friction and disagreements in the Latvian Islamic Community, a splinter congregation, the Latvian Muslim Consultative Centre, was established in Riga. The second largest congregation in Latvia is the Daugavpils Islamic Centre, founded in 1994 and also dominated by Volga-Ural Tatars.

Arguably, the most visible sign of Muslim presence (and normative Islam) in an area is mosques, especially those which are purpose-built. While in several former Soviet republics, foremost Russia and Ukraine, Islamic revival expressed itself in the boom of mosque restoration and construction, the Baltic States trail behind on the matter of mosque building – not a single purpose-built mosque has been constructed in any Baltic state since their regaining of independence. This may in part be explained by the purported absence of demand – the size and distribution of Muslim communities may be taken as not calling for urgent measures to increase prayer space. However, the reality on the ground shows that Muslims in the Baltic States lack sufficient prayer space, especially on Fridays.

As indicated above, in the three Baltic States, only Lithuanian Tatars historically had purpose-built mosques. Currently, there are four historic Tatar-owned mosques, of which, however, only the one in Kaunas is used regularly. The muftiate has been negotiating for two decades with Vilnius Municipality over a plot of land for a new purpose-built mosque in the capital city but has not yet settled on one. Neither Estonia nor Latvia had purpose-built mosques, and local Muslims had been holding their Friday prayers either in rented apartments and halls or on private premises. However, both the Estonian and Latvian Muslims had also been contemplating building a mosque in the capitals of their respective countries. In Estonia, some tentative plans to build a mosque in central Tallinn had been announced in the 1990s by local Muslim businessmen and in the early 2000s by prospective foreign donors, but were not implemented. However, finally, in early 2009 the Estonian Islamic Congregation purchased (with a Saudi sponsor's money) a three-storey 1,000-square-metre former office building on the outskirts of Tallinn, which now houses the Islamic Cultural Centre 'Turath' (with rooms for lectures, a small library, and a reading room), the office of the head of the Estonian Islamic Congregation, and a prayer hall. Similarly, in 2005 the Latvian Islamic Community settled on a purchased apartment-turned-mosque on one of the major thoroughfares of Riga. The Lithuanian muftiate also followed suit and in 2013 acquired new space to accommodate worshippers.

However, even with these recent developments, the religious activities of Muslim communities in the Baltic States remain minimal. First of all, like elsewhere in the former USSR, this is because a significant share of nominal Muslims, and particularly autochthonous Muslims and those of colonist background, are secularised to the point that if they consider themselves to be Muslims at all, they rarely perform any religious rituals or otherwise take part in community activities. The leader of the Latvian Islamic community back in 2009 estimated the number of Muslims to be in the range of 5,000, but added that only 10 per cent were practising. If mosque attendance on Fridays could serve as a criterion for measuring religiosity, one may conclude that the number of practising Muslims in Lithuania and Estonia is around the same as in Latvia. In all three countries, the majority of practising Muslims appear to come from the immigrant and convert segments. The converts, in fact, are representatives of revivalist Islam in the Baltic States with some among them openly identifying as Salafi (Račius and Norvilaitė 2014).

So, while the official Muslim organisations in the Baltic States nominally represent normative Islam (in Lithuania, the muftiate identifies with the classical Hanafi tradition), converts shun (or are denied, as in Estonia) membership in these organisations, and often choose to individually and in groups (through forming virtual communities) position themselves as representatives of what they themselves consider 'true' Islam. Thus, the spectrum of forms of religiosity in the Baltic States lacks two essential classical dimensions – Sufism and folk Islam. While the first has never historically existed in the territory of the Baltic States and has not yet been introduced in the post-Soviet era, at least not in its classical forms, the second, having been the main form of Islam practised among Lithuanian Tatars for centuries, all but disappeared during the Soviet period and has never recovered. Its carriers, the Tatars, though numerically still the majority, are (along with those of colonist background) the least religious among Lithuania's inhabitants of Muslim background.

Belarus

Belarus remains (or rather, since the coming to power in 1994 of Alexander Lukashenko gradually became) the most reclusive state not only in Eastern but in all of Europe. The authoritarian regime of Lukashenko, due to its consistent and numerous violations of human and citizen rights, led to the country being regarded by the Council of Europe as unfit for membership. Due to censorship and other restrictions on academic, media and other information freedoms, there is a dire lack of reliable information and data on Muslims in Belarus. Therefore, all information in this section should be treated as tentative and with caution.

The presence of Muslims in the territory of the present-day state of Belarus dates back to the same time as in Lithuania, because in the Middle Ages the Belarusian territory was the central part of the Grand Duchy of Lithuania. Therefore, historically speaking, Belarusian and Lithuanian Muslims are the same people – Lithuanian Tatars – who until the demise of the Russian Empire in the 1910s formed a single community. However, while the Lithuanian (and Polish) Muslims were able to nurture their distinct ethno-confessional culture in the twenty-year period between the two world wars, the Belarusian (then called Byelorussian) Muslims, almost immediately following the removal of the tsarist regime, found themselves under the suffocating rule of Bolsheviks and later communists, which they, like other Muslims of the USSR, had to endure to the very end of the Soviet empire.

With the shifting of borders westwards in the aftermath of the Second World War, even more Tatars found themselves within the borders of Soviet Byelorussia, though some were forcefully repatriated to Poland or went into exile in the West. The fate of those who remained did not differ essentially from that of other Muslim communities of the USSR: all but one of their historical mosques were closed or destroyed (for example, the brick mosque of the capital city Minsk, built in 1902 in place of a wooden mosque first built at the end of the sixteenth century, which was demolished in 1962), imams dismissed and some prosecuted, religious education practically banned. The Belarusian Muslim religious practices survived only in the folk Islam form, practised by local Tatars.

Like other European constituent Soviet republics, Byelorussia received its share of colonists from Muslim-majority regions of the USSR. By 1989, next to over 12,500 Tatars (apparently, including autochthonous Tatars), there were over 5,000 Azerbaijanis, 3,500 Uzbeks, 2,200 Kazakhs and almost 800 Turkmen, most, if not all, of whom must have been of Muslim cultural background. However, as elsewhere, even when believers, the colonists did not exhibit their religion and did not attempt to form religious communities. Instead, the devout among them individually performed their religious duties in private or joined the Tatars in their religion-related celebrations. Byelorussia also hosted some of the student-turned-immigrants from the Middle East and other Muslim-majority countries in Asia and Africa. A few of them settled down and even started families. Though in the aftermath of the collapse of the USSR some of the colonists and their progeny repatriated (notably, the Tatar community shrank to just over 7,300 by 2009), the majority stayed. Thus, the Muslim population of post-Soviet Belarus is comprised primarily of three constituent segments: the autochthonous Tatars, Central Asian and Caucasian colonists and their progeny, and recent immigrants from the Middle East (1,330 Arabs in 2009) and further afield. There are also some estimated 300 Slavs who have converted to Islam. Though there are no official numbers, the estimated number of people of Muslim background in Belarus might be up to a few tens of thousands, with the majority of them of Soviet colonist background. The overwhelming majority of Muslims in Belarus are of Sunni origins (with Tatars nominally of the Hanafi legal tradition), though Shi'i Azerbaijanis have their own registered religious community.

For the first few years of independence after the demise of the USSR, when both state and society seemed to be on a democratisation and liberalisation course, autochthonous Tatar Muslims proceeded with the reconstitution and official registration of their religious groups (with only one having functioned during the Soviet period), and also reclaimed part of their communal property, including any mosques that were still standing. To replace the Soviet-demolished mosque in Minsk, Belarusian Muslims started building a new mosque. Though the whole process took almost two decades (with the construction itself having taken more than a decade), the mosque, with a capacity of 1,500, was finally completed in 2016.

In 1994, the first umbrella organisation uniting two dozen, chiefly Tatar-controlled Muslim communities – the Muslim Religious Association in the Republic of Belarus (MRA) – was established, headed by a mufti. However, it split in 2002 and a rival Muslim Spiritual Board of the Republic of Belarus (MSB) was registered. Yet, the latter attracted just one fifth of the twenty five Muslim communities in the country. The MRA, as a representative of normative Islam, during its two decades of existence established close relations with both Russian Islamic administrations (particularly in Tatarstan) and Muslim (Tatar) organisations in Poland, Lithuania and the Ukraine/Crimea. The MSB, in turn, though not known for having any Muslim Brotherhood leanings, has established working relations with the Ukrainian SAUM-Ummah. Several registered local Muslim communities chose to function independently of the two umbrella Islamic administrations.

The Belarusian state recognises Islam as one of the traditional faiths in the country (very much like in Lithuania and Poland, it is understood to be represented, if not 'owned' by indigenous Tatars). However, due to its authoritarian nature, the regime seeks to closely monitor and control the communal activities of Muslims, like other religious communities. With this in mind, the regime seeks to ensure that the Islam practised in the country is the accepted 'traditional' Islam (for this reason, only citizens may be the heads of Muslim religious organisations) and it persecutes any forms deemed deviant. For instance, in the early 2000s, the state authorities refused to register the Ahmadi community.[2] In 2015, the security services made public information on the arrests of some twenty persons who allegedly belonged to an informal Muslim revivalist group (a crime in itself, as the law prohibits the functioning of non-registered religious groups) variably presented as either Salafi or Hizb at-Tahrir. This was not only the first time in Belarusian history that revivalist Muslims had been arrested but also the first time it became publicly known that there are Muslim revivalists in the country. Any revivalist tendencies are met with suspicion not only by the state but also by the Tatar community, which on the one hand jealously guards its 'traditionalist' Islam and on the other wants to make sure the state does not start associating them with any unacceptable (illegal) innovations in beliefs and practices.

Furthermore, the regime has on some occasions instrumentalised local Muslim organisations and their leaderships in its drive to suppress political and social opposition: for instance, in 2006, when the regime sought to punish the chief editor of an oppositional newspaper and get it shut down for reprinting the famous drawings of the Prophet Muhammad originally published in a Danish daily. It pressurised the mufti of the MSB to file a suit against the editor and, although the editor had apologised to both the mufti and all Belarusian Muslims and the mufti himself had asked the court for a more lenient punishment, the regime-controlled court both sentenced the editor and closed the newspaper.

Centuries-practised Tatar folk Islam barely survived the Soviet period and became, as in Lithuania and to a certain extent Poland, more of an ethnographic feature of the local Tatar community. Though there is insufficient research-based evidence, it is believed that the Tatar and colonist segments of the Belarusian Muslim community exhibit as little religious interest as those in Lithuania, Latvia, Estonia and Poland. On the other hand, the cult of Kuntus, a local shepherd-turned-saint, has survived and not only among Belarusian Tatars; some of the Lithuanian and Polish Tatars also regard him with esteem and perform improvised pilgrimages to his grave. Therefore, one may say that for the past quarter of a century Islam in Belarus has been almost insulated and conserved in a sort of indigenous quazi-legalist-cum-folk form acceptable to the state but also the overwhelming majority of local Tatars.

Moldova

When it comes to the presence of Muslims in its territory, Moldova shares a number of similarities with Ukraine but also with the Central European countries. Apart from the modest number of Muslims of student-turned-immigrant background and 'colonists' from other Soviet regions who started coming to Moldova (then still called Moldavia) in the last decades of the existence of the USSR, it has not had any historical Muslim community. Since its independence (1991), Moldova took in even more students from the Middle East and beyond, many of whom chose to stay in the country after their graduation. Like elsewhere in Europe, marriages with local women followed, producing Muslim progeny of mixed parentage. Therefore, as in the Central European countries, today the majority of Moldova's Muslims are of immigrant (Soviet-time 'colonist' and from the Middle East) background with a segment of converts.

Though the Moldovan population censuses do include questions on religious identity of its inhabitants, the available 'precise' figures are not at all reliable. This is not least because the most recent publicly available official figures are from 2004 but also because the official number of 1,667 Muslims is considered (by local Muslims and researchers alike) to be way too low even for the year of the census and was definitely outdated by the mid-2010s. The reality on the ground suggests that the real numbers might indeed be closer to 5,000. The 2004 census results indicate that the overwhelming majority of Muslims in Moldova in 2004 came from the ethnic groups of the former USSR, namely Tatars (974), Azeris (891), Uzbeks (416), Kazakhs (256), Turkmens (220), Tajiks (211) and Chechens (108) but also from among the Turks (269) and Arabs (259).

In the context of the post-communist Eastern European countries, Moldova is rather unique in terms of institutionalisation and acceptance of Islam in its territory. As Moldovan laws favour the Orthodox Church and they regard Orthodox Christianity as the national religion, all other faith communities have a hard time attaining official recognition by the state as religious entities, though may function as NGOs with few constraints. The path to formal recognition (through official registration) of the first Muslim religious organisation, the Islamic League of the Republic of Moldova, proved to be exceptionally long and bumpy – it was finally registered only in 2011. Its leadership reported harassment from the security services when still unregistered and practically considered illegal; Islam was publicly vilified as not only an alien religion but as a dangerous 'sect', particularly by the Moldovan Orthodox Church. The institutionalisation of its status, however, did not spare the Islamic League from being continually treated by some segments of society – the Orthodox Church and some political parties (like the Communist Party) – as a 'terrorist-breeding nest'. This was evident in the protests organised by the Orthodox Church against the establishment of the League's Islamic Centre in a building it had purchased in an industrial area on the outskirts of the capital city Chişinău.

Although the Moldovan Muslim *umma* is numerically tiny, it nonetheless is diverse, and not only in ethnic terms. As Moldova has not had any experience or presence of classical forms of Islam – legalist, mystical or folk – Muslims in post-communist Moldova mainly represent the part of the theologico-ideological spectrum ranging from moderate revivalist to Salafi Islam. The Islamic League of the Republic of Moldova – the sole Muslim organisation registered as a religious entity, whose membership is multi-ethnic comprising mainly Arabs and local converts – appears to be leaning towards the ideology of the Muslim Brotherhood. Its close cooperation with a sister-organisation SAUM-Ummah in

Ukraine, also of a Muslim Brotherhood leaning, attests to this inclination of the Moldovan Islamic League.

The Foundation for the Support of the Islamic Culture and Traditions in Moldova, which opened a six-storey headquarters in central Chişinău in 2015, has been around since at least the early 2000s (it was registered as an NGO in 2001). Besides being an exclusively Turkish group, it appears to be either a direct branch of the Gülen movement or at least closely related to it. What strikes a visitor to its premises, and to those owned by the League, is their spaciousness – the prayer halls in both may accommodate hundreds of worshippers at one time and dining facilities are also available for up to a hundred people. The League plans to open a kindergarden on the upper floor of its headquarters and the Foundation has a number of classrooms including a computer lab.

Moldova hosts a small but vibrant Salafi community registered (in 2006) as an NGO, Gardens of Peace. However, the Salafi community has been far less fortunate than the above mentioned organisations, particularly the Islamic League. It has been unable to acquire its own premises, has not been allowed to register as a religious organisation and the leader of the community – a Tatar originating from Russia – has been taken to court by the authorities on a number of charges. The membership of this organisation appears to come predominantly from the Middle East. Though the Islamic League has invited the Gardens of Peace to unite with the League under its leadership, this way increasing the Muslims' bargaining power with the state, the Gardens' leadership perceive the League to be not Islamic enough in its ideology and practical implementation of Islamic requirements. By refusing to unite with the League the Gardens risk not only remaining in a legal limbo – it does not expect to be registered as a religious organisation – but also risks becoming increasingly vulnerable in the face of the securitisation of the 'Islam question' in the country, related to the perceived threat stemming from ISIS and similar groups.

Linguistically, the Moldovan population can be divided into two broad groups – the Romanian-speaking majority (there is no distinct 'Moldovan' language and Romanian is the mother-tongue of ethnic Moldovans) and the Russian-speaking minority. However, while the Russian speakers tend not to be able to communicate in Romanian, the overwhelming majority of Moldovans speak Russian. The liguistic and cultural affinity, as well as physical proximity, allows Moldovan Muslims to maintain close relations with Muslim organisations in Romania (many Moldovans also hold Romanian passports) but also in Ukraine and even Russia. Thus, in a broader picture, the religious activities of the Moldovan Muslim communities, and chiefly the Islamic League (particularly, their Romanian-speaking members), may be seen in effect as being part of the larger Romanian-speaking Muslim scene.

CHAPTER 4

Successor states of Yugoslavia

The Socialist Federal Republic of Yugoslavia and its legacy

From the emergence of the South Slav (Yugoslavian) state in 1918, which united Slav-inhabited lands in the Western and Central Balkans formerly held by the Ottoman Empire and also parts of the extinct Austro-Hungarian Empire, in absolute numbers its Muslims were the largest population in all of South-eastern Europe. They were mainly comprised of two distinct ethnic groups – Serbo-Croatian and Albanian speakers – who not only lived in different, albeit bordering, regions of the country, but also had distinct ethno-confessional cultures. Therefore, one should think of them in terms of two major distinct Muslim communities. Institutionally, this difference in the Socialist Federal Republic of Yugoslavia (SFRY) was both acknowledged and reinforced by the division of the Yugoslav Muslim spiritual-administrative authority into four organisations: one based in Sarajevo (for Bosnia, Croatia and Slovenia), others in Skopje (Macedonia), Podgorica (Montenegro) and Prishtina (for Serbia, including Kosovo).

One also should bear in mind that in socialist Yugoslavia, officially identifying as Muslim, from 1961, meant identifying as 'Muslim in the ethnic sense' and, from 1971, as 'Muslim in a national sense', whose mother tongue was held to be Serbo-Croatian. Being religious or not was officially an irrelevance. Consequently, a Muslim by ethnicity/nationality could have been a non-Muslim by religion – an atheist or at least an agnostic – while an Albanian could have been a Muslim only by religion and not by ethnicity/nationality. As is shown below, Muslim as ethnicity has survived socialist Yugoslavia and is still in random use in practically all post-Yugoslav states.

Socialist Yugoslavia, which emerged in 1946, comprised practically the same territories as the pre-Second World War kingdom and inherited not only the same Muslim populations but also their institutional structures. Very much like elsewhere in communist-ruled Eastern Europe, socialist authorities in Yugoslavia proceeded with the persecution of religion, which in the first decade of the regime was particularly virulent. In 1946 the regime abolished the Shari'a courts, then in 1952 shut down primary religious schools, placed a virtual ban on Sufi activities and proceeded with the expropriation of *waqf* properties (Merdjanova 2013: 31). Of over forty madrasas in pre-Second World War

Bosnia, by 1949 the communist authorities only allowed one to continue offering Islamic education in the entire SFRY. There were also forced migrations of Yugoslav Muslims akin to those in the wake of the secession of the former Ottoman provinces in Europe. So,

> the 'voluntary' migration treaty between Tito and Prime Minister Menderes led to the exodus of 300,000 Muslims of all ethnic groups in Yugoslavia, via Skopje to Turkey, between 1953 and 1960. The 1953 migrations broke the back of the Turkish communities in Macedonia, also substantially reducing the numbers of other Muslim communities, particularly in the Sandžak, the homeland of most of Turkey's Bosniaks. (Öktem 2011: 157; see also Pačariz 2016: 97–161)

However, having parted ways with the USSR back in 1948, and within the framework for founding the bloc of 'non-aligned' states in 1961 – among which was a number of Muslim-majority or large Muslim-minorities-containing countries – from the 1960s the Yugoslav government adjusted its religious policies by relaxing restrictions on religious organisations and practices. The Islamic Community – the official Islamic body – was given more power in the actual administration of internal Islamic affairs and its officials made to represent the Yugoslavian Muslims abroad; censorship was relaxed, Islamic religious education and public propagation of Islam allowed (inter alia through the IC's bi-weekly newspaper *Preporod*, 'Renaissance', the first issue of which appeared in 1970); and Muslims permitted to travel abroad for pilgrimage and religious studies (Karčić 2015: 100–18). In the early 1970s, the authorities even allowed the creation of two Sufi organisations, one of which, the Community of Islamic Dervish Orders of Yugoslavia (ZIDRA, established in 1974), covering mainly Albanian Sufi brotherhoods in Kosovo and Macedonia, was not only independent of the Islamic Community but also somewhat antagonistic towards it. The other organisation, Tarikatski Centar, based in Bosnia-Herzegovina, was under the formal supervision of the Bosnian Islamic administration. Finally, in 1977, the government even allowed a Faculty of Islamic Studies to be opened in Sarajevo.

The disintegration of the SFRY began in late 1990, when Slovenia's population overwhelmingly voted in a referendum in favour of secession from the SFRY. Slovenia's independence in 1991 was followed the same year by that of Croatia and Macedonia and, the next year, by that of Bosnia. That left the Federal State of Yugoslavia composed of only Serbia and Montenegro; the latter split in 2006 leaving Serbia on its own, which itself had been downsized by secession of its province of Kosovo in 1999. Out of the ruins of Yugoslavia, seven sovereign nation states emerged, each with its own titular ethnicity forming a clear majority of the population, the exception being Bosnia and Herzegovina where ethnic Bosniaks are just over half (50.11 per cent according to the 2013 census) of the population.

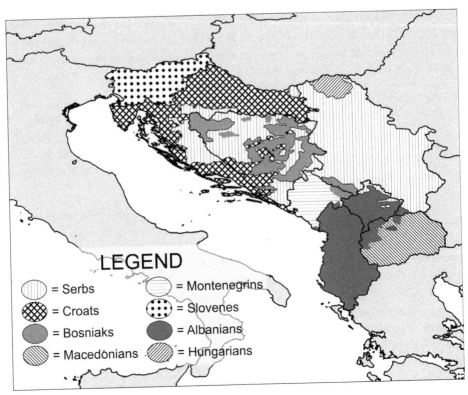

Map 4.1 Ethnic composition of Yugoslavia and Albania
Compiled by Davide Calzoni

As for the Muslim populations in these successor states, Kosovo has the highest volume, where (Albanian) Muslims make up the absolute majority (over 90 per cent), followed by Bosnia (almost 51 per cent), Macedonia (estimated at between 30 and 35 per cent) and Montenegro (around 20 per cent). Serbia has significantly fewer Muslims (between 3 and 4 per cent) and Slovenia and Croatia (the only two Catholic-majority and incidentally, EU member states as of 2017) have an even lower share (2.5 and 1.5 per cent respectively). In practically all the successor states, there are both Bosniak and Albanian Muslim minorities, though ethnic Albanians as indigenous minorities concentrate primarily in Macedonia, Montenegro and Serbia, while autochthonous Bosniaks dominate in the Serbian and Montenegrin parts of Sandžak. Roma Muslims are also to be found across the region. Turks are found mainly in Macedonia and Kosovo, which are also home to indigenous Slavic-speaking Muslim groups – Torbeshis in Macedonia and Goranis in Kosovo.

Though in the SFRY Islam had never been banned and all Muslims – not only those adhering to normative, but also mystical Islam – could openly practise their religion, one still may talk of revival and reappearance of Islam in post-Yugoslav lands. Faced with the resurgence of Muslim religiosity and the rise of their religious (and political) consciousness, the governments of the new states had to create adequate policies pertaining to governance of Islam (and ultimately the national groups associated with it). Elbasani argues that

> [a]lthough the management of Islam depended upon the demographic and historical particularities of each entity, the use of state's muscles to discipline it remained the same. Communist style centralization and modernization thus bequeathed vestiges of largely interventionist and occasionally hostile state policies to the post-Communist institutional models of managing Islam. (Elbasani 2015: 3)

This shared communist Yugoslavian legacy notwithstanding, due to a number of circumstances (the main among which concern the nature, identity, size and aspirations of respective Muslim populations) the institutionalisation and governance of Islam in them differs significantly. Ultimately, the status and position of Muslim communities also differ from country to country. This will be made evident in the following sections. However, there are also common traits.

One common trait in the post-Yugoslav space, arguably shared with other post-socialist Balkan countries, particularly Bulgaria and Albania, is that in a number of cases the new political elites (among them even in Muslim-majority Kosovo) took to view Islam and Muslims as 'some kind of ethnic "fifth column", remnants of a bygone era' (Elbasani and Roy 2015: 461); in other words, an inherited headache. In the Eastern Balkans, Islam had been and remains associated politically with Ottomanism and culturally with Turkishness, both of which are despised and rejected by Balkan non-Muslims. Consequently, the local Muslim communities instantly came to be suspected by ex-Yugoslav non-Muslims of harbouring, if not revanchist, then at least separatist and irredentist aspirations. Some of them proved to be true – Serbia lost Kosovo and has been experiencing problems with the loyalty of Muslims of Sandžak and the Preševo Valley, and Macedonia was shaken in 2001 by an inter-ethnic (which some would see as also inter-confessional) conflict.

Another common trait is that, in the wake of the collapse of the SFRY, Islam was nationalised in practically all the former constituent units; Muslim communities in every former Yugoslav Republic proceeded with founding autonomous (autocephalous) Islamic administrations. Admittedly, they arose from the communist-era branches of the pan-Yugoslavian Islamic Community but the determining factor in their emergence was the ethnic divisions, if not cleavages, among Yugoslavia's Muslims. So, while nationalising Islam, Muslims of the crumbling SFRY also effectively ethnicised it, a notable exception being the Montenegrin case.

Though it was not undertaken by the states, nationalisation of institutionalised Islam became useful to governing elites as among other things it also meant the taming of Islam/Muslims – the officially recognised (and they expected, co-opted and easily controlled and coerced, if be need) national institutions were to serve as (sole) representatives and custodians of 'acceptable' Islam and were entrusted by the state to 'issue binding decisions in all administrative and spiritual issues pertinent to the Muslim community' (Elbasani and Roy 2015: 461). At the same time, arguably, '[p]olicies of nationalization-cum-etatization of Islam often served worldly interests of subjecting religion to the service of concrete political projects and agendas' (Elbasani 2015: 3). As an example of this, Abazović argues that the

> early postsocialist period in Bosnia and Herzegovina has been characterized by powerful 'nationalization of sacral' and 'sacralization of national'. In other words, national political ideologies have requested (and have been granted) the support from religious doctrines in order to legitimize new establishments. Bosnian Muslims were no exception. Such interdependence ('symbiosis') of new ruling elites and religious leadership resulted in an understanding that solving 'religious issues' can be done in the field of politics, while position of religious institutions (in this case Islamic Community) in politics becomes more and more central. (Abazović 2007: 54–5)

One may argue, however, that the emergence of national autocephalous Islamic administrations in fact is nothing new in the Yugoslav space – it had all started with the founding of the first Islamic administrations independent of the political or religious authorities in Istanbul towards the end of the nineteenth century in both Bosnia (then under Austro-Hungarian rule) and (by then, sovereign) Montenegro, and continued through the monarchical and communist periods in the form of pan-Yugoslav Islamic administrations with their republican branches.

On the other hand, there has been a development in the opposite direction: some of those newly emergent, ethnically based Islamic administrations (chiefly Bosniak, as those in Slovenia, Croatia and the Serbian part of Sandžak) sought to cluster around the strongest among them (in this case, the Bosnian Islamic Community), even if that meant allegiance to a *de jure* foreign Islamic administration. This way, the vestiges of the pan-Yugoslav Islamic administration have survived to a certain degree in the Western Balkans, but also brought friction not only between state and local Islamic administrations but also between the concerned states.

Despite, or rather as a reaction to, the processes of institutionalisation-cum-nationalisation of Islam and the bureaucratisation of its administrative structures in the post-Yugoslav countries, a dissenting major tendency revealed itself in practically all the states – that of the individualisation of religiosity. This dissention took the shape of alternative forms of religiosity to those promoted by the official Islamic administrations and presented as 'traditional' to the land. They encompassed chiefly revivalist beliefs and practices, many of which, though not new in the broader world, until the collapse of socialist Yugoslavia were unheard of in this region, much less cultivated. Muslim groups independent of, and at times hostile and even rival to, the officially espoused Islam emerged to manifest an experience of religiosity that has become 'detached from organized religion and official doctrinal prescriptions' (Elbasani and Roy 2015: 458). In the words of Elbasani and Roy (2015: 458), the result of this ongoing novel turn 'is the revival of Islam as faith, not as a collective identity or organized form of "belonging"'. Therefore, the 'return of the Sacred' to the post-Yugoslav states has been accompanied not only by the resurgence of institutionalised Islam but also of its opposite: individualisation and privatisation, with the emergence of 'autonomous "faith communities", informal structures where members of an ethno-national group or subgroup endeavour to build a community of believers within a larger group of "cultural Muslims"' (Elbasani and Roy 2015: 466).

Ultimately, as argued by Elbasani and Roy, the 'gap between state-organized religion featuring its own actors, ideas and mechanisms of diffusion, on the one hand, and informal faith communities embracing alternative ideas, sources and networks, on the other, represents the emergence of different visions of Islam' (Elbasani and Roy 2015: 469) in the post-Yugoslav space, this way revealing the ever-widening spectrum of forms of Islamic religiosity on national, communal and individual levels.

Bosnia and Herzegovina

Statistically, Bosnia and Herzegovina (BiH) has the largest population of Muslim background not only among the ex-Yugoslav states but in the entire Balkan region. In fact, its 1,790,000-strong Muslim community is the second largest among the post-communist/post-socialist Eastern European states – only Russia has a bigger community. Percentage-wise, Bosnia ranks the third in Eastern Europe, trailing behind the two Albanian- (and Muslim-) majority countries: Kosovo and Albania.

For a long time the exact numbers and distribution of Muslims in the country remained obscure as there were no censuses conducted and the results of the census of 2013, the first in twenty years of independence, were withheld for some three years from the public. The previous census, from 1991, when Bosnia was still part of the SFRY, had returned 43.5 per cent Muslim. However, as 'Muslim' then meant 'nationality' rather than religious identity (therefore, Muslim Albanians were counted as 'Albanians', not 'Muslims') and there was no question in the census on religious affiliation, one cannot conclude with any confidence how many Muslims 'in the religious sense' were living in Bosnia in the last days of the SFRY.

With the results of the 2013 census made public, it became evident that Muslims constituted 50.7 per cent of the population in that year. The over-whelming majority of BiH Muslims are Bosniaks, officially recognised as a separate ethnic – and indeed the titular – group since 1993, distinct from both Serbs and Croats. Until then, in socialist Yugoslavia, most of them were identified as 'Muslims in the ethnic sense' (from 1961) and later (from 1971) as 'Muslims in a national sense', held to be speaking the same Serbo-Croatian language as Serbs and Croats. Though, ideally speaking, neither the socialist-era designation of 'Muslim' nor the current 'Bosniak' carry by default a religious identity and affiliation (there have been numerous atheist Muslim communists in the SFRY and there are many Bosniaks who do not identify with Islam) there nonetheless is a tendency, both internally and outside of the country, to associate Bosniaks with Islam. Bougarel argues that 'the adoption of the national label "Bosniak" went hand in hand with a sustained effort by the SDA [then the major Bosniak political party] and the religious institutions to put Islam at the heart of this new Bosniak national identity' (Bougarel 2005: 14). The ideological basis for this was 'The Islamic Declaration: a Programme for the Islamization of Muslims and the Muslim Peoples' written by Alija Izetbegović, the leader of the SDA and the first Bosnian president. Indeed, nowhere else in post-communist Eastern Europe has Islam been nationalised as it has in BiH. In the words of Alibašić,

> [r]eligious and national identities in their [Bosnian Muslim] case are reinforcing each other and it is often difficult to say where Islam stops and national culture begins. Sometimes it seems that Islam is at the service of Bosniak nationhood as much as the other way around. (Alibašić 2014: 439)

Therefore, Catholic or Orthodox Bosniak would sound a contradiction in terms. However, there is a completely religious-background-free supra-ethnic designation: Bosnian, that is, a national of Bosnia and Herzegovina. Consequently, there may be Muslim non-Bosniak Bosnians – for instance, Albanians, Roma, Turks, but also Croat and Serb converts. The difference between the numbers of Bosniaks and Muslims in the 2013 census attests to this distinction: there were 21,000 more Muslims than Bosniaks in the country. The number of agnostics, atheists and non-declared, according to the census results stood at almost 78,000.

Though there had been a Muslim presence for more than half a millennium, the birth and formation of autonomous Bosnian Muslim religious institutions could be traced back to the Austro-Hungarian period (1878–1918). After having been part of the ruling Muslim majority in the Ottoman state for over 400 years, Bosnian Muslims found themselves a double (ethnic and religious) minority, effectively cut off from the Islamic authorities in Istanbul, in an overwhelmingly Catholic state. Though a number of Muslims (estimated to have been up to 150,000) moved to the remaining parts of the Ottoman Empire in both Europe and Anatolia, the majority stayed and reconciled with becoming Austro-Hungarian subjects and later, after the 1908 annexation, its citizens. But before that, Bosnian Muslims were accorded their own religious institutions; in 1882, the imperial government created something resembling the Russian practice: the office of *reis ul-ulama*, the supreme administrative and spiritual leader of all Muslims in the territory of Bosnia. Appointed by the Habsburg monarch, the *reis* presided over the council of the men of religion (*medžlis ul-ulama*), which was in charge of religion-related Muslim affairs. It also had the power to nominate regional muftis who, as Habsburg state employees, were paid out of the coffers of the state. Their primary tasks were issuing fatwas (legal opinions) to individual and corporate petitioners as well as overseeing religious educational establishments in the areas under their jurisdiction (Merdjanova 2013: 30).

In 1909, a new 'Statute for Autonomous Administration of Islamic Religious, Waqf and Educational Affairs in Bosnia and Herzegovina' was promulgated by the imperial government, arguably 'in response to a growing Bosniak movement for greater religious, cultural, and educational autonomy in the framework of the Austro-Hungarian Empire' (Merdjanova 2013: 30), which accorded more freedom to Muslims in not only choosing their leader but administering their religious affairs (Karčić 1997). Finally, not long before the First World War, in 1912 the Austro-Hungarian state even formally recognised Islam through a special law, *Islamgesetz*; this was the first time in Europe that a non-Muslim state had done that.

After the First World War, in the aftermath of the collapse of the Austro-Hungarian Empire, the Bosnian territory was incorporated into the Kingdom of Serbs, Croats and Slovenes (renamed in 1929 as the Kingdom of Yugoslavia – the kingdom of 'southern Slavs'). Besides the Bosnian Muslims, there were several other sizeable Muslim communities living elsewhere in the territory of the new state, so initially, the government proceeded with creating four separate autonomous Islamic administrations, one of them, naturally, in Bosnia. However, with a turn toward authoritarian rule with centralising tendencies, a central Islamic administration with headquarters in the kingdom's capital Belgrade was created in 1930, relegating the Sarajevo- (the Bosnian capital) based administration to a lesser, subordinate status (Sorabji 1989: 121). The central Board of Elders itself was firmly under state control. However, moving the headquarters of the Islamic administration away from Sarajevo and '[t]he imposition of the concept of Yugoslavism, with its centralization impulses, compromised the territorial integrity of Bosnia and fostered a stronger communal solidarity among Bosnian Muslims, even though this shared communal identity did not solidify into national self-determination' (Merdjanova 2013: 31). Nonetheless, political and other pressure from the Bosnian Muslim side led to yet another reform of the Islamic administrative bodies and resulted in the office of *reis ul-ulama* being returned to Sarajevo, which then 'regained its status as the religious and cultural center of Muslims in this part of the Balkans' (Merdjanova 2013: 31).

With the emergence of the communist-ruled post-Second World War SFRY, like the rest of Yugoslavian Muslims, Bosnian Muslims had to endure years of repression with severe restrictions on the activities of their spiritual-administrative institutions, though these were eased from the 1960s. However, even if the Bosnian Islamic institutions did not endure the same level of pressure from the communist regime during the later decades of the communist period as their counterparts in the USSR, the Islamic Community was still expected to follow the state's stance on religion and its place and role in both socialist Yugoslav society and the state. Through self-censorship it did indeed outwardly mimic the state's line – which prevented it from being truly representative of local Muslim believers. As Sorabji discovered during her fieldwork research in 1980s Sarajevo, the Islamic Community was

> treated by Muslims very much as they treat secular authorities. Thus when one asks what the Islamska Zajednica [Islamic Community] is or what it does, no-one suggests that it provides guidance in matters of faith, that it protects or represents Islam in Bosnia or that its members are the wisest and best of Muslims . . . Like the secular authorities the Islamska Zajednica is seen as a body to be contributed to, benefited from and otherwise dealt with; it is not taken as the spiritual or social centre of religious life, just as the secular authorities are not taken as embodying the political will of the people. (Sorabji 1989: 148)

Therefore, the survival of living Islam in communist-era Bosnia, as elsewhere in Eastern Europe, depended to a great degree on devout Muslim individuals. It has been suggested (Bringa 1996) that it was primarily women who preserved Islamic beliefs and practices on a personal level. Not being tied to outwardly atheist communist structures as much as men were, women purportedly had more liberty not only to practise Islam themselves but to also teach it to their children.

The independence war of 1992–5 significantly altered the demographic balance and distribution of the country's constituent ethnic groups. In certain areas (foremost in the eastern part of the country bordering Serbia, which after the war became a separate entity, 'the Republic of Serbs' – RS), due to ethnic cleansing of genocidal proportions, forced evictions and other means of intimidation, the share of Muslims was reduced to a negligible level (according to the 2013 census, the Muslim population in RS was only 14 per cent), while it significantly rose in other areas due to the departure of non-Muslims (for instance, in the national capital Sarajevo and its vicinity). The war also profoundly affected the Islamic infrastructure of the country – hundreds of mosques (well over 800; Smajić 2014: 114) were completely destroyed, with many more partially. Likewise, *tekke*s and *turbe*s and even religious schools (almost seventy; Smajić

2014: 114) suffered the same fate. For all this to be rebuilt, foreign aid was inevitable. But rebuilding the infrastructure had to follow the new demographic reality – in many places rebuilding mosques did not make sense as there were no longer any Muslims in the vicinity.

The newly founded Bosnian state was soon recognised by a score of key Muslim-majority states, and, under the leadership of its first government, in the midst of its independence war, it proceeded to establish itself in the pan-Islamic organisations, foremost of which is the Organisation of Islamic Cooperation, which Bosnia and Herzegovina joined as an observer in 1994. The Bosnian Constitution does not prioritise Islam and the regime for the governance of religion formally treats all religions equally, including the three major religious communities: Muslim, Orthodox and Catholic. However, while both Christian churches managed to sign comprehensive agreements with the state that formalised their status in and relations with it (the Catholic Church in 2006 and the Orthodox in 2008), the Muslim community, represented by the Islamic Community, has (as of 2016) failed to achieve this, although it submitted the first draft of the agreement back in 2010. The adoption of the agreement has been reportedly blocked by Bosnian Serb politicians, who insinuated that the agreement would 'introduce shari'a in the country', something they deemed to be anachronistic and inappropriate in a European country in the twenty-first century (Smajić and Fazlović 2015: 119). Therefore, when compared with the Bosnian citizens of Christian background, the Muslim situation remains more precarious and vulnerable.

With the secession from the SFRY, Bosnian Muslims could finally mould their religious institutions into national ones, independent of any outside tutelage. However, as Alibašić argues, '[t]he way Islamic affairs are administered in Bosnia is, in fact, a combined legacy of Ottoman, Austrian, and Yugoslav periods' (Alibašić 2014: 440). The sole official Muslim religious institution in BiH is the Islamic Community in Bosnia and Herzegovina, which arguably, has been continuously functioning since its inception in 1882. Today the Islamic Community is a complex bureaucratic apparatus made up of a number of departments, each in charge of different fields of administration of Bosnia's Muslim affairs. The basic structural unit of the Islamic Community is the *jama'a* ('community of at least 100 households'; Smajić 2014: 112); no less than seven *jama'as* in one municipality or city form *majlis*; cantons have their regional muftis – there are nine muftiates; the muftis form the Council of Muftis. The highest representative and legislative body of the Islamic Community is the Assembly while the main executive body is the Rijaset, which serves in the capacity of top administrative organ. Both the Council of Muftis and the Rijaset are presided over by an elected *reis ul-ulama*, popularly referred to as the Grand Mufti (Alibašić 2014: 441; Smajić 2014: 112). All other muftis and indeed all *ulama* are formally subordinate to him. Therefore, the administration of Muslim religious affairs in BiH is strictly hierarchical.

However, the flock of the Bosnian Muslim institution is formally much larger than the number of Muslims in the country. This is because the Bosnian Islamic Community (BIC) sees it as its prerogative to oversee the religious institutions of Bosnian Muslims/Bosniaks (presuming that all Bosniaks are Muslim, even if some only nominally) outside the borders of the country, firstly in the successor states of Yugoslavia – to which most of those institutions acquiesced. Thus, formally, Bosniak Muslim religious authorities, locally called *meshihat*, in Slovenia, Croatia and Serbia, but also the diaspora, are all subordinate to the Rijaset in Sarajevo, and are represented by the BIC governing bodies.

It should be noted that the Islamic Community of BiH positions itself as the custodian of 'the Islamic tradition of Bosniaks' (Article 3 of the Constitution of the IC in B&H, 2014), which 'is listed, after the Qur'an and Sunnah, as one of the sources serving as the basis for the structure of bodies and institutions of the IC in B&H and its work' (Karčić 2006). However, this 'Islamic tradition of Bosniaks' is not defined in the fundamental documents of the Islamic Community. Karčić, himself a Bosnian Muslim scholar, has attempted to explain it in these words:

> Firstly, 'the Islamic tradition of Bosniaks' is not a theoretical construct but reality of understanding and living of Islam by our people for the last five centuries . . . Second, 'the Islamic tradition of Bosniaks' is comprised by static and developing elements. These two types of elements have a dynamic relationship which includes tensions too. Thirdly, in terms of these developing elements, we think that the following two elements should have an important role in further development of the Islamic tradition of Bosniaks – development of Islamic thought which needs to ensure Islamically legitimate responses to the challenges of time, and institutional development which will guarantee individual and collective expression of belief and preservation of identity to Muslims. (Karčić 2006)

Karčić (2006) lists six elements, which he sees collectively to make up the 'Islamic tradition of Bosniaks':

1. *Ahl al-sunnah* branch of Islam, including application of Maturidi thought in *aqaid* and Hanafi *madhhab* in *fiqh*, with respective Sufi orders (*tariqats*) . . .
2. Belonging to Ottoman-Islamic cultural zone . . .
3. Existence of elements of 'Islamized' practice of inhabitants of pre-Ottoman Bosnia . . .
4. Tradition of Islamic reformism (*islah*) in interpretation of Islam . . .
5. Institutionalization of Islam in the form of the Islamic Community . . .
6. Practice of expression of Islam in a secular state.

One may argue that such an understanding of the 'Islamic tradition of Bosniaks' is not only very inclusive but also makes it very syncretic, as besides a form of strictly legalist Islam it not only includes Sufi brotherhoods but even allows for non-defined "'Islamized" practice', akin to folk Islam. Finally, it includes features of revivalist Islam in the form of Islamic reformism. On the other hand, all or most of these six elements could be successfully applied to a hypothetical 'Islamic tradition of Albanians'.

The BIC, in its nature being the institution of Bosniak Muslims, sees itself (as stated in Article 1 of its Constitution) as the sole warden of all Muslims not only in the country but also in Croatia, Slovenia and Serbia. The BIC vigorously objects to the establishment and functioning of alternative religious authorities and insists that all – even non-Bosniak – Muslims in BiH submit themselves to its supervision. This is reminiscent and indeed a continuation of its stance from the communist period, when, in the late 1980s, the Islamic Community argu-ably saw

> itself as the only truly legitimate religious authority of Muslims. It attempt[ed] to present itself as such to the Muslim population, to obtain this population's alle-giance, to monopolise the control of the practice of Islam and to combat rivalling religious leaders and orientations. (Sorabji 1989: 119)

Today, the BIC primarily supervises legalist Islam-related affairs – it runs and staffs the mosques, administers religious educational institutions and issues publications. The education of both mosque imams and Islamic catechists for Muslim school pupils is undertaken by the Faculty of Islamic Studies of Sarajevo University, and two other Islamic Religious Pedagogy faculties around the country. It also runs six madrasas (high schools). Many of the graduates of these institutions serve as imams in the mosques of neighbouring countries where there are Bosniak Muslim communities, like Slovenia, Croatia and Montenegro. Nonetheless, alongside being an institution of dispensation and administration of legalist Islam, by having included (or co-opted) Sufi brother-hoods into its apparatus (it has a separate 'Sufi brotherhoods department', with Sufi shaykhs sitting on the Islamic Community's governing bodies) the BIC has effectively also become the upholder of mystical Islam, albeit, admittedly, only of those forms that do not blatantly contradict the norms of legalist Islam and apparently fit into the notion of the 'Islamic tradition of Bosniaks'.

Retrospectively, Sufism is indeed as old a feature of Bosnian Islam as Islam in Bosnia itself. Several Sufi brotherhoods were so deeply entrenched among Bosnia's Muslims during Ottoman (and even Yugoslavian) times that the number of Sufi lodges (tekkes) could have been well into the hundreds (Lelić 2006:16–19). It is reported that in the first part of the nineteenth century there were no less than '74 tomb cults in and around Sarajevo', of which '42 were the tombs of dead sheikhs and dervishes to which pilgrims came in the hope of being cured by the power of the saintly dead' (Sorabji 1989: 166).

During the communist period, particularly in the first decades of the SFRY, Sufism, like other forms of Islamic religiosity, was suppressed. So, 'all tekijas were to be closed and their property to fall to the Islamska Zajednica . . ., the

Kadiri tekija of Sarajevo was to be used as a museum for dervish artifacts, the others were to be employed as mesdjids' (Sorabji 1989: 163). However, as Sorabji points out, 'this measure was ordered by the Islamska Zajednica, and not by the state' (Sorabji 1989: 163), which purportedly sought to be the sole representative of Islam in the federal republic. In the 1970s, institutionalised Sufism rebounded: in 1977 the 'Centre of Sufi brotherhoods' was legally recognised as a subordinate part of the institutions of normative Islam. It is reported that in the late 1980s, '[o]f the five regularly functioning tekijas in Bosnia one [wa]s Kadiri and four Naqshbandi but of the latter four, one house[d] Kadiri zikr alternately with its own and the other (in Sarajevo) Mevlevi' (Sorabji 1989: 165). In the years leading upto the disintegration of the SFRY, public *dhikr* is reported to have been willingly attended by Bosnian Muslims (Bringa 1996: 220–4). However, as the independence war had left many of their *tekkes* (no less than four) and *turbes* (at least thirty seven) in ruins (Smajić 2014: 114) and Sufi brotherhoods dispersed, reinstating Sufi practices proved as daunting, if not more difficult a task, as rebuilding the infrastructure of legalist Islam.

Today Sufism in Bosnia is practised by local Muslims adhering chiefly to the Naqshbandi and Kadiri traditions. It is reported that there are over 100 known 'places of *dhikr*' of which some thirty are Sufi lodges (*tekkes*; Alibašić 2014: 449). Three quarters of known Sufi communities are affiliated with the BIC (Alibašić 2014: 450). The rest function outside official BIC tutelage. This, arguably, is for two main reasons: groups either do not meet the criteria (are not orthodox enough) to be accepted into the Islamic Community system or their leadership does not want their groups to be part of the system. Some of the latter are the heirs of the 'new mystics' (Sorabji 1989: 171–83) of the 1980s, groups of 'non-denominational' mystics not affiliated with any Sufi brotherhood that started emerging in still-communist-controlled Bosnia. In any case, adherence to Sufi groups has become and remains a marginal phenomenon among Bosnian Muslims; a recent survey has found that only 2 per cent of Bosnia's Muslims identify themselves with Sufi brotherhoods (Pew 2012: 31).

The picture of the forms of Islamic religiosity in Bosnia and Herzegovina would not be complete without including folk Islam. Though it is not known how widespread among Bosnian Muslims folk Islam is today, it is documented to have survived the communist period. As Bringa discovered during her field-work research just before the break-up of socialist Yugoslavia, the practice of folk Islam among rural Bosnian Muslims was fairly common, with visiting the resting places of 'holy men' or other 'sacred places' as well as religious healers and diviners, and the writing and wearing of amulets widely and openly prac-tised (Bringa 1996: 213–17). The independence war, which caused massive loss and displacement of people and destruction of devotional sites, must have affected these practices. Yet, the results of a recent survey suggest that today many among the country's Muslims do not object to such typical practices of folk Islam as the visiting of shrines (68 per cent consider it 'acceptable'; Pew 2012: 96). On the other hand, few Muslims in Bosnia have 'objects against evil eye' (11 per cent; Pew 2012: 77) or 'use religious healers' (16 per cent; Pew 2012: 80).

With the numbers of immigrant and convert Muslims (still) being negligible, the BIC's claim to unite all, and not only Bosniak, Muslims under its wings is not challenged by any alternative ethnicity- or country-of-origin-based organisations. However, the challenge has come from within, from revivalist-leaning Bosniak Muslims, particularly Salafis, who see the BIC as too traditionalist and even liberal. The accusations of being too liberal stem inter alia from the fact that the BIC, though a custodian of classical legalist Islam of the Hanafi tradition, accepts Sufism as an integral part of the Bosniak Muslim heritage and also as an institutional part. This, naturally, bodes ill with revivalists. There also are those who are sceptical of the older generation of *ulama* and the Islamic Community's rank and file, which is seen by some to have been staffed during the communist period with collaborators, some of whom have remained in the power structures of the Islamic Community to this day.

In independent Bosnia today there is 'almost every Islamic group (and religious practice associated with them) represented from the followers of Nursi to salafis, to revivalists, . . . at least on the internet' (Alibašić 2005: 3). In other words, the spectrum of forms of revivalist Islam and its representatives in Bosnia is as wide as anywhere else that sizeable Muslim communities live, be it Muslim-majority countries or diaspora settings in the West. But Islamic revivalism came to Bosnia in an infantile form even before the independence war (Sorabji 1989: 184–5; Karčić 2015), and therefore earlier than to most other places in Eastern Europe. The first revivalist-leaning Muslims in Bosnia were mainly individual intellectuals who, from the late 1970s, pondered over and wished for a more prominent role for Islamic morality in Bosnian society. The more outspoken among them earned such titles as (pan)Islamists and even fundamentalists.

Revivalist ideas in Salafi/Wahhabi[1] guise arrived in Bosnia in the early 1990s, when, in the midst of the independence war, numerous revivalist Muslim organisations showered Bosnia's Muslims with their attention through both material and spiritual support. Alongside humanitarian assistance, many Muslim NGOs brought literature and personnel permeated by Salafi ideas of how Muslim (in this case, Bosnian) societies should look. The participation of several hundred foreign fighters (mujahidin) in the Bosnian war of independence brought an additional side to the development of Salafism in the country. Not only were the soldiers' ways willingly emulated by some local youth fighting alongside them but, having settled in the country after the war, these mujahidin-turned-naturalised immigrants started families and, together with like-minded locals, even formed small communities with a very conservative lifestyle. This was also the time when an increasing number of Bosniak Muslim women started donning not only hijab but even niqab. The Active Islamic Youth, founded in 1995, was arguably the most prominent of the Salafi groups; it engaged in numerous diverse activities aimed at instilling in the Bosnian Muslim youth a commitment to the Salafi ideology and way of living. At its peak, between 1997 and 1999, the movement is believed to have had a following of several thousand.

Salafis operated practically unhindered until the fateful year of 2001, after which, under pressure from the US, the Bosnian authorities started looking closely into their activities and past. In the wake of anti-terror campaigns, several dozen former mujahidin who had settled in the country and even formally become citizens were stripped of their Bosnian citizenship and deported. With patrons gone and donors in short supply, the cash-stricken Active Islamic Youth gradually fell into oblivion and was eventually closed down by its leadership.

This, however, did not bring Salafi activities to an end as by that time a number of Bosniak Muslims had been indoctrinated into Salafi ideas; they even made serious attempts to take control of several dozen mosques in different parts of the country. However, the crackdown by the civil authorities gave the BIC the opportunity to try and rein in the segment of the Muslim flock that in their eyes had gone astray. The BIC leadership was determined to win back the mosques 'lost' to Salafis. With the tacit support of the state authorities, in the late 2000s the BIC started squeezing Salafis out of the mosques, unless they 're-joined' the BIC-led congregations.

This Salafi–legalist Islam tension and rivalry, however, has little bearing on the majority of Bosnia's Muslims, since, as research findings suggest, the majority of the country's Muslims are very secularised, to the point that they do not even fulfil the essential Islamic duties, like praying and fasting. Only a little more than a third (36 per cent) of surveyed Muslims indicated that 'religion is very important in their lives' (Pew 2012: 40). Though regular daily prayer is arguably one of the most essential religious rituals of Islam, in the Bosnian case, survey results reveal that only 14 per cent of the country's Muslims claim to pray all five times, with another 4 per cent claiming to pray several times but short of the required five (Pew 2012: 43). On the other hand, the arrival and entrenchment of revivalist Islam might have partially contributed to the Bosnian Muslims' self-designation as 'just Muslim' (54 per cent) as opposed to the relatively low share (38 per cent) of those who self-identify as 'Sunni' (Pew 2012: 30). One may be reminded that the 'Islamic tradition of Bosniaks' is explicitly associated with Sunnism.

Montenegro and Serbia

For fifteen years after the start of the disintegration of the Socialist Federal Republic of Yugoslavia, Serbia and Montenegro formed a reconstituted federal state, out of inertia officially called Yugoslavia. For this reason, but also because these two constitutive parts of post-socialist Yugoslavia shared the Bosniak-Muslim-dominated region of Sandžak while in areas along their eastern borders having ethnic Albanian minorities, in an analysis of the development of Islam one may talk of these two by-now-sovereign states as making up a separate sub-region among the post-Yugoslav states. Historically, the territories of both countries had been under Ottoman rule for several centuries before becoming independent in 1878, only to be reunited in post-First World War monarchical Yugoslavia and continue so until the complete erradication of Yugoslavia from the world map in 2006, when Montenegro went its own way.

Though both Serbia and Montenegro were part of the Ottoman Empire for some 350 years and their cities were fairly Islamised, unlike in neighbouring Bosnia and the Albanian lands, the bulk of their Slavic population remained Christian Orthodox. During numerous incursions by Austrians and uprisings of locals, much of the Islamic infrastructure in the form of buildings (including mosques, madrasas, *tekkes* and *turbes*) was destroyed and whatever remained was wiped away at the end of the nineteenth century, when both countries won independence from the Ottoman suzerainty. While during the Ottoman period the Montenegrin capital city Podgorica had not been an urban centre of any importance, the Serbian capital city Belgrade was one of the largest Ottoman cities in Europe. As such, it was full of Islamic architecture and Muslim inhabitants, with close to 100 mosques in the heyday of the Ottoman period in the seventeenth century. Today Belgrade has only one surviving historical mosque, but even that was torched by assailants in 2004 (this not being the first time it was attacked), in an apparent revenge act for the burnt Christian sites in Kosovo. With its four historical mosques and several other Muslim religious establishments, Podgorica today thus has more Islamic architecture than Belgrade.

After it annexed Kosovo and Macedonia in the aftermath of the 1912–13 Balkan wars, Serbia became the possessor of sizeable Albanian Muslim communities. During the socialist Yugoslavian period, when Macedonia was made into a separate federal republic, the Serbian Muslim population shrank significantly to encompass Albanian-inhabited Kosovo, Albanian-dominated Preševo Valley and the northern part of Sandžak, inhabited by Slavic-speaking Muslims, the future Bosniaks. Montenegro, for its part, swallowed the southern part of Bosniak-inhabited Sandžak while its eastern border went deep into Albanian-populated areas, bordering what after the Balkan wars became monarchical and later republican Albania.

In the post-communist era, with Kosovo gone since 1999, the Serbian Muslim community consists of two geographically distant parts – the majority Bosniaks are concentrated in Raška district (called Sandžak of Novi Pazar by the Bosniaks) bordering Bosnia and Herzegovina, and the minority Albanians inhabit the Preševo Valley straddling the Macedonian border. The two Muslim enclaves in Serbia are physically separated by independent Kosovo. Since Bosniaks and Albanians have always led rather distinct cultural lives, in contemporary Serbia one may as well talk about these segments of its Muslim population as two distinct communities.

The Albanian population, the second largest ethnic community of Muslim background, is viewed with particular suspicion by the Serbian state, as it is suspected of harbouring irredentist hopes – either to join with the Kosovan state (something that had been attempted through a referendum in the early 1990s, when Kosovo was still part of Serbia) or with the Macedonian Albanians, who are also known to have been entertaining the idea of secession from Macedonia. Tellingly, Albanians of the Preševo Valley practically en masse boycotted the last Serbian population census and have been maintaining minimal contact with the Serbian state authorities. Away from the southern part of the country, there are many fewer Muslims, with the capital Belgrade being a notable exception. Next to Bosniak and Albanian Muslims, this is where immigrant and convert Muslims dwell, officially (according to the census results) exceeding 30,000 but estimated to actually amount in total to between 40,000 and 50,000 (Kostić 2015: 511).

The situation in Montenegro in regards to the composition and distribution of its Muslim population somewhat resembles that in Serbia: the majority of Muslims are Bosniaks with Albanians making up a minority. Like in Serbia, these two Muslim communities in Montenegro inhabit different compact regions in the north-east (Bosniaks) and the south-east (Albanians) with most of the country's territory (in the centre, north, west and south-west) with practically no Muslim presence, the exception, naturally, being the capital city Podgorica, where Muslims of different ethnic backgrounds reside and where the national Islamic administration is headquartered.

However, while in absolute numbers the size of the Muslim population in Serbia is double that of Montenegro – anywhere between 223,000 (officially) and 350,000 (estimated) in Serbia as opposed to less than 120,000 in Montenegro – the share of the population of Muslim background in Montenegro is five to six times higher than that in Serbia – almost 20 per cent and just 3–4 per cent, respectively. The last population census in both countries took place in 2011. The design of the questionnaire with regards to ethnic and religious identity of the population bears significant commonalities – both states included the categories of 'Muslim in ethnic/national sense' and 'Yugoslav', both relics from the times of socialist Yugoslavia. In Montenegro though, besides 'Bosniaks' they also had such categories as 'Bosnian', 'Bosniak-Muslim', 'Montenegrin-Muslim' and even 'Muslim-Bosniak' and 'Muslim-Montenegrin'! This cacophony of ethnic labels made counting the Muslim population in Montenegro particularly difficult as there were some Muslims 'in ethnic sense' who religiously identified themselves as either atheists or even Catholic or Christian Orthodox (sic!).

Of the total number of almost 118,500 inhabitants of Montenegro who in the census results are counted under the category of Islamic faith, 53,453 are Bosniaks, 22,267 Albanians, 20,270 'ethnic' Muslims (practically all of whom may be regarded Bosniak), 12,758 Montenegrins, 5,034 Romany and 2,003 Egyptians (arguably, another self-designation of Roma people). If Muslims 'in ethnic sense' were to be treated as synonymous with Bosniaks, the Bosniak population of Montenegro would be over 73,700, which would make it the majority (over 62 per cent) of the population of Muslim background in the country, while Albanian Muslims make up less than 19 per cent. It is intriguing to discover that ethnic Montenegrins (including 'Montenegrin-Muslims' and 'Muslim-Montenegrins') make up the third biggest (11 per cent) community; though there certainly may be Montenegrin converts to Islam and their progeny among them, it would be reasonable to assume that a fair number of them are of Bosniak origin.

The results of the Serbian census reveal that there were over 222,800 adherents of Islam in the country at the time of the census in 2011. However, as it has been pointed out by the Serbian researcher Kostić (2015: 511), this census was boycotted by Albanians of the Preševo Valley: while in the earlier census of 2002, the Albanian population of Serbia (excluding Kosovo, which since 1999 was no longer under Serbian rule) numbered over 61,000, the 2011 census counted less than 6,000 Albanians in the entire country. As the overwhelming majority of Serbia's Albanians are of Muslim background, the official results of the 2011 census for the Muslim population in Serbia are short by at least an estimated 50,000 individuals of Muslim background. Kostić indicates that a number of Bosniaks also boycotted the census, while many Muslim Romas were not even included in the census as they are without either documents or a known place of residence. Taking all these considerations into account, Kostić argues that the actual number of Muslims in Serbia at the time of the 2011 census might have been at least around 350,000 (Kostić 2015: 512). In any case, Bosniaks are the largest ethnic group of Muslim background in Serbia, with almost 145,300 recorded in the census results. Additionally, some 22,300 of Serbia's inhabitants identified themselves as 'ethnic Muslims'. Following the pattern of considering 'ethnic Muslims' as synonymous with Bosniaks, the total number of Bosniaks in Serbia at the time of the 2011 census could have been closer to 168,000. Using this number, at the time of the census, Bosniaks made up three quarters of the official number of followers of Islam in the country. If the missing 50,000 Albanian Muslims are added, the Bosniaks' share would still be comfortably over 60 per cent, with the estimated share of Albanians being around 19 per cent and that of Romas 12.5 per cent (Kostić 2015: 512). However, it might also be mentioned that another 23,300 inhabitants of the country identified themselves as Yugoslavs by ethnicity but it remains unknown how many of them could have been of Bosniak origin and/or Muslim background.

Though Serbia is formally a secular state, it recognises the Muslim community along with seven other religious communities as 'traditional', thus arguably privileging it and other traditional religious communities over the 'non-traditional' – though no other traditional community compares with the actual status and influence of the Serbian Orthodox Church. Thus, the Serbian situation is a formal division of religious communities into traditional (including Muslims) and non-traditional, with actual preference still clearly on the side of the religious community associated with the titular ethnicity – which is reminiscent of that in several other Eastern European countries, particularly Lithuania and Belarus. In Montenegro, which like Serbia is a secular state, though the Montenegrin Orthodox Church is also the strongest of the country's religious communities, the bargaining power of the Muslim community is evidently stronger, in part because of its numerical strength but also because of the more accommodating stance of the state and the non-Muslim majority. It might also be noted that, unlike Serbia, Montenegro has not experienced secessionist and irredentist movements among its Muslim populations, although secession of Kosovo from Serbia also meant its secession from the joint Yugoslav republic of which Montenegro was then still a part.

As the majority of Serbia's Muslims are based in the southern part of the country, the first Islamic administration in post-communist Serbia (then still part of Yugoslavia) – the Islamic Community of Sandžak – was founded there in 1993 in the administrative centre of the Serbian part of Sandžak, Novi Pazar. Its jurisdiction was seen to encompass Sandžak in its entirety, including that part of the region in the Montenegrin territory. As Montenegro and Serbia at that time still formed a single, albeit federal state, this might look logical. However, by 1994, Montenegrin Muslims had set up a separate Islamic community in the territory of the constituent republic. Also in 1994, another Islamic administration was set up in Belgrade, while regional Islamic communities also emerged in the northern Vojvodina region and the Preševo Valley in the south-east.

Initially, the Islamic Community of Sandžak, being part of the Bosnian Islamic Community's system, served as a regional institution. However, by 2007, apparently in reaction to the new law on religious communities adopted in 2006 (which among other things stipulated that there may be only one state-recognised Muslim religious organisation in the country with the words 'Islamic Community' in its title) and with the emergence of a rival aspiring national organisation (the Islamic Community of Serbia), the Islamic Community of Sandžak claimed to have become national, thus changing its name to the Islamic Community in Serbia. To prove its national reach, it announced the establishment of its four constitutive muftiates: besides the Sandžak muftiate, there was to be a muftiate in the Albanian-inhabited Preševo Valley and another two, for Belgrade (and the central part) and Novi Sad (the northern part). However, though founded and staffed by Serbian citizens, the Islamic Community in Serbia recognises the spiritual authority of the Sarajevo-based *reis ul-ulama* of the Rijaset of the Islamic Community in Bosnia and Herzegovina. The election of the mufti of the Islamic Community is confirmed by the Bosnian *reis ul-ulama* and he also serves on the Board of the Rijaset.

This is seen by the Serbian state (and the majority population) as a problematic affiliation: the Islamic Community in Serbia (ICiS), though physically based in the country, is under the jurisdiction of an organisation that is based outside Serbia. To offset the unwanted ramifications arising from the ICiS's institutional subordinate affiliation with a foreign organisation beyond the control of the Serbian authorities, but also to have the headquarters of a more conciliatory Muslim spiritual-administrative institution closer to the seat of power, the Serbian government tacitly supported the initiative to reconstitute the Islamic Community of Serbia (ICoS) as a national Islamic administration independent from the Bosnian Islamic Community, that is with *rijaset* status rather than the subordinate *meshihat* held by the ICiS. The technical switch from 'in' to 'of' carries a profound symbolic meaning – the ICoS is claimed to be a truly Serbian Muslim institution, unlike the ICiS, which is portrayed as a mere branch of a foreign (Bosnian) organisation.

The two institutions proceeded to violently clash with each other so that even outside actors like Ahmet Davotoğlu, the Minister of Foreign Affairs of Turkey, sought to calm down the flaring animosity. For a period of time between 2010 and 2014, through its inspired Unification Initiative, Turkey was instrumental in the promotion of an alternative institution to both Islamic Communities; however, this attempt failed and the enmity continued unabated.

This rivalry between the two religious institutions spilled over into political infighting among Serbia's Bosniaks. The two major Bosniak political parties, neither of which espouses religious sentiments let alone ideology, sided with opposing spiritual-administrative authorities, further splintering both the Bosniak electorate and the Muslim community. In the words of the Serbian researcher Kostić,

> due to their close links with political parties, as well as open political engagement by some of the imams and muftis, both organisations are often thought of by other Muslims as mere mouthpieces for various political parties. This is particularly the case with the ICoS [Islamic Community of Serbia], which is closely linked with the Party of Democratic Action (SDA) and the government. (Kostić 2015: 504)

It may be argued that the disunity in Serbia's Muslim population and animosity between the two Islamic Communities has led to none of them being recognised in the ten years since the passing of the law on religious communities by the state as the (sole) official representative of normative Islam in the country, something that arguably has been detrimental to the spiritual and social development of the Muslim community.

With Montenegrin independence in 2006, Muslims in this brand new country escaped the squabbles between the two Islamic administrations in Serbia, though there were attempts in 2014 to draw them (particularly Bosniaks of the Montenegrin Sandžak) into the competition between the Serbian Islamic administrations by subordinating them to the muftiate of the Serbian Sandžak. The leadership of the unitary Islamic Community in Montenegro withstood the onslaught from the Sandžak mufti and remained steadfast in its determination to keep their institution independent of Serbian tutelage. In 2012, the Islamic Community in Montenegro signed the Memorandum of Understanding formalising its (and Islam's in general) institutional status in the state. The Memorandum enshrined the religious rights of the country's Muslims ranging from dress and diet, Islamic education, days off during Islamic holidays and time off for Friday afternoon communal prayer, to spiritual care in state facilities like prisons, and many more.

Moreover, unlike its Serbian counterparts, the Islamic Community in Montenegro has so far managed to keep united not only both major ethnic groups – Bosniak and Albanian Muslims – but also include and thus represent all other Muslims of the country, despite the ethnically (and, arguably, culturally) double nature of the Montenegrin Muslim population. There is no other parallel or rival Islamic administration in the country. Though this is not unique in Eastern Europe or even the Balkan states, the Montenegrin case is exceptional as the Muslim community there is primarily composed of two different ethno-linguistic groups. The same two groups appear to have little in common in neighbouring Serbia, where they lead virtually separate parallel lives, running their own mosques and establishments of religious education.

As elsewhere in the Balkans, in Ottoman Serbia Sufism was widespread and very visible. There are historical accounts claiming that in the seventeenth century there were at least seventeen *tekkes* belonging to an array of Sufi brotherhoods (Vukomanović 2007). However, Sufi practices, as indeed any Islamic practices, shrank to negligible levels with the mass exodus of Muslims in the wake of Serbian independence in the nineteenth century. Sufism 'returned' to Serbia via Kosovo, when in the aftermath of the Balkan wars of 1912–13, Sufi-saturated Kosovo came under Serbian control. However, though Sufism thrived in Kosovo in the interwar period and survived the communist era (for more details, see the relevant section on Kosovo), in Serbia proper it never regained strength. Therefore, in today's Serbia, Sufi practices may be observed only very locally: in Sandžak, where there are four *tekkes*, all in the administrative centre Novi Pazar (Pramenković 2014: 531), and in Niš, where there are two *tekkes* used by Sufis of mainly Roma ethnicity (Đorđević and Todorović 2007). Non-denominational neo-Sufi practices may be found among the few Serbian converts to Islam.

The protracted institutional infighting in Serbia's Muslim community between the two competing Islamic administrations, particularly in Sandžak, must have contributed to the strengthening of the revivalist alternative there, but also elsewhere in the country. Dismayed by what they saw as a politically motivated brawl between institutions whose primary, if not sole, aim was supposed to have been to take care of Serbia's Muslims' spiritual needs, some local devout Muslims turned to alternative forms of Islamic religiosity. To many this meant turning to Wahhabism and Salafism. Though, arguably, Islamic revivalism (in its ideologically light and institutionally loose form) came to Serbia around the same time as to elsewhere in the former SFRY (that is, in its last decade), it made deep and more sustained inroads during the early 1990s, at the height of the war in neighbouring Bosnia, and has been present in the country ever since. Seizing the opportunity in the mid-2000s when the two Islamic communities were at each other's throats, revivalist-leaning local Muslims established or took over some of the mosques where they started preaching their ideology, at times bordering on jihadism. This was also the time of violent clashes between groups of revivalist and 'moderate' Muslims as well as arrests of alleged terrorists in Sandžak (Zdravkovski 2014: 221). Since then, however, the intra-communal violence has subsided.

The Salafi presence in Sanžak's administrative centre, Novi Pazar, has remained very visible into the mid-2010s – one can easily spot men in short pants and with long beards on the town's streets. Only one other place in the whole of Eastern Europe may match this public visibility of Salafis and that is Macedonia, in its Albanian-inhabited urban centres. The appeal of Islamic revivalism in Serbia may also partially be explained as some Muslims' reaction to the persistent Muslimophobic stance of the majority Serbian population and many of its politicians, who are not happy about Bosnia's and particularly Kosovo's independence.

Though Montenegro also has its share of revivalist-leaning Muslims, neither their volume nor visibility matches those of the Serbian or Macedonian groups. This may be credited to both the ability of the leadership of the Montenegrin Islamic Community to satisfy the spiritual and other needs of the majority of the country's Muslims (and the unitary nature of its Islamic administration is of utmost importance here) and to the state's welcoming stance toward the Muslim population, enshrined in the earlier-mentioned Memorandum of Understanding between the Islamic Community and the state, which guaranteed wide-ranging rights to Muslim believers. In other words, in terms of grievances and un-met expectations, there is little of what might be used by revivalists to advance their cause in Montenegro. However, this does not mean that the situation may never change – the *hijra* of several dozen Montenegrin Muslims to the Islamic Khilafa State indicates a pending trend in possible radicalisation of some local Muslims.

Kosovo

While the state-building process in Kosovo effectively only started after 1999, the development of the Muslim community there dates back to Ottoman times. Being the youngest European nation state in the making, Kosovo is also not only another Albanian but a nominally Muslim-majority state in South-east Europe. Kosovo was part of the Ottoman Empire for some half a millennium before it was annexed by Serbia in 1912, later to become an integral part of consecutive Yugoslavias, albeit within the constitutive Serbian entity. In 1974, it was even upgraded to the status of an autonomous province within the SFRY with wide-ranging political and administrative rights, but the new Serbian Constitution of 1990 stripped Kosovo of this status and attached rights. The Kosovar reaction was swift and decisive – the newly established Assembly of the Kosovo Republic, backed by the majority of the territory's population proclaimed Kosovo independent from Serbia in 1991, when many of the Yugoslavian republics had already declared establishment of their statehood. The real break with the Serbian state had to wait until 1999 though, when, in reaction to the Serbian military campaign, US-led North Atlantic Treaty Organization (NATO) forces effectively detached Kosovo from Serbia. So, although embryonic attempts at Kosovan statehood and, in parallel, nationhood may be pushed back to the early 1990s, in reality, Kosovo started turning into a state with a distinct nation only after the independence war of 1999. However, it took almost another decade before, in 2008, Kosovo unilaterally declared founding a sovereign state without Serbia – which continues to consider Kosovo a part of its territory.

Although it was by far shorter than the Bosnian war, the independence war in Kosovo was nonetheless as brutal and bore many of the same patterns, including ethnic cleansing, forced evictions and intimidation, as well as the systematic destruction of Muslim religious infrastructure. Thus, like in Bosnia, mosques, madrasas, *tekkes*, *turbes* and other religio-cultural objects of Kosovan Muslims were particularly targeted by Serbian forces before they were pushed out by a NATO-led coalition. There are reports that over 200 mosques out of some 500 active in the 1990s were damaged or destroyed by Serbians, among them a dozen or so dating from the fifteenth and sixteenth centuries (Krasniqi 2011: 196; Mehmeti 2015: 72). On the other hand, the Serbian Orthodox population and its property, including religious objects and sites, were also targeted by Albanian armed groups. Due to this but also because of the *de facto* changed status of the territory, many Serbs chose to leave thus diminishing the non-Muslim and particularly Christian Orthodox share in the Kosovan population. Those Serbs who remain continue to refuse to accept that they now live in a different country and mainly live in protected segregated enclaves.

Kosovo's Muslim population, according to the 2013 census, stood at 96 per cent. However, since the census was boycotted by the Serbian minority, had they participated the share of Muslims would have been somewhat lower, possibly around 92 per cent. Though the overwhelming majority of Kosovo's Muslims are Albanians, it also has small Bosniak, Turkish, Roma, Ashkali and Gorani communities, each around or below 1 per cent of the country's population. Traditionally, the overwhelming majority of Kosovan Muslims have been Sunni, with small numbers of Bektashis. Naturally, as elsewhere in the Balkans, Sufi brotherhoods were widespread. However, a 2012 survey found that only a quarter (24 per cent) of Kosovo's Muslims still self-identify as 'Sunni', with 58 per cent identifying as 'just a Muslim' (Pew 2012: 30).

Due to a high share of its citizens identifing with Islam in one or another way, it would not be unthinkable to expect Kosovo's legislation to recognise this by, if not making Islam a state religion, then at least acknowledging its historical and contemporary place. However, in reality, Kosovo's legislation is far from promoting Islam – the country's Constitution not only makes no mention of Islam but is very explicit about Kosovo being a secular state. The reasons behind this might be traced to an attempt to placate both the Serbian minority and Serbia. Also, because it was the EU and other international institutions, European countries and experts who set up the Kosovan legal framework (or at least assisted in the process), drawing on common European practices they have refrained from prioritising a particular religious tradition and instead promote equality among the religious groups vis-à-vis the law. It might also partially be due to the fact that Kosovan Albanians themselves had no appetite for religion being enshrined in their new country's legislation. Discussions and decisions made in the Kosovan parliament favouring a ban on religious instruction in schools, on hijabs and loud calls to prayer attest to the deeper level of secularisation of the Kosovan polity and broader society (Krasniqi 2011: 198; Mehmeti 2015: 67).

It should also be recalled that neither the Kosovo Liberation Army (UÇK) as the leading guerrilla organisation in the Kosovan Albanians' fight for independence, nor the political elite of Kosovars ever emphasised their religious (read, Muslim) identity. As argued by Krasniqi,

> [in] the 1990s, no Kosovar Albanian political party or association of any importance rallied around Islamic symbols . . . in opposition to the Serbian regime. Religious motives – in this case Muslim ones – did, however, play a role in defining and constructing the self-image of many Albanians in opposition to the Serbian (Orthodox) 'Other'. Yet this Islam was a 'Popular Islam', not an 'Official Islam'. (Krasniqi 2011: 196)

Research findings show that in independent Kosovo, the share of devout Muslims among the pool of citizens of Muslim cultural background is fairly low – some observers estimate that the religious part of the Muslim population may constitute only a tenth of them. Indeed, in the larger cities, like the capital

Prishtina and the second largest city Prizren, even on Fridays life does not differ from any other European city, with people busy with their daily chores during the day and hanging around numerous bars and restaurants at night. Results of a 2012 survey show that 39 per cent of the surveyed Kosovo Muslims admitted to 'never attend mosque' (Pew 2012: 47), while the share of those who claimed to attend it at least once a week (for communal Friday prayer) is reported to be 22 per cent (Pew 2012: 46). Of course, low mosque attendance on its own does not imply low religiosity as believers may resort to religious practices outside of the framework of mosque-centred rituals, be it of Sufi or folk Islam nature. However, admittance to abstention from prayers at mosque confirms the generally held impression that Kosovan Muslims are not particularly normative Islam oriented.

Though Kosovan Muslims may not be as religious as one would expect them to be (and certainly, less religious, if compared with Bosniak Muslims in Bosnia, Sandžak or elsewhere, or Albanians in Macedonia), Kosovo has had a long tradition of Muslim institutions, and not only of normative Islam. For instance, even during the socialist Yugoslavia period, Kosovo had its own Muslim religious authorities (both of normative and Sufi Islam), effectively setting its Muslim population and development of Islam apart from the rest of Muslims in Yugoslavia. Also, from 1967 when all religions, including Islam, were banned in atheist Albania, Islamic literature in the Albanian language was published in the SFRY, chiefly in Kosovo, and then smuggled into Albania. But even more importantly, with the Islamic tradition almost obliterated, in the 1990s Albania had to 'import' Islamic knowledge anew, and much of it initially came from Kosovo. Therefore, the Kosovan Islamic institutions through their publications, educational institutions and foremost *ulama* helped to reintroduce and revive Islam in neighbouring Albania.

Today, legalist Islam in Kosovo is represented by the Islamic Community of Kosovo, which formally split from the Yugoslav Islamic administrative structures in 1993, when

> [f]ollowing the dissolution of socialist Yugoslavia, the Supreme Council of the Yugoslav Islamic Community for Serbia, which was based in Prishtina, changed its name to the Islamic Community of Kosovo . . . thus taking full responsibility of organizing Muslim religious life in Kosovo. (Krasniqi 2011: 195)

However, its status within the sovereign Kosovan state has not been decisively established. Though Islam is recognised by law as one of the traditional religions in the territory of Kosovo, with no relevant law and no comprehensive agreement with the state, the Islamic Community of Kosovo has been functioning as a mere NGO. Such a status is arguably detrimental to the development and rights of the country's Muslims and puts them on the defensive, in the position of the weaker and vulnerable actor in deliberations pertaining to the place and role of religion in the country.

Tellingly, the Islamic Community of Kosovo claims to represent Muslims of the Preševo Valley in Serbia, the majority of whom are ethnic Albanians. As indicated in the section on Serbia, Albanians of the Preševo Valley have very strained relations with the Serbian state and also appear to keep their distance from the Bosniak-dominated Islamic administrations in Serbia.

As elsewhere among Albanian Muslims, in Kosovo, non-legalist forms of Islam have thrived throughout the centuries. Sufism in the form of half a dozen brotherhoods even survived the communist period more intact than elsewhere in Yugoslavia. In 1973, the Albanian dervishes set up their own organisation, ZIDRA (Community of the Islamic Dervish Orders of Ali), virtually independent of the Yugoslavian Islamic administration. With all restrictions on practising Sufi Islam in post-communist Kosovo removed, its revival could have been expected. However, a recent survey found that only 3 per cent of the surveyed Kosovo Muslims indicated belonging to a Sufi brotherhood (Pew 2012: 31). The low level of Kosovan Muslims' attachment to Sufism may be partially explained by the general trend of secularisation observable throughout the former Yugoslavian region and beyond in Eastern Europe.

Nonetheless, a new draft law on religious communities introduced in 2014 includes Sufis among the six 'religious communities in the Republic of Kosovo, which constitute the historical heritage, cultural and social life of the country'. The Sufi community in the draft law is referred to as the Tarikate Community of Kosovo as separate from the Kosovan Islamic Community. Though such an organisation has been functioning in Kosovo for quite some time, the official, state-endorsed separation of Sufis from Muslims would have several consequences. First of all, it would follow the path of Albania, where Bektashis are recognised as a separate religious community, different from that of Muslims, with its own religious administration independent of the Islamic Community. With the Sufi community formally separated from the Islamic Community, the number of Muslims (that is, those who identify with the Islamic Community of Kosovo) would go down, even if, admittedly, not significantly. But the most symbolic consequence would be that Sufis would cease to be identified and potentially self-identify as Muslims. While in the case of Bektashis it might still make sense, in the case of most Sufis, and certainly among those whose brotherhoods are closer to normative Islam, this would cause unnecessary if not altogether harmful confusion. Furthermore, the divorce would also have certain financial consequences as the two communities would not only run separate budgets but would compete among themselves for the resources and funding from the state and private donors.

It remains to be seen whether the Kosovan Bektashi community will be included in this newly proposed community, and whether it would be content with such a status: it is known that Bektashis in Kosovo have been harbouring expectations to be recognised as a separate religious community, like their co-religionists in Albania (where, admittedly, numbers are significantly higher). Bektashis in today's Kosovo make up only a fraction of its population and are reported to run just one *tekke* in Gjakova, where they are concentrated (Ismaili 2014: 352). Other Sufi brotherhoods are more numerous and together may have a sufficient following to constitute a separate, though numerically small, religious association if not a full-fledged community with a single religious administration. However, it is hard to believe the share of Sufis, and with it the strength of their community, would grow in any foreseeable future.

Unlike the Sufis, revivalist Islam may gain in strength in Kosovo. As in Bosnia, when rebuilding the annihilated infrastructure, local Muslims had often to rely on the same foreign Islamic NGOs as Bosnian Muslims had done. This led to similar consequences, one of which is the emergence of a Salafi segment among Kosovan Muslims.

Former Yugoslav Republic of Macedonia

As elsewhere in the post-communist Balkans and further afield in Eastern Europe, religious communities in Macedonia, and among them Muslims, could start breathing freely after the collapse of the communist system. However, while legal and other freedom to practise religion in many post-communist countries did not necessarily translate into high religiosity of the local populations, according to some polls (Gallup 2012), Macedonia's inhabitants are some of the most religious of all Eastern Europeans (closely followed by the Romanians). Though the publicly available poll results do not differentiate between Muslim and non-Muslim respondents, it may be inferred that even with some variations across different religious communities, Macedonia's Muslims would still rank high among other, in general, religious, and in particular, Muslim communities. The level of religiosity, if judged by the appearance of Macedonia's Muslims, differs strikingly from that observed on the streets of other Eastern European settlements with sizeable populations of Muslim background – women in hijabs and even niqabs are a common sight. The only other region with such a high level of 'Islamic attire' is Serbian Sandžak, while in both neighbouring Kosovo and Albania the public display of such attire is significantly lower.

Unlike other former constituent federal units of the SFRY, Macedonia experienced no political violence or armed conflict at the time of its secession, with no claims made on its territory by either Yugoslavia/Serbia or neighbouring Bulgaria and Greece. Yet, one may be reminded that Macedonia had been a prize for which Serbia, Bulgaria and Greece vied at the beginning of the twentieth century. At that time it went to Serbia, later to become a separate constituent republic of the SFRY. More recently, it was peacefully let go by the Yugoslav authorities in 1991, who at the same time were engaging in attempts to suppress by use of armed force the independence of both Slovenia and Croatia. With no destruction and other war-associated upheavals or losses, Macedonia had a rather good starting position from which to proceed with building a nation state.

However, since its independence, it has been bombarded by obstacles of a different nature to its development as a sovereign nation state. The very name of the state became the object of a bitter dispute between the new state and Greece, which strongly opposes the former Yugoslav republic's self-designation as Macedonia, because Greece already uses that name for its northern province. Therefore, the universally used name remains 'The Former Yugoslav Republic of Macedonia'. Secondly, the status of the Macedonian language as an independent language is contested by Bulgarians who maintain that Macedonian is a dialect of the Bulgarian language. Third, as the majority of Macedonia's citizens are Orthodox, the question and status of which church they are members of also remains a contested issue: the Serbian Orthodox Church does not reconcile with the existence of the autocephalous Macedonian Orthodox Church and blocks its membership in the family of Orthodox churches. Finally, from the start, the building of the Macedonian nation appears not to have taken the expectations of the country's large Albanian minority into full consideration. Making up more than a quarter of its population, the Albanians have been constitutionally marginalised in the new state, which identifies the Macedonian nation almost exclusively with Macedonian ethnicity (and by extension Christian Orthodoxy).

The simmering dissatisfaction of the Albanians, who incidentally also make up the majority of the country's Muslim population, in 2001 spilled over into a brief armed conflict between rebellious Albanian armed groups, supported by sympathetic Kosovan Albanians, and the Macedonian security forces. Though for a moment it might have looked like Macedonia would follow the Bosnian path (some sixty mosques were reportedly attacked in the brief period of armed hostilities), a swift world community's reaction and the willingness of both warring sides to move from the battlefield to the negotiations' table not only spared the country the pending devastation and possible split but also granted increased citizens' rights to the country's Albanian (and by extension Muslim) population making, at least formally, the project of nation- (and state-) building more inclusive and comprehensive. The new Constitution, inter alia, acknowledges the status of Islam as one of the five 'traditional' religions.

Though the overwhelming majority of Macedonia's Albanians are of Muslim cultural background, Albanians are not the only Muslims in Macedonia. As in neighbouring countries, Roma, Ashkali, Gorani, Turkish and Torbeshi[2] Muslims inhabit the territory of Macedonia. Together with Albanians, these ethnic minorities of Muslim cultural background make up a third of Macedonia's inhabitants. The Pew Research Center even predicts that by 2030 Muslims in Macedonia could increase to over 40 per cent of the population (Pew 2011: 162).

Of some 660,000 Muslims in 2002, the year for which the last official census figures are available, over half a million Albanian Muslims made up over three quarters of Macedonia's Muslims, followed by 78,000 Turks (12 per cent) and 54,000 Roma (8 per cent). Macedonian-speaking Muslims, in the scholarly literature collectively referred to as 'Torbeshis', fall through the census net and are not accounted for. However, they are estimated to number no less than 20,000 (Jahja 2014: 398) and are reported to live 'predominantly in the western and southern parts of Macedonia and in Kosovo, with limited numbers in Greece, Albania and Turkey' (Dikici 2008: 28). Though in the census of 1981 there were almost 40,000 'Macedonian Muslims' in the republic when still part of the SFRY, according to the 1994 census conducted in by then independent Macedonia, only just over 15,000 of them remained. The fall in numbers of those who self-identified as 'Macedonian Muslims' (aka Torbeshis) might be partially explained by the alleged fact that '[a]lthough most of the Torbeshes are not able to speak Turkish, they claim to be Turks' (Dikici 2008: 27). If this is the case, the total figure for Turks might include some 'Slavic-speaking Turks', that is, Torbeshis. Additionally, the 1994 census introduced the category of Bosniak, with over 7,200 returns (Dikici 2008: 33). In the 2002 census, there were already over 17,000 Bosniaks, with the 'Macedonian Muslim' category eliminated altogether.

The ethnic roots of Torbeshis in Macedonia, very much like Pomaks in Bulgaria and Goranis in Kosovo, remain a contested issue with

> [s]ome scholars say[ing] that the Gorans of Kosovo and the Torbeshes of Macedonia are closely related to the Pomaks of Greece and Bulgaria, and that the Torbesh community is a subgroup of the Muslim Pomak ethnicity in Bulgaria, and so the Pomaks are called Torbeshes in Macedonia and Gorans in Kosovo and Albania. (Dikici 2008: 28)

Their situation as Macedonian-speaking Muslims sets Torbeshis apart from the majority ethnic group of Muslim background, Albanians, if not in religious terms, then certainly in nation-building terms. While Albanians have been sidelined by the Macedonian Orthodox majority in the nation-building process, there have been numerous attempts to include Torbeshis into the more inclusive understanding of the Macedonian nation, where, besides Orthodox Christianity, Islam 'spoken and practised in Macedonian' is accepted. In fact, one may observe a long-term policy of the state to nationalise Islam and to extract an 'ethnically Macedonian' version of it – but making sure this is separate from the 'Albanian' version. To this end, even back in communist times in the 1970s, the government supported an organisation explicitly catering for the needs of 'Macedonian Muslims' – the Republican Community for Cultural and Scientific Events of Macedonian Muslims.

In any case, the numerically largest and arguably politically most powerful segment of the Muslim population in Macedonia are the Albanians, most of whom live in the western and south-western part of the country, along the borders with Kosovo, Albania and the Preševo Valley of Serbia, all Albanian and Muslim majority. This physical proximity facilitates cross-border communication and cooperation in religious matters, though the Islamic administrations in Albania, Kosovo and Macedonia are independent of each other.

The national organisation claiming to represent all the country's Muslims is the Islamic Religious Community of Macedonia, headed, as in most other post-Yugoslav or even post-Ottoman Balkan states, by the *reis ul-ulama* (the Grand Mufti). It emerged out of ruins of the pan-Yugoslav Islamic administration in 1994 as a single united institution representing all Macedonia's Muslims. In reality, however, it has been dominated by Albanians and the organisation is popularly seen to favour the 'Albanian cause'. Although no serious rival Islamic administration has so far emerged (despite several aborted attempts by disgruntled imams and their following), the Islamic Religious Community has experienced internal divisions and rivalries with different groups of imams promoting competing claimants to the post of mufti, particularly in the mid-2000s. Dissatisfaction with the policies of the mufti have also recently (in 2015) led to a brief expulsion of him and his staff from the organisation's headquarters, by force, to which he was then returned only by a court order.

The internal strife in the Islamic Religious Community of Macedonia (and by extension in the broader Muslim community of the country) is reminiscent of that in Serbian Sandžak, where there are even rival Islamic administrations closely linked to rival ethnic (Bosniak) political parties. In Macedonia, the Albanian (and to a large extent Muslim) electorate is split along party political lines: while some Albanians support and vote for the Democratic Union for Integration, others prefer its rival, the Democratic Party of Albanians (Barišić 2007: 38). The chronic turmoil inside the main (and aspiring to be the sole) custodian institution of normative Islam in Macedonia is arguably very unhealthy; it divides and thus weakens the Muslim community as a social and political actor in the face of continuing and new pressures from the state, particularly in the face of the upsurge in radicalisation of Albanian Muslim youth, some of whom have even left Macedonia for the Islamic Khilafa State.

The leadership of the Islamic Religious Community of Macedonia has found itself between a rock and a hard place. On the one hand, it has been embroiled in constant wrangling and negotiations with the state over the rights of the country's Muslims, starting with the property rights to Muslim sites and land that had been nationalised by the communist Yugoslavian regime and since independence, appears to have been encroached upon by the Orthodox Church and the state working in tandem. On the other hand, it struggles to keep its claimed flock under its wings, as a number of mosques (and their imams) are actually out of its control. Often, these are the mosques where revivalist (and/or even radical) Islam is preached and practised, but adherents of mystical Islam also shy away from the tutelage of the Islamic Religious Community of Macedonia.

It goes without saying that mystical Islam had been as widespread in Macedonia as everywhere else in the eastern Balkans and it also survived the communist period. Alongside several other Sufi brotherhoods, Bektashism has likewise been present among Macedonia's Albanians. Today however, as in Kosovo, Bektashis in post-communist Macedonia make up only a fraction of the inhabitants of Muslim background – estimated to be around 5,000 (Jahja 2014: 400) – and are in control of just a few establishments. Nonetheless, the Macedonian Bektashis, following the example of their Albanian brothers-in-faith, aspire for spiritual and institutional independence from national Muslim authorities. However, as both the official Muslim institutions and the state regard Bektashis as part of the national Muslim population, Bektashis in Macedonia have attained a mere status of 'religious group', a far cry from the 'independent religious community' that they dream of (Clayer 2012: 191). The tensions between Bektashis and Sunni Muslims reached their apogee in 2002: an armed incident took place in a dispute over a precious historical property in the Albanian-majority town of Tetovo. Sunnis took over the property used by the Bektashis, jeopardising, if not altogether putting an end to Bektashi religious practices there.

Revivalist Islam ideas must have reached Macedonia's Muslims as far back as the 1980s, when they started spreading in the SFRY, particularly in Bosnia and Sandžak but also among Albanians in southern Serbia (Kosovo and the Preševo Valley). However, it was not until the late 1990s, during the Kosovo war for independence, that a string of aid and humanitarian NGOs of a revivalist nature, catering for the needs of Kosovo's Muslims (among them refugees sheltered in Macedonia), arrived in Macedonia and raised the presence of revivalist Islam, not only to a level hitherto not seen in the country but arguably, hardly matched in other Eastern Balkan Muslim communities. It is reported that from the late 2000s to the beginning of the 2010s, revivalists (locally popularly referred to as Wahhabis) were in control of at least five mosques in the capital Skopje along with many more across the country, something that the Islamic Religious Community of Macedonia itself does not deny (Krasniqi 2011: 203; Jahja 2014: 401).

The rise in and persistence of the revivalist presence in Macedonia may be partially explained through the close interaction of Macedonia's Albanian Muslims with their co-religionists across the border in Kosovo, where revivalist NGOs with origins in Saudi Arabia and other Persian Gulf states have been functioning unhindered for practically the entire post-Serbian period. One might even be tempted to consider Kosovan and Macedonian revivalists as a single cluster rather than two separate 'national' communities.

Slovenia and Croatia

Slovenia and Croatia, the two countries that split from the socialist Yugoslavian state the earliest, besides being Catholic-majority and EU member states, share commonalities in regards to their Muslim populations. First of all, the presence of Muslim communities of any significant size in their territories is a relative novelty as the territories they evolved from had either never been conquered by the Ottomans or the period of their rule over some regions (like north-eastern and south-eastern parts of today's Croatia) was too short to translate into Islamisation akin to that in neighbouring Bosnia or elsewhere in the Central and Eastern Balkans. Though up to a quarter of the population of 'Ottoman Slavonia' in the sixteenth century might have been Muslim, they were primarily colonists from Bosnia or even further afield (all the way to Anatolia) and, after the conquest of the territory by the Austrians, their traces disappeared. Apparently, most of them chose to relocate (or were expelled) to lands still under Ottoman rule, the closest being Bosnia (Mujadzevic 2014: 146). So, between the beginning of the eighteenth century and the first half of the twentieth century, neither Slovenia nor Croatia had Muslim communities in their territories, and with an absence of Muslim communities, there was little need for their institutions.

Bosniaks started coming to the territories of Slovenia and Croatia during the Austro-Hungarian period (the late nineteenth–beginning of the twentieth centuries) as itinerant workers, some of whom settled permanently, the bulk of them in and around the Croatian capital Zagreb. In interwar Yugoslavia, local Muslim communities, amounting to several thousand members, were entrusted to the care of the Bosnian Islamic administrations, a practice that would continue throughout the socialist Yugoslavian period. It should be mentioned that during the brief period of its existence in the 1940s, the Independent State of Croatia included Bosnia. This was the time when, due to the high number of Muslims, the authorities had to come up with their own policies of governing Islam within the wider framework of the Second World War. Like the overlord Nazis, the Croatian Ustaša regime made numerous overtures toward the national Muslim community (among them, the building of a mosque in the capital Zagreb in 1944), which it then considered to be of ethnic Croat origin as opposed to other non-Croats, Muslim or non-Muslim (Banac 1996: 141–4). The regime managed to co-opt some of the Muslim leaders to throw in their lot with the Ustaša (and by extension, the Nazis), though it never succeeded in luring the Muslim masses to its side as the Germans did during the same period both in the Crimea and the Caucasus.

The mass immigration of Bosniaks and Albanians to Slovenia and Croatia dates back to the times of the SFRY, and particularly from the 1970s, when tens of thousands of people from less-developed regions of the country were attracted to the faster developing and more affluent western republics. This internal migration is reminiscent of that experienced at around the same time by the Baltic republics within the USSR, when scores of 'colonists' of Muslim background arrived from inner Russia, Caucasus and Central Asia. In both instances, the majority of 'settlers' were low-skilled labourers, with a few high-skilled professionals. Most of the newly arrived settled in the industrialised urban areas, first of all in and around the two capitals, Liubliana and Zagreb. The period of the SFRY was also the time when the nascent Muslim communities started institutionalising their religious organisations, albeit still under the aegis of the Bosnian Rijaset.

Bosniak Muslims, this time as war refugees, also arrived in large numbers during the Bosnian war of 1992–5. Though many moved back once hostilities had ceased, some stayed and settled permanently as immigrants, joining the earlier arrivals and together becoming the nucleus of the national Muslim communities in the newly independent states of Slovenia and Croatia. With Slovenia joining the EU in 2004 and Croatia in 2014, the legal situation of Muslims in the two countries acquired an EU dimension: both countries had to comply with the *acquis communitaire* required of all candidate countries and accordingly change their legislation, inter alia, pertaining to governance of religion. From this point of view, the legal and also social position of Muslims in Slovenia and Croatia may arguably be seen as much more secure and stable than that in the rest of the post-Yugoslav states.

A second similarity between this pair of countries is that, compared to other Balkan states, their Muslim communities comprise a rather negligible share of the population – just 2.5 per cent in Slovenia (though Muslims are the second largest faith community in the country) and a mere 1.5 per cent in Croatia. In this regard, Slovenia and Croatia are comparable to most Western and Central European countries where the share of Muslims hovers around the same figure. Furthermore, in regards to the ethnic composition of the population of Muslim background, in both countries Bosniaks are the biggest ethnic group of Muslim cultural background (in Slovenia, they make up three quarters of all Muslims; in Croatia, over 56 per cent). As the Bosnian language is Slavic and arguably close to Croatian, though ethnically different, linguistically Bosniaks do not differ significantly from the titular ethnicities of the two countries. Likewise, in both countries, Albanians are the second largest Muslim ethnic group – 11 per cent in Slovenia and 15 per cent in Croatia. It might also be noted that Muslims who identified themselves with the titular ethnicity of their respective countries – 6 per cent in Slovenia and a staggering 15 per cent in Croatia – are a curious group. Though there is no doubt that some ethnic Slovenes and Croats have converted to Islam, it is hard to believe that their numbers are that high. It may, thus, be reasonable to speculate that at least some from among those who identified as Slovene and Croat Muslims actually hail from other (arguably, Slavic-speaking) ethnicities, chiefly Bosniaks.

In both countries, Muslim spiritual-administrative institutions – the Islamic Community in the Republic of Slovenia and Islamic Community in Croatia – are under the formal hierarchical framework of the Islamic Community of Bosnia and Herzegovina. In other words, the two Communities hold the status of *meshihat* as subordinate Islamic administrations of the Rijaset of Bosnia. This institutional subordination was proposed by the Bosnian Islamic authorities, to which the two Communities acquiesced. So, formally, although they are legally registered religious organisations in, respectively, Slovenia and Croatia, spiritually they pledge allegiance to an institution outside of the respective national jurisdictions. In this regard, the Croatian and Slovenian Islamic Communities are sister organisations to the Serbian Sandžak Islamic Community in Serbia and together with the Bosnian Islamic Community form what Mujadzevic has called the 'Bosniak Islamic transnational network' (Mujadzevic 2013: 1).

However, such spiritual, if not legal, affiliation with the Bosnian (aka ethnic Bosniak) Islamic administration has proven to be more of an obstacle than an asset to the development and internal cohesion and health of both Islamic Communities. The Slovenian Islamic Community experienced a shake-up when a splinter organisation, the Slovenian Muslim Community, was formed in 2006 by a former mufti of the Slovenian *meshihat*, who had been dismissed by the Bosnian Rijaset. Naturally, the new organisation is not only legally but also spiritually independent of the Bosnian Rijaset. Although it is reported to have a negligible membership (Moe 2015: 533), the very fact of the emergence and survival of such an alternative and rival Islamic administration is not only reminiscent of the Serbian Sandžak case but also an indication that the 'Bosniak Islamic transnational network' may not be sustainable in other post-Yugoslav countries, such as Croatia.

In fact, the Croatian Islamic Community came close to splintering in 2012 when it had to choose a new leader – the mufti. Since the mufti is elected, the election campaign of 2012 divided Croatia's Muslim community along ethnic but also conceptual lines, with the Bosniak candidate being supported mainly by Bosniaks while the Albanian candidate was supported by not only Albanians and Muslims of non-Bosniak background but also by a segment of the Bosniaks. According to Mujadzevic, the supporters of the Albanian candidate for the mufti's post considered that

> the interests of Muslims in Croatia cannot be any longer identified with Bosniak interests in Croatia. If done so, they reckon[ed], the ICC would face more tensions on ethnic lines. They were fully supportive of keeping the distance towards ICBH (although not completely break with it). (Mujadzevic 2013: 4)

In the end, however, it was the Bosniak candidate who secured the majority of the votes thus so far preserving the status of the Islamic Community in Croatia as the unitary Islamic administration in the country, yet at the same time being a Bosniak Muslim organisation subordinate to the Bosnian Islamic administration.

It remains to be seen if this relationship changes in the future, whether the spiritual umbilical cord is cut and the Islamic Community in Croatia ceases to be a part of the 'Bosniak Islamic transnational network' and instead becomes a 'multi-ethnic Croatia-centered Muslim organization' (Mujadzevic 2013: 1). But until any changes to the composition and orientation of the Islamic Community in Croatia happen, it is not only the sole *de facto* pan-Muslim organisation in the country (though, it should be mentioned that the Ahmadi community, seen by most non-Ahmadi Muslims as being heterodox if not altogether heretical, registered its own organisation in 2013) but also the organisation which has signed a comprehensive agreement with the state regulating the rights of the country's Muslims, the implementation of which is entrusted by the state to the Islamic Community.

In the Slovenian case, though there are two parallel Islamic administrations in the country, it is the older one, the Islamic Community in Slovenia, with whom the state has signed (in 2007) an agreement similar to the one signed by the state and the Islamic Community in Croatia. As in the Croatian case, the agreement stipulates the rights of the country's Muslims and regards the Islamic Community in Slovenia as the designated custodian and representative of (normative) Islam in the country.

Unlike in the Central and Eastern Balkans, where it had been widespread, Sufism has never historically been present in Slovenia. In Croatia, its presence was restricted to the north-eastern part, which was under Ottoman control for a while in the sixteenth and seventeenth centuries, and where, it is claimed, Sufi *tekkes* functioned (Mujadzevic 2014: 146). There are reports that in today's Croatia some of its Muslims are adherents of several Sufi brotherhoods, including the Bektashiyya (Mujadzevic 2014: 146).

Though there are reports of a Salafi presence in Slovenia, where it is represented by the Resnica-Haq Society, their activities have not reached any noticeable levels to draw any wider attention or concerns from either the state or the Islamic administrations.

CHAPTER 5

South-eastern Europe

The three countries of South-eastern Europe that were not part of the Yugoslavian state, namely, Albania, Bulgaria and Romania, had also been part of the Ottoman Empire and thus share this legacy not only among themselves but also with most of the successor states of Yugoslavia. When they emerged as independent nation states (Bulgaria and Romania in the second half of the nineteenth century, Albania after the Balkan wars of 1912–13), they had inherited sizeable Muslim communities, with Albania being nominally a Muslim-majority state (and at that time, the only one in the whole of Europe). However, as the majority of Muslims in Romania and particularly Bulgaria were of Turkish origin, due to a number of factors, a mass exodus of Turks (and also Muslims of other ethnicities) to Anatolia began almost immediately. For example, the proportion of Muslims in Bulgaria at independence in 1878 stood at around a quarter of the population, yet within a couple of decades it fell to half of that and subsequently declined even further. Likewise, the Muslim population in Romania shrank from several hundred thousand in 1877 to just tens of thousands by the turn of the century. In Albania, where the indigenous Albanian Muslims made up (and still make up) the majority of the population, no major emigration processes were observed, though some Muslims (ethnic Albanians and of other ethnicities) did leave the newly independent country for territories remaining under Ottoman rule.

In the second half of the twentieth century, following the Second World War, all three countries failed to escape the nightmare of communist rule. It might be argued that the communist period in these three countries was even more detrimental to the development of local Muslim communities than in either socialist Yugoslavia or the USSR: while the Muslim minority in Bulgaria was subjected not only to atheist policies but also to forced Bulgarisation by their communist government, in Albania all religions were banned in 1967. In communist Romania, the Muslim community, chiefly comprised of Turks and Tatars, was also heavily targeted by atheist policies. Turks of both communist-ruled Bulgaria and Romania were additionally targeted as a fifth column. The authorities suspected them of harbouring sentiments towards Turkey, which was not only a Muslim country with the potential to spread pan-Turkic and pan-Islamic ideas but also a member state of their adversary the NATO alliance. In the end, at the fall of the communist regimes in the beginning of the

1990s, Muslim communities in the three countries emerged much weakened, disoriented and disorganised and had to rebuild their religious institutions almost from the scratch.

Though all three post-communist countries experienced internal perturbations, social upheavals and unrest caused by the disintegration of the communist system, none of them was drawn into anything even remotely resembling the tensions and violence that ravaged some of the post-Yugoslavian states in the immediate aftermath of the collapse of the communist system in Southeastern Europe. Consequently, the development of local Muslim populations in the three countries was neither interrupted (as in the case of Bosnia) nor particularly burdened (as, arguably, in Serbia/Kosovo and Macedonia). And while Albania's Muslims, being ethnic kin of both the neighbouring Kosovan and Macedonian Muslims, were to a degree drawn into events affecting Muslim communities there, the Muslim communities in both Bulgaria and Romania had practically no connection/relation not only to the Muslim communities in the former Yugoslavia but also Albania, with which none of them shares a border. On the other hand, the 'Turkish factor' weighed heavily in Bulgaria and to a lesser extent in Romania, which suggests they should be treated together.

The joining of the EU in 2007 by Bulgaria and Romania also suggests another commonality as they had to implement *acquis communitaire* at the same time, which inter alia includes issues of minority rights protection (including religious rights). Additionally, all three countries joined NATO (Bulgaria and Romania in 2004, Albania in 2009), with Albania becoming the second (after Turkey) Muslim-majority member state in the Alliance.

Albania

Albania is exceptional if not altogether unique in view of the development of religion and its governance: to this day, it is the sole European state to have completely forbidden the practice of any religion in its territory. This happened in 1967 at the high point of communism in the country and lasted until the communist regime's collapse in 1990. Therefore, the development of the Muslim community in the modern Albanian nation state may be conditionally divided into three periods: (1) the pre-1967 period, when Muslims, making up the majority of Albania's population, enjoyed a somewhat privileged status in the country; (2) the period of state atheism between 1967 and 1990, marked by brutal suppression of religiousness; and (3) the post-communist era continuing into the present.

Though on its independence from the Ottomans, Albania nominally became a Muslim-majority state, it has since been of a secular nature – from the start, the politico-legal system has been both secular and accommodating of all religious communities. In the nascent independent state, religious differences were downplayed in favour of nation-building, the foundational block of which was belonging to the Albanian ethnicity. As argued by Merdjanova, '[a]lready in the 1920s, the Albanian state adopted a strong secularist tendency to downplay the role of religion in the name of a form of civic nationalism broadly described as "Albanianism"' (Merdjanova 2013: 39). One might also compare the etatist stance of the Albanian political elite of the 1920s to that of Kemalist Turkey, whose political reforms had a lasting impression on Albania's ruling political establishment of the time (Clayer 2010: 54–5). Among the 'modernising' measures, a law banning the veil and other conspicuous (traditional) religious attire in public was promulgated by parliament in 1937.

Albania, as the only Muslim-majority country in Europe at that time, proceeded with what was then regarded as modernising reforms in both the governance of Islam and the internal structures of the country's Muslim community. On the first count, the state embarked on what may be regarded as not merely secularisation (in the sense of separation of religion and politics) but all the way to laicisation (when the state directly controls and dictates its will over the religious authorities), emulating the Turkish example. As argued by Merdjanova,

> [i]n line with the strong nation-building impulses of the new state, the Sunni Islamic Community was proclaimed independent from the Ottoman Caliphate in 1923, one year before the abolishment of the Caliphate by Kemal Atatürk. Therefore, while Muslims in other post-Ottoman countries in the region sought to uphold their communal autonomy by preserving their links with the Caliphate, Muslims in Albania pursued autonomy by breaking with it. (Merdjanova 2013: 39)

On the second count, directly stemming from the first, the Muslim spiritual-administrative institutions and their subordinate establishments, foremost educational institutions, were shaped to meet 'the demands of the modern age'.

In principle, this trend continued into the communist period, until 1967, when the government moved decisively against religion in all its forms. The banning of religion in the country led to actions meant to eliminate religion not only from the country's public but also private space by both physically destroying its material side – buildings (over 2,000 mosques, *tekkes* and *turbes*), libraries, institutions, religious symbols and artefacts – as well as criminalising any religious activity, even to teaching it to the younger generations. A great number of 'men of religion' of all faith communities found themselves behind bars with scores of them sentenced to long periods of imprisonment or even death. With this drastic move by the communist regime, Albania's Muslim community not only formally ceased to exist but haemorrhaged people capable of providing spiritual guidance. However, it would be naive to assume that a centuries-long religious tradition like Islam could have disappeared overnight as the communists might have hoped. Many Muslims not only continued practising Islam in secrecy but also organised clandestine communal activities to perpetuate the traditions and to convey them to the younger generation despite the looming danger of being prosecuted. With the religious situation much better in neighbouring socialist Yugoslavia, and particularly Albanian-speaking Kosovo, though border control and censorship were severe, there was still a narrow window for Islamic ideas to seep across the border. Nonetheless, the level of religious knowledge and along with it religiosity in Albania gradually declined so that by the late 1980s Albanian society in general, and its Muslim component in particular, had indeed approached a state of widespread agnosticism if not atheism.

The exceptionally brutal treatment of Islam and Muslims at the hands of the communist government between 1967 and 1990 left the Albanian Muslim community severely crippled; in the end, it had neither knowledgeable men nor institutions, nor even places of worship, the majority of which had been destroyed in the anti-religious frenzy of the 1960s and 1970s. For instance, of the dozens of mosques in the capital city Tirana before 1967, only one, admittedly very beautiful, mosque survived, though even it was not used for prayers but served as a museum of atheism. The ridiculousness of the Albanian state atheism is symbolised in the label of a Tirana beer company on which the surviving historical mosque is pictured.

Of all the former communist countries in Eastern Europe, it is of Albania where one can truly talk of the 'return of the Sacred' in the wake of the tectonic transformations following the collapse of the communist system in this part of the Old Continent. The return of religion and public displays of religiosity reached unprecedented levels with hundreds of thousands of followers of different religions gathering for public religious rituals of their respective faiths. Due to the proportion of Muslims in the country, the re-emergence of the Muslim community was even more visible than that of the other faith communities. Albania was soon internationally recognised as a Muslim (majority) country and joined the Organization of Islamic Cooperation in 1992, though has since (in 1997) downgraded its status from a full member to that of an observer state, leaving Bosnia and Herzegovina the only European member state in the organisation.

Also, though nominally a Muslim-majority country, the Constitution (adopted in 1998) of post-communist (and post-atheist) Albania establishes it as a secular state with not only no formal preference for any religion but also with no indication of Islam's role in its history. In this regard, post-communist Albania follows in the footsteps of the monarchical state of the interwar period, but at the same time breaks with the prevailing tradition of mentioning the role of the Orthodox Church found in neighbouring countries like Macedonia, Serbia and Bulgaria. Non-recognition in the Constitution of any historical role for religion (of Islam) may also be read as an indication that though the majority of Albania's inhabitants are nominal Muslims – the 2011 census revealed that 1,587,608 (56.70 per cent) of respondents identified themselves as Muslims – the level of religiosity may (still) be relatively low and therefore there might be no pressure even from Muslims for such recognition.

Indeed, a recent survey found that only 15 per cent of Muslims indicated that 'religion is very important in their lives' (Pew 2012: 40). Moreover, undertaking regular daily prayers among Albanian Muslims appears to be particularly low – only 4 per cent of the country's Muslims claimed to pray all five times with another 3 per cent claiming to pray several times but short of the required five (Pew 2012: 43). Likewise, attending mosque at least once a week (for the communal Friday prayer) is exceptionally low – a mere 5 per cent claim to do this (Pew 2012: 46), while 44 per cent answered that they 'never attend mosque' (Pew 2012: 47). Though these figures should not be overstated, they nonetheless indicate that the Albanian population of Muslim background has been and remains thoroughly secularised.

The Albanian situation is also exceptional when talking about Islam in that Bektashis are officially recognised as a separate independent religious community, next to the Sunni Muslim community formally represented by the Muslim Community of Albania (though survey results suggest that only a tenth of Albania's Muslims self-identify as 'Sunni', with 65 per cent identifying as 'just a Muslim'; Pew 2012: 30). In the national census, which includes a question on religious affiliation, Bektashis are put in a separate category from Muslims: the 2011 census revealed that 58,628 (or 2.09 per cent of the total population) presented themselves as Bektashis. Bektashis have their own spiritual-administrative institution, which, however, aspires to a status well beyond national borders. Its very name, the World Bektashi Center, betrays the organisation's claim to be the central Bektashi institution in the world. Though most of the Albanian-speaking Bektashi communities appear to endorse this claim, there are numerous Bektashi communities worldwide which dismiss it.

The designation of Bektashism as a religion separate from Islam has boded ill with the Albanian Muslim institutions, which are reported to have protested against this separation of Bektashism from Islam:

> [i]n the 1990s, members of the official Islamic institutions repeatedly asserted (in the press or in books) that Bektashism was not different from Islam, as some Albanian intellectuals claimed, generally stressing that there were only three religions in the country. They claimed that Bektashism is not a separate religion, but a 'sect', arguing that various Bektashis had already presented Bektashism as such. (Clayer 2012: 190)

However, even Albania's Bektashis are not unanimous in seeing themselves as a separate faith community from Muslims – a minority of Bektashis in Albania continue to regard themselves as Muslims, though, admittedly, very different from Sunnis.

In 1991, the Sunni Islamic community (officially called the Muslim Community of Albania, MCA) reconstituted itself and immediately proceeded to rebuild the Islamic infrastructure of the country. On its own, this would have been virtually impossible but '[w]ith foreign aid, Muslims built or rebuilt some 520 mosques (about half of those existing in the country until 1967) and opened eight medreses and two mektebs' (Merdjanova 2013: 40). However, the rush to build mosques in the 1990s had led to a significant number of them (counted in the hundreds, with some thirty in and around the capital Tirana alone) not being officially registered and officially without a formal owner. The registration process has been so protracted that hundreds of mosques, some of them in use for twenty years or more remain unregistered into the mid 2010s. Many of these mosques remain outside the control of the MCA, with one classified secret services document of 2015 putting the number at eighty-nine (Jazehxi 2016: 21). A similar phenomenon is reported for Kosovo where mosques started springing up on donated money in the early 2000s, when the international status of the region had not yet been determined and the country had no effective state institutions. But even with this seemingly large number of new mosques, in the 2010s Albania's capital Tirana witnessed the execution of the project to build the Grand Mosque, which would dwarf the nearby parliament building.

Albania's situation is peculiar in yet another respect: its official Islamic administration is claimed to have been effectively taken over by sympathisers of Fethullah Gülen, if not altogether by his movement Hizmet (Jazehxi 2016: 21). Even if this were not the case, the presence and influence of the Gulenist movement is undeniable: Bedr University is under its control and has an Islamic studies programme through which it prepares graduates to take on positions in MCA institutions (Jazehxi 2016: 31). The influence of Hizmet within the Islamic administration in Albania has arguably 'become a source of concern not only for the local Salafi-Arab educated imams who want to have a share in the direction of "official Islam", but for the Turkish government as well' (Jazehxi 2016: 21). The latter is particularly concerned and during his visit to Albania in 2015 the Turkish President reportedly 'asked the Albanian government to remove the Gülen movement from Albania, since this movement was considered a terrorist organisation in Turkey' but his request was rebuffed by high-standing Albanian officials, who argued that Hizmet is not a terrorist organisation and its activities in the country are perfectly legal (Jazehxi 2016: 22).

Up until the total ban on religion in 1967, Sufism was an integral part of the Albanian Islamic landscape. In the 1920s and 1930s, several Sufi brotherhoods even formed their own organisation within the broader structure of Islamic institutions. During the decades of official atheism, Sufi practices were also banned and prosecuted with Sufi lodges and shrines desecrated or even destroyed and adepts dispersed while their leaders were imprisoned. But it would be wrong to believe Sufism in Albania to have fallen into oblivion – a recent survey found that in the early 2010s, 13 per cent of the surveyed Albanian Muslims claimed to belong to some Sufi brotherhood (Pew 2012: 31). Without further qualification, however, this figure tells us little as it is not clear whether the Bektashis fall into this category – though since 1945 Bektashis in Albania have been formally treated as a separate religious community from Muslims, there is no denying that their historical roots lie in mystical Islam. It is reported that in the mid-2010s, Bektashis had almost 140 lodges, with other Sufi brotherhoods running close to 400 (Jazehxi 2016: 30; Merdjanova 2013: 40).

Though there is little available information on Albanian practices of folk Islam, it appears to have survived the atheist period: 47 per cent of the recently surveyed Albanian Muslims admit to having 'objects against evil eye' (Pew 2012: 77) and 38 per cent to using 'religious healers' (Pew 2012: 80).

Islamic revivalism in Albania, like pretty much elsewhere in the Eastern and Central Bakans, was initially fostered by foreign state and non-state actors in the form of the numerous NGOs who came to Albania in the early 1990s to rebuild the Islamic infrastructure. It was revivalist- (Salafi/Wahhabi) leaning imams who were placed to preach at the newly built mosques and teach at establishments of religious education sponsored by foreign donors. The US-supported anti-terrorist campaign of the early 2000s severely curtailed the operations of foreign organisations, and financing of revivalist activities sharply decreased. With Albania seeking to join NATO, which it did in 2009, securitisation of 'the Islamic issue' was upgraded even more. However, with the alleged takeover by Gülen followers of the MCA's infrastructure, this gave a new impetus to the spread of alternative (chiefly, revivalist) forms of religiosity from those propagated by the MCA. The revivalist imams even created an informal League of Albanian Imams as a counter-balancing force, which however, has not attracted much following. Nonetheless, the spread of radical and even extremist ideas among the country's Muslim population, particularly its younger generation, has reached unprecedented levels with several hundred of them having gone to the Middle East to join the jihadi groups there.

Bulgaria

Nowhere else in Eastern Europe has the national historiography given so much attention to the question of the origins of their Muslim population as in Bulgaria. Since the Muslim population in Bulgaria is heterogeneous, comprising at least three distinctive 'ethnic' groups, the debate about their roots has also been a complex one. Compared to other Balkan (post-Ottoman) countries, Bulgaria has an exceptionally high percentage (and in absolute numbers) of the population which identifies itself as ethnically Turkish (and Muslim) with, naturally, Turkish as the mother tongue. From practically the birth of the independent

Bulgarian state in 1878, that is, for almost a century and a half now, Bulgarian historians and politicians have been swinging from one extreme to the other in their designation of this part of their population, either including it into the Bulgarian nation (and even ethnicity) or excluding it as an ontological alien, the 'Other'. Similarly, the Bulgarian-speaking Muslims (known as Pomaks) have also been regarded as either a 'lost tribe' of ethnic Bulgarians or Bulgarian-speaking aliens (Turks, by virtue of being Muslims but also because some among them self-identify as Turks) – or even as an altogether autonomous ethnic group. While discussions about the Pomaks origins closely echo the ones on the origins of Torbeshis in neighbouring Macedonia (who sometimes are also identified as Pomaks of Macedonia) and to a much lesser extent those on the origins of Bosniaks (particularly among Serbs), the question of belonging to and inclusion of Bulgarian Turks in the Bulgarian national body has no precedent anywhere in Eastern Europe.

In a nutshell, the essential question in this discussion is to decide whether Bulgarian Turks are Turks at all (read, descendants of Turkish 'colonists') or rather Islamised and 'Turkified' Slavs (read, proto-Bulgarians). In the latter case, the following question is of the crucial importance: had the original conversion to Islam been forced or voluntary? Depending on the prevailing (official) position in this regard, state policies vis-à-vis the Muslims in Bulgaria would oscillate between relatively benevolent and discriminatory. This, in its turn would directly affect the Muslims' lives, including their religious activities.

The initial perception of Turks in independent Bulgaria was that they were nothing less than aliens, that is, descendants of colonist Turks who had come to the Bulgarian territory with the invading Ottoman troops and settled the land as overlords. Such an attitude, coupled with actions (coercion, threatening or even outright violence), caused the first exodus of Turks from Bulgaria that would later become numerous waves of emigration. It is reported that up to '198,000 Muslims left Bulgaria during the struggles for national liberation in the mid-1870s, while another 350,000 emigrated between 1878 and 1912' (Merdjanova 2013: 10). However, hundreds of thousands stayed and became citizens of the country, whose rights to a high degree were regulated by international treaties imposed on Bulgaria. Apparently, in compliance with the stipulations of the treaties,

> [i]n 1885 a law was passed giving Bulgarian Turks autonomy in education, which allowed them to preserve their own schools in which the language of instruction was Turkish. In the beginning of the 20th century there were more than 1,300 such schools in Bulgaria. (Marushiakova and Popov 2004: 4)

The status of Bulgarian-speaking Muslims (Pomaks), however, was more vulnerable than that of Bulgaria's Turks. In the early 1910s they were subjected to the first, albeit aborted, campaign coordinated by a 'special state committee' to 'Bulgarise' them through baptism and the forced changing of names of Turkish and Arabic origin into Slavic. It is reported that the campaign affected up to 200,000 people (Merdjanova 2013: 22). However, due to resistance by the target group and external pressure, the campaign, which started in 1912, was not only discontinued in 1913 (after the Balkan wars) but Pomaks were also allowed to reclaim their 'Islamic' identity, including their names. In post-First World War Bulgaria, governance of Islam was further conditioned by new international and, later, bilateral treaties, so that new legislation had to safeguard Muslims' right to autonomy in not only their religious but also social affairs (Marushiakova and Popov 2004: 6).

With the Ottoman Empire dismembered and the Caliphate abolished, Istanbul ceased to be the spiritual centre of the Bulgarian Muslims. However, since the overwhelming majority of Bulgaria's Muslims were Turkish speakers, they could not have been immune to what was going on in the nascent Turkish Republic. Moreover, some Turks, who were not content with the political course of the Turkish state, emigrated to Bulgaria. The sweeping political and social reforms initiated by the new republican regime in Turkey effectively split the Bulgarian Muslim (Turkish) population into two opposing camps: supporters of secularist reforms (and by extension, Turkish nationalism) and their opponents (Merdjanova 2013: 15–17). The latter were, among other things, religious conservative traditionalists.

The religious conservatives were soon picked by the Bulgarian regime as its partners in suppressing the rise in Turkish nationalism in the country, which could have threatened Bulgaria's territorial integrity. By the early 1930s, with tacit support from the state, this group was organised into the Association of the Defenders of Islam in Bulgaria in order to fend off the Kemalist propaganda and activities spearheaded by the pro-Turkish association Turan. The anti-Kemalist forces prevailed and Islam in interwar Bulgaria remained traditional/'Ottoman', with several dozen Islamic courts functioning practically until the beginning of the Second World War (Merdjanova 2013: 15).

For a time, it might have seemed that the life of Bulgaria's Muslims would follow a normal course with religious institutions to take care of the spiritual needs of the believers. Unfortunately, a subsequent *coup d'état* and dictatorial regime proved to be detrimental to the development of the Muslim community and '[s]ome 200,000 Turks left Bulgaria between 1925 and 1939' (Merdjanova 2013: 10). Though emigration of Muslims continuously diminished their numbers and share in the state, in 1940 when Bulgaria annexed the southern Romanian Dobruja region, 'approximately 150,000 additional Turks were added to Bulgaria's Turkish Muslim population' (Nitzova 1994: 102).

The coming to power of communists in Bulgaria in 1944 was followed by patterns of governance of religion universally recognisable throughout Eastern

Europe of that period with policies aimed at the complete eradication of religion from the public life of countries and attempts at ousting it from citizens' personal lives. To pursue this aim, in 1949, Quranic schools were nationalised and turned into secular state schools and, at the beginning of the 1950s, 'the study of religion was banned from all public schools' (Marushiakova and Popov 2004: 5). Later in the 1950s, the authorities turned against what may be referred to as traditional (Muslim) clothes, including head covering, both female (hijab/scarf) and male (fez and other male headgear). The press at that time was ripe with articles ridiculing Islamic religious practices like fasting during the month of Ramadan or Islamic festivities as 'antiscientific', 'unhealthy', 'reactionary' and 'anti-social'. In the end, the two most important Islamic celebrations were banned. Instead, in the late 1970s, the communist regime, following the Soviet example, introduced alternative 'socialist' rituals (including name-giving instead of circumcision, and for marriage and burial) and holidays to replace the old religion-related ones. As argued by Nitzova,

> [t]he Communist Party's campaign against all forms of Islamic religious expression among Turks, Pomaks and Gypsies was built up upon the following rationale: (a) Islam was an alien religion forced on Bulgarians against their will; (b) Islam had played a reactionary role in Bulgarian history; (c) Islam had been used by foreign reactionary elements (i.e. Turkey) to promote bourgeois nationalism and religious fanaticism in Bulgaria; (d) Islam was an obstacle to the integration of Turks and other Muslims into Bulgarian society. (Nitzova 1994:101)

If anti-religious (anti-Islamic) policies of the Bulgarian communist regime may be easily recognised in other Eastern European states of the time, particularly, in the USSR, anti-Turkish policies by the Bulgarian communist authorities hardly have an analogue in the region. Though some of these policies, like the banning of 'Turkish' clothes, may be seen as being tied to anti-Muslim campaigns, banning the Turkish language in public in the early 1980s quickly followed by an unprecedented campaign of forced Slavisation of Turkish (and Arabic) names, known as the 'process of rebirth', were clearly exclusively of ethnic (nationalist) character.

In result and as a reaction to these and other anti-Muslim (and anti-Turkish) policies of the communist regime, over 600,000 Bulgarian Muslims are reported to have left communist-ruled Bulgaria, with over 200,000 in 1950–1, 130,000 between 1968 and 1978, and over 300,000 in 1989 alone (Merdjanova 2013: 10). The latter emigration wave, known as the 'Big Excursion', was provoked by the communist regime just before its collapse later the same year when it opened its border with Turkey and allowed, and in fact actively encouraged (by liberalising the acquisition of foreign travel passports for Bulgarian Turks) those willing to leave. It should be added, though, that around half of those who left

Bulgaria soon returned to the post-communist state. The return was facilitated by a legislative act in the last days of 1989, allowing the resumption of Muslim names. In a period of just a couple of years, the government had to deal with over half a million requests to restore original names.

Formally, like all other countries in Eastern Europe, post-communist Bulgaria is a secular state with religion separated from politics. Its Constitution's (adopted in 1991) paragraph 4 of Article 13 declares that 'Religious institutions and communities, and religious beliefs shall not be used to political ends.' However, the preceding paragraph 3 of the same article establishes Eastern Orthodox Christianity as 'the traditional religion in the Republic of Bulgaria' with no other religions mentioned. So, unlike neighbouring Macedonia, which amended its Constitution to include Muslim and other faith communities, Bulgaria remains firm in refusing to acknowledge any positive role of Islam in its history or contribution of its Muslim population to its development.

The difficult relationship between the Bulgarian state (and ethnic Bulgarians) and its Muslim population, when viewed from the state's (and majority non-Muslim population's) perspective, has been both caused by and based on several, seemingly immovable principles, such as a deep conviction that besides being an alien religion that had been forcefully imposed on Bulgaria by the Ottomans, Islam had stifled, if not altogether prevented, the development of the Bulgarian nation. Moreover, perceived to be a reactionary religion, it had compelled local Muslims, at the instigation of outside actors (read, first the Ottoman Empire and later the Turkish Republic), to resist modernisation and development and to move in the direction of religious conservativism, if not fanaticism. Though the official rhetoric would change with time and depending on the nature of the regime in power, the basic notions toward the country's Muslims arguably remained intact into the post-communist period, if not on the legislative level, then at least on practical politics and social levels.

On the other hand, in an apparent rebuff to the Constitution, in post-communist Bulgaria, a political party created by and for Muslims of the country made a very early entry into national politics. Since its founding in 1990, the Movement for Rights and Freedoms has been a heavy-weight player not only taking part in all national and municipal elections but also on several occasions making it into government positions. Though neither its name nor its programme suggest it, the party has been equally perceived by its electorate and outsiders as being representative of, first of all, the Turkish-speaking segment of the country's population and, since most of the Turks are (seen as) Muslims, the party is also thought of as representative of all Muslims irrespective of their ethnic origins. However, the party's leadership has 'been very careful to avoid any identification with Islamist or pan-Turkist ideas. They use an essentially secular and moderate language in their programs and statements' (Merdjanova 2013: 19).

Despite the high volume of emigration of Turks/Muslims,

> in 1900, there were 531,240 Turks in Bulgaria or 14.2 percent of the total population; in 1920, 520,339 Turks or 10.7 percent of the total population; in 1946, 675,500 Turks or 9.6 percent of the total population; in 1956, 656,025 Turks or 8.6 percent of the total population; in 1965, 780,928 Turks or 9.5 percent of the total population; in 1975, 730,728 Turks or 8.4 percent of the total population, and the census of 1992 registered 800,052 Turks or 9.4 percent of the Bulgarian population. (Marushiakova and Popov 2004: 45–6)

Emigration (and assimilation) of Muslims from post-communist Bulgaria was halted for some time (though Marushiakova and Popov claim that '[f]or the period 1992–2002 . . . estimates range from 200,000 to 300,000 persons' (Marushiakova and Popov 2004: 47) to have left the country), only to resume with force in the second half of the 2000s after Bulgaria joined the EU and its citizens were granted the right to travel, reside and work without restrictions in most of the member states of the bloc. So, though the 2001 census recorded almost 967,000 Muslim residents, the 2011 census counted only just over 577,000. However, it needs to be pointed out that since answering the question on religious identity and affiliation was not obligatory in the 2011 census, almost 22 per cent of respondents did not reply to it, among them, for instance, close to 40,000 ethnic Turks.

Another shortcoming in calculating the Muslim population in Bulgaria is the phenomenon of the 'preferential ethnic affiliation', when '[s]ome population groups (Gypsies, Tartars, Bulgarian Muslims) sometimes, for various reasons, prefer to declare themselves as belonging to another ethnic group (most often 'Turkish' because of the syncretic concept of ethnic and religious affiliation in the Balkans)' (Marushiakova and Popov 2004: 44). As Marushiakova and Popov point out, this phenomenon is observable not only in Bulgaria – Slavic- and Roma-speaking Muslims in Macedonia, Kosovo and Greece are noted to sometimes identify themselves as either Turks or belonging to the titular ethnicity. Due to this, the statistical numbers of Turks may be inflated and those of Roma, Pomak, Gorani or Torbeshi be too low.

Of all the Muslims in the 2011 census, over 131,500 declared Bulgarian to be their mother tongue. Since it is hard to believe that many Turks could have chosen to indicate Bulgarian as their mother tongue, it must be Pomaks and Roma who have done so. Pomaks, like similar Slavic-speaking groups of Muslim background elsewhere in the Eastern Balkans, are a curious group. Throughout the history of the Bulgarian statehood, Pomaks have been denied an independent identity. In fact,

> since the 1920s the official line has been that Bulgarian Muslims are Bulgarians who were converted to Islam – thus they are not a minority, they are part of the majority. Much of the scholarship on this population from the 1950s onward has set out to prove this thesis. (Osterman 2013: 16)

Though forced attempts to Bulgarise Pomaks have ceased in post-communist Bulgaria – its membership in the minority-rights-championing EU preventing the Bulgarian state from contemplating such policies – the discussions on where Bulgarian-speaking Muslims belong in the nation and the state have continued. With their origin remaining a contested issue, lately a somewhat more concerted effort to lobby for the official recognition of Pomaks as a separate ethnic group has emerged from within the Pomak community (Osterman 2013: 6–7).

Another ethnic group in Bulgaria, which historically has been Muslim, is the Tatars. Besides Bulgaria, where their official number hovers just around 5,000 (it might be expected that a share of Tatars self-identify as Turks), Tatars are also found in larger numbers in neighbouring Romania. In fact, Bulgarian and Romanian Tatars have the same roots: their ancestors migrated to the Romanian and Bulgarian territories in the eighteenth century (after the annexation of Crimea by Russia) and the nineteenth century (after the Crimean war), when they were still part of the Ottoman Empire. The number of Tatars who had fled Crimea in several waves must have been in the tens of thousands. However, on the founding of the sovereign Bulgarian and Romanian states with their expressly unfavourable view of Turks/Muslims (with whom Tatars were often identified and themselves identified with), many Tatars joined the Turkish exodus, so that today there are fairly sizeable Tatar communities in Turkey who are descendants of Bulgarian and Romanian (and by extension Crimean) Tatars. Nonetheless, though in the 2001 census, only '4,515 persons declared themselves to be Tartars, and 7,883 persons declared Tartar to be their mother tongue', Marushiakova and Popov maintain that their 'actual number is probably between 10,000 and 15,000' (Marushiakova and Popov 2004: 5).

Though Muslims may be found across the country, there are several areas of higher concentration: in the region of the Rhodope Mountains in the south of the country (where Pomaks are mainly concentrated) and the Dobruja region in the north-east of the country (dominated by Turks and Tatars). The majority of Bulgaria's Muslims reside in rural areas, though inner migration to large cities has led to the emergence of sizeable communities in the country's industrial centres.

Though the overwhelming majority of Bulgaria's Muslims are Sunni like their co-religionists elsewhere in the Balkans, the 2011 census results revealed that over 27,000 (that is just below 5 per cent) identified themselves as Shiʿi. This is a sharp decrease from 1992, when the share of Shiʿis (Alevis) was found to be 7.7 per cent of the total Muslim population in Bulgaria. Nowhere else in the Balkans is the proportion of Shiʿis in the national Muslim population so high, and of all Eastern Europe, it is only Russia which has such a significant share of Shiʿis. Shiʿis in Bulgaria are associated with Alevis (also called Kizilbash), who are suggested to have come to the Bulgarian territory from Western Asia. Marushiakova and Popov report that '[t]he popular belief is that the majority of their forefathers migrated (or were forced to migrate) from Iran and Asia Minor between the 15th and 17th centuries' (Marushiakova and Popov 2004: 2). During her fieldwork research, Maeva discovered that Pomaks, who tended to identify themselves as Bektashis or Kazilbashis, while Turks identified as Alevi or Aliani, 'revealed small practical and ideological differences in the local religious rituals' (Maeva 2015: 83).

With the communist system gone, in the early 1990s Bulgarian society experienced a sudden return of religion to the public sphere. The Turkish-dominated Muslim community of the country proceeded to rebuild its infrastructure, the institutions and facilities. The first step was to secure a favourable legal status for Muslims in the country and to formalise their relations with the state. To this end, the spiritual Islamic administration had to renegotiate both its and its represented community's status. Parallel to this, the Muslim religious establishment had to undergo its own rejuvenation. However, this process of rejuvenation, reportedly very much influenced by the then governments (Barišić 2007: 37), had effectively led to a split inside the Muslim community and the ultimate emergence of rival spiritual administrations claiming to represent normative Islam in the country. By 1995, there already were two rival Muslim religious institutions headed by 'grand' muftis, who were both officially recognised in such capacity by the state (Marushiakova and Popov 2004: 34). Notably, one of them was headed by a former communist-time Grand Mufti who, though dismissed from his position in the first years after the change of regime, with the return of (by then reformed) communists, seized upon the opportunity to reclaim his status. The impasse lasted until the end of 2000, when a sole new Grand Mufti was elected and the leadership of legalist Islam passed into his hands with no more rival claimants (Marushiakova and Popov 2004: 37).

As many of the mosques had been closed and became derelict or were even destroyed during the communist era, the revival of Islamic religiosity in postcommunist Bulgaria made their restoration a priority. Next to the historical mosques, new ones were being built in locations with larger concentrations of Muslims, with over 400 built between 1990 and the mid-2010s (Shakir 2016: 158). And all this, despite a steady decline in the number of people in the country who identify with Islam.

Nominal official numbers also do not tell anything about the *de facto* levels of religiosity. But there are surveys that may be used to get a picture of how religious Bulgaria's Muslims are. For instance, according to the findings of one of the pan-European surveys in the early 2000s, 'just 28% of the Turkish population is deeply religious, 47% is religious to some extent, and 19% is mostly unreligious' (Maeva 2015: 88). Such surveys, however, often fail to grasp the spectrum of religious practices of those who consider themselves religious. If praying and fasting can be seen as the key points in legalist Islam-related religiosity, religious rituals of non-normativist nature cover a much wider spectrum.

As Islam arrived in Bulgaria early and remained the official religion in the land for almost 500 years, it is natural to expect heterodox forms of it to have been widespread. And indeed, both Sufi and folk forms of Islam had been very widespread before the emergence of the sovereign Bulgarian state (Gramatikova 2011). Unfortunately, due to the tectonic shifts that befell the Muslim population in independent Bulgaria, the presence of Sufism in the country has shrunk to negligible levels with the communist authorities reported to have cracked down on the last Sufi practices in the early 1980s (Marushiakova and Popov 2004: 21). In post-communist Bulgaria, just over fifty *tekkes* are known to have survived (Erolova 2016: 50). But even those surviving hardly have a community of Sufi adepts attached to them; instead, those *tekkes* that contain *turbes* continue serving as sites of pilgrimage. Some half a dozen of the *turbes*, like the one in Akyazılı Baba *tekke*, have a dual function of being sacred sites for both local Muslims and Christians. It has been reported that lately, '[a] new vision of tekke "Akyazılı – St. Athanasius" as a cultural object has started to come into being and to be advertised with the purpose of developing tourism and investments' (Erolova 2016: 61).

One may observe that the abandoned and often derelict former Sufi *tekkes* with their *turbes* have effectively become the sites of rituals and practices of folk Islam, like seeking healing. In one of them, the *tekke* in Obrochishte, visitors are reported to 'lie on the sarcophagus and spend the night there. They leave gifts (towels, scarves, socks and other items) on it, light candles and pray' (Erolova 2016: 58). Another commonly observed practice at the same *tekke* is tying

> a cloth or piece of a cloth, a thread on the trees nearby the tomb believing that this action will bring them health. Trees in that area are considered an integral part of the sacred place. They connect the visible world of life and the invisible one of death. (Erolova 2016: 58)

Folk Islam has survived in the Bulgarian hinterlands, where relatively isolated rural Muslim communities had not been affected to the same degree by secularisation as in the cities. In Pomak-inhabited villages, to this day a number of communal festivities include religious rituals with elements of folk Islam next to purely lay practices. So, for instance, folk dancing and singing may be supplemented by recitations of religious character or include religious lyrics. There are reports that

> [i]t was not an uncommon practice among the Pomaks in the Smolyan region to seek out local 'fortune-tellers' in times of confusion and uncertainty, and then to ask for amulets from local hodzhas in order to protect themselves from the dangers predicted for them. (Ghodsee 2010: 19)

Like Muslim communities elsewhere in Eastern Europe, Bulgaria's Muslims had not been immune from inroads by revivalist Islam, though this started, admittedly, much later than in the then neighbouring Yugoslavia. The revivalist forms of Islam came to be identified in popular parlance in Bulgaria as 'Arab Islam', as the revivalist ideas were seen to be originating in the Arab Middle East and brought over to Bulgaria either by Arabs themselves (via charity and aid organisations) or through those Bulgarians who studied at religious universities in the Arab world (Ghodsee 2010: 14). There are reports that Pomaks have been susceptible to revivalist ideas coming from and through organisations based in and hailing from the Gulf:

> the hybridity and fluidity of Pomak identity and the political powerlessness that accompanied it caused some Pomaks to embrace forms of Islam that diverged significantly from those practiced by the Turks . . . By establishing closer links (even through an imagined ethnicity) to the Saudis or Gulf Arabs and practicing more 'orthodox' forms of Islam, the new Pomak religious leaders also strategically positioned themselves to take advantage of the generous resources available from wealthy Saudi charities or other foreign sources of Islamic aid. (Ghodsee 2010: 22)

However, although the Grand Mufti is reported to have said that 'Salafism does not mean anything frightening or dangerous, it is purely and simply a current [within Islam]' (Osterman 2013: 10), the activities of more radically inclined revivalist Muslims have already raised the concern of the state. For instance, in 2012, over a dozen imams were arrested and charged with 'spreading radical Islam in Bulgaria' (Osterman 2013: 10).

Romania

When it emerged as a sovereign state in 1877, Romania had a sizeable Turkic-speaking Muslim population compactly settled in the south-east of the country, which, however, neither in absolute numbers nor percentage-wise matched those of other newly founded states in the eastern Balkans. Independent Romania was distinct from the other Balkan states – whose Muslim populations were composed of indigenous Slavic- and/or Albanian-speaking Muslims and/or descendants of Turkish colonists – in that it 'inherited' a sizeable community of Crimean Tatar Muslims, along with Turks who had come to its territories from Asia Minor as colonists in Ottoman times.

Though Muslim Tatars first came to Romanian lands back in the seventeenth century as (it turned out, temporary) immigrants from the Grand Duchy of Lithuania (and there are also suggestions of Tatars arriving at the turn of the thirteenth and fourteenth centuries, even before the Ottoman conquest; Grigore 1999: 34), the bulk of them had settled in Romania as refugees and immigrants from the Crimean Peninsula after it had been annexed by Russia at the end of the eighteenth century. The number of Muslim refugees/immigrants who moved to the Romanian territory (and specifically, the Dobruja region strad-dling the border of Romania and Bulgaria) in the decade between the 1850s and the 1860s alone, as a result of the Russo-Ottoman war, is estimated to have been up to 120,000. The majority of them would have been Tatars, though there certainly must have been some Turks among the newly arrived. However, with ethno-confessional policies of the independent Romanian state resembling those of its neighbour Bulgaria, many of its Muslim inhabitants chose (or were forced to choose) to relocate to Ottoman/Turkish lands. There are reports that while at the time of Romanian independence the proportion of Muslims in the Dobruja region was well above half of the population, in some thirty years it shrank by five times (Vainovski-Mihai 2016: 570). There are also reports sug-gesting that between 1913 and 1930 some 36,000 Muslims left Romania for Turkey, to be followed in 1937–9 by up to 150,000 others (Eminov 2000: 134). Bulgaria's annexation of the southern part of the Dobruja region in 1940 further diminished the number of Muslims in Romania.

The communist period was not as harsh for Romania's Muslims as for those in Bulgaria or Albania, though, like Muslims (and indeed any other religious groups) elsewhere in communist-ruled Eastern Europe they had to bear the brunt of the local regime's anti-religious/atheist policies. With the only religious college closed by the communist regime in the mid-1960s, the local Muslims were stripped of the possibility to renew their body of *ulama*, and with the decrease in availability and quality of spiritual guidance, levels of religiosity, and particularly of normative Islam, gradually declined. As argued by Eminov, '[l]ack of religious instruction, shortage of well-trained religious personnel, scar-city of functioning mosques, and anti-religious propaganda combined to create a generation of Tatars and Turks ignorant about the fundamental principles of their religion' (Eminov 2000: 135–6). There were also lukewarm attempts to Romanise Turks and Tatars; however, literature in both Turkish and Tatar was allowed to be imported and also published locally (Eminov 2000: 135).

On the other hand, like in most communist-ruled Eastern European states, including the USSR, the Islamic administrative structures in Romania were allowed to function throughout the communist period, though not indepen-dently of the state. In fact, as in most other communist-ruled Eastern European countries, Romania's Muslim leadership were co-opted by the state and may be seen to have been no more than the state's instruments and mouthpiece, both for communicating the regime's messages to common believers and for present-ing the regime's religious policies in a favourable light to the outside world. All this inevitably diminished the credentials and relevance of the official Islamic administration, presided over by the mufti. Though Tatars comprised just a third of Romania's Muslim population, they were the preferred choice of the communists to serve in the Islamic administration: muftis and their staff during the communist period are reported to have been Tatars (Eminov 2000: 136).

Eminov explains this by suggesting that Tatars were seen by the communist authorities as more loyal than the more numerous Turks (Eminov 2000: 136).

With the abrupt and violent collapse of the communist regime in 1989, Romania's Muslim community re-emerged as a public, and even political, actor. Though the majority of Romania's Muslims are still concentrated in their historical regions (for example, Dobruja, where two thirds of the country's Muslims are concentrated, with 90 per cent of all the Turks and 96 per cent of Tatars living there), new congregations have emerged in urban centres, comprised of both local Turks and Tatars who have moved there as well as newly immigrated and also local Romanian converts, with the country's capital city Bucharest hosting one seventh of the country's total Muslim population. Like those of some other former communist Eastern European countries, Romania's larger cities during the 1980s had become the adopted home of students-turned-immigrants from 'friendly' Muslim-majority countries in the Middle East.

Though the Great Mufti's Office of the Muslim Community of Romania on its website claims that the number of Muslims in the country is around 70,000, the latest (2011) census' official data shows that there were over 64,330 Muslims in the country that year, of whom almost 27,000 were Turks and 20,000 Tatars, followed by over 6,200 who identified themselves as Romanian Muslims, while some 3,350 identified themselves as Roma Muslims. Roma Muslims are not unique to Romania; they are found throughout the Balkans and in particular in neighbouring countries like Bulgaria and Macedonia. Practically everywhere in the region, they have been stigmatised and marginalised by the majority societies and states to the point that many among them identify (and are also often identified by non-Muslims) with Muslim groups of other ethnic backgrounds, particularly Turks. Romania's Roma Muslims are no exception – many pretend to be Turks and are seen by non-Muslim Romanians as such; Romanian Turks, however, do not necessarily recognise Roma Muslims as being part of their community (Alak 2015: 154). In the end, 'Rroma Muslims were and are still pariah in the Romanian society. Accused of refusing to integrate in and adjust to mainstream social life, they are unilaterally blamed for their traditions' (Alak 2015: 156).

In general, as in other Eastern European countries like Poland, Lithuania and even Belarus, the Muslim population in Romania may be seen as composed of two broad groups: the 'old' Muslims, representing indigenous/autochthonous ethnic groups inhabiting a particular region, and a widely dispersed group of 'new' Muslims, consisting of Muslims of immigrant and convert background. These two groups hardly ever interact and in fact lead lifestyles that often are if not incompatible then at least distinct, with the role played by religion in them also differing sharply. In the words of Vainovski-Mihai, newly emerged segments of immigrants and converts 'have not joined the old Muslim communities in Romania, and the two groups live almost parallel lives. Discussions do not revolve around the question of who is a Muslim, but rather what kind of Muslim someone is and to which extent' (Vainovski-Mihai 2016: 571). The differences in lifestyles not only encompass personal and intra-communal levels but also pertain to inter-communal relations.

With the overwhelming majority of the 'old' Muslims concentrated in the Dobruja region, when talking about this category of Romania's Muslims some observers came to refer to a 'Dobruja model of incorporation'. In the words of Kozák, this model

> promotes symbolic and corporate ethnicity and religion meaning that it circum-scribes the activities that are taken as a group. These activities are managed by ethnic and religious institutions in the institutional space of the nation state. The main characteristics are their institutional and local embeddedness, coopera-tion between local/regional political and religious institutions and/or with state institutions . . . in performing activities related to the preservation of tradition, language, customs and religion. Religious holidays, pilgrimages, traditional fights, a soccer league, festivals of ethnic cuisine, dance and music are jointly supported reproducing folklore based ethnic affiliation and sense of belonging. Traditions and customs are also basic building blocks for the kind of Islam pro-moted by religious leaders: 'We practice our religion according to what we have seen from our parents and grandparents, according to our customs'. Moreover, in certain contexts ethnic affiliation supersedes religious ones . . . Given the pow-erful regional and ethnic dimension of Muslim identity Muslims of other nation-alities or living in other regions of Romania are not fully, if at all, incorporated in this model. (Kozák 2009: 13)

Furthermore, 'old' Muslims are represented in the Romanian parliament on a quota basis by two political organisations: the Democratic Union of Turkish-Muslim Tatars in Romania and the Turkish Democratic Union of Romania. Though the two organisations as political parties are officially regarded as representatives of their respective ethnic constituencies, with the overwhelming majority of Romania's Tatars and Turks being at least nominally Muslim or of Muslim cultural background they are also regarded as 'Muslim'. However, neither of the parties has any overt religious agenda and thus may be regarded as representing Tatar or Turkish Muslims only inasmuch as Tatar/Turkish interests coincide with religious ones. On the other hand, representatives of both organisations sit on the board of the collective body governing Islamic affairs in the country.

The administration of Islamic affairs in Romania, as pretty much elsewhere in the Balkans, is entrusted to an officially recognised organisation: the Muslim Community of Romania. The Community is one of eighteen officially recog-nised religious organisations in the country that can seek financial assistance from the state for their activities, like the maintenance of religious communal property. The collective body governing the Community is its Synodal Council, comprised of the Grand Mufti, fifteeen regional muftis, representatives of the two political parties and the director of the Muslim school. The executive branch of the Community, the Muftiate, is headquartered in the Dobrujan city of Constanta. The Grand Mufti, in his capacity as chairperson of the Muftiate, is recognised as the supreme leader of the country's Muslims. There are rather strict qualification criteria: the aspirant for the post of mufti must not only be a current Romanian citizen but have been born in Romania and have no other citizenship; he also has to be a graduate of an Islamic theological institution in Romania. The latter requirement is somewhat tricky as there is no Islamic studies/Shariʿa faculty in the country and all theological higher education is of a Christian Orthodox nature.

Though the Community/Muftiate is officially regarded as the sole representative Islamic administration in Romania, which has the exclusive right to supervise Islamic affairs in the country (such as opening mosques and appointing imams to them), one may argue that since it is dominated by the 'old' Muslims of either Turkish or Tatar ethnic background, in reality it is representative of them, and mainly those among them who subscribe to its version of Islam. This resembles the situation in many other Eastern European countries where the officially recognised Islamic administrations (often one per country) are tightly connected to one or several particular ethnic groups while 'new' Muslims – immigrants and converts – are inadvertently marginalised if not discriminated against.

As in other countries in the Balkans and elsewhere in Eastern Europe, in Romania the line between normative and folk Islam is often blurred so that some practices of a folk Islam nature are tolerated by the Muftiate. Though traits of folk Islam may be found across all ethnic groups comprising 'old' Muslims in Romania, Roma Muslims in particular are reported to have retained such folk Islam practices as charms with 'divination and the belief in demons' being 'strong religious representations that might externally contradict the Islamic faith but nevertheless are integrated in the Horahane Rroma (Turkophone Roma) spiritual life' (Alak 2015: 155). At a particular festivity Hâdârlez ('Turkish' or 'Gypsy' Easter),

> a very syncretic spring festival that unites many Christian and Muslim symbols . . ., Muslim Gypsy invested the practice of jumping over the fire set in front of their houses with purifying qualities, considering it an expiatory ritual and also, reminiscence of their ancestral beliefs, as a powerful method of expelling the bad spirits. They also light candles, give alms and receive alms; lambs are slaughtered for protection from diseases and good fortune. (Alak 2015: 155)

The survival of such practices among the Roma is explained through the fact that they 'did not have churches or mosques in Romania, they were no attracted to an institutionalized method of experimenting the closeness to divinity' (Alak 2015: 156). Instead, arguably,

> trance, different forms of meditation similar to Islamic dhikr, music and dance were values of the general Rroma spirituality and means of ecstatic union with divinity in a world that is just a Purgatory (sin is not eternal). These Rroma practices and their mystical view of life and God resemble deeply, in the author's opinion, the Sufi type of spiritual, interior culture. (Alak 2015: 156)

The mystical dimension of Islam in today's Romania, however, is neither part of the official Islamic administration (as it is in Bosnia and Herzegovina) nor a direct continuation of this tradition from Ottoman times, when Sufism flourished all over the Balkans. Today, Sufism in Romania is represented by

> either intellectual Romanian converts who approach Islam from an esoteric metaphysical perspective, in the line of Rene Guenon's perennialism, or Sufi Turkish Muslims that attend special mosques centered on a more intense ritualistic Sufi practice, or converts and immigrants that follow a special Sunni-Sufi interpretation of Islam promoted in Romania by the Fattabiouni. (Alak 2015: 161)

While the normative and folk forms of Islam in Romania dominate the religious scene in the Turkish, Tatar and Roma Muslim communities, both in Dobruja and elsewhere, besides (neo)Sufi forms of Islamic religiosity Islamic revivalism is widespread among the Muslims of immigrant and convert background, who tacitly despise and even oppose the Muftiate. Through their own established NGOs, which are active in translating into Romanian and publishing texts authored by revivalist thinkers, Romania's Muslims with revivalist leanings aim to break the Muftiate's monopoly over the administration of the spiritual life of the country's Muslims. Revivalists do not fail to publicly point to the perceived failures of the Muftiate to 'correctly' administer Islamic affairs in the country accusing the Muftiate of incompetence. In return, the Muftiate reminds the revivalists that their advocated Islam is alien to Romania and its indigenous (read 'old') Muslim population. The ensuing antagonism between the two extremes of the Muslim body

> represents a strife for authority and power to control the discourse about Islam in Romania and it is a paradoxical situation as the legitimate, nominal credibility belongs with the Muftiate, but the concrete influence and impact on the less numerous non Turkish-Tatar communities can be attributed to the much more well-endowed and active NGOs. (Alak 2015: 152)

As Islamic revivalism remains a little investigated side of the Islamic presence in Romania, '[t]here are no statistics regarding the predominance of the different Islamic interpretations within the new Muslim groups, but it can be said that the most vocal and the most visible virtual public discourse belongs to the Salafi groups' (Alak 2015: 163). Though Muslims hailing from the Middle East and further afield are very prominent in Romania's Islamic revivalist scene in general, the converts (like in other, and not only Eastern European countries) are also very active, particularly in the Salafi groups for, as argued by Alak, 'most of the Romanian converts [are] familiarized with Islam, at first, through the Salafi lens' (Alak 2015: 163).

The spread of revivalist ideas and practices may in part be attested to by the proliferation of *musallas* in the urban areas outside of Dobruja, particularly in the capital city Bucharest, which is thought to have a 9,000-strong Muslim population served by a sole (historical) mosque built back in 1900 that can accommodate only one hundred worshippers. The twenty or so known *musallas* in Bucharest are all outside the Muftate's control and thus served by self-appointed imams whose understanding of 'proper' Islamic religiosity may be at variance with that professed by the Muftiate. However, rather than try to co-opt those imams and bring them and their flock into the fold of the official Islamic administration, the Muftiate in 2015 opted to build a brand new mosque in Bucharest, reportedly to be spacious enough to accommodate all the worshippers willing to pray in it. The Muftiate also used the mosque-building project as a trump card in its argument that it could serve not only as a community uniting factor but also as a bulwark against possible radicalisation tendencies, particularly among Muslims of immigrant and convert background.

CHAPTER 6

Central Europe

Though the history of Islam in their territories predates the formation of nation states in Central Europe (there were tiny Muslim communities in the first part of the twentieth century in Hungary, mainly made up of Bosniaks and Turks, and in Czechoslovakia, of local converts and expatriates; Rozsa 2013: 243; Mendel 1998), the significant increase (if not reappearance) of Muslims in the Central European states of Hungary, the Czech Republic, Slovakia and to a certain extent in Poland is somewhat paradoxically connected to the communist period (Hannova 2014). The present Muslim communities started slowly taking shape from the 1970s, when predominantly male students from what were then seen as 'friendly' Arab and other Asian and African states with significant Muslim populations started coming to local universities to study. It was the most religious among these expatriates who set up informal Muslim student communities centred around dormitories later, in the last years of communism and especially after the change of regimes and ideologies, to become (often the first) formal institutions of Muslims in these countries. Though the majority of graduates would leave the countries at the end of their studies, some would settle, often marrying local women, some of whom converted to Islam.

From the 1990s, many more students-turned-immigrants from the Middle East and beyond came to study and settle, and to eventually form the backbone of the present Muslim communities in the states that became known as the Višegrad Four. Numerically, the converts are a significantly smaller segment of the Central European Muslim communities. However, as citizens of the respective countries, some individual converts are either accepted by the states as interlocutors, thus empowering them vis-à-vis non-naturalised immigrants, or have themselves attained established positions as imams, muftis or presidents of local Muslim religious communities and their organisations.

In terms of demographic (but also historical) processes related to the emergence and development of Muslim communities, the four Central European countries straddle an invisible border between Western Europe, which historically had no Muslim presence but has for the last half a century been experiencing the mass immigration of people of Muslim cultural background, and Eastern Europe, which had indigenous Muslim communities yet not only remains unattractive to immigrants but actually 'sends' its Muslims as economic migrants and refugees to Western Europe. Some Eastern European Muslims, both from the

Balkans and the territories of the former USSR, have become immigrants and refugees in Central European states, which due to relatively higher standards of living are becoming more and more attractive to migrants from Eastern Europe. Since all four Central European countries are EU member states, ultimately the governance of religion within them is in part influenced by EU regulations.

Poland

For centuries, the only Muslims in Polish territories were the Tatars (not taking into account Russian officials and soldiers of the tsarist period) who, with the emergence of the modern Polish state at the beginning of the twentieth century, came to be referred to as Polish (or Lithuanian-Polish) Tatars. Between the fourteenth and twentieth centuries, the Tatar Muslim communities lived in a single state: first, the Grand Duchy of Lithuania; then, between the mid-sixteenth and the end of the eighteenth centuries, the Commonwealth of the Two Nations; and, finally, until the beginning of the twentieth century, the Russian Empire. The numerous shifts in the national borders in the first half of the twentieth century have led to local Tatars' change in citizenship status over the course of several decades, chiefly from Polish to Lithuanian or Byelorussian (Soviet), but also the other way around. Therefore, it is right to consider the history of Polish Tatars as being an integral part of the wider community of the Tatars, originally of the Grand Duchy of Lithuania, which unites the communities of today's Lithuanian, Belarusian and Polish Tatar Muslims. Polish Tatars historically lived in a discrete area of the north-eastern corner of the country where they were in close physical proximity to the Lithuanian and Belarusian Tatars with whom they shared the same vernacular and intermingled through marriage, so that today's Polish Tatars have either close relatives still living on the other side of the border, or at least their graves. Historically, however, like in neighbouring Lithuania, the inhabitants of the rest of the country were hardly aware of the presence of Muslims in the state.

With the birth of the Polish nation state in the aftermath of the First World War, the development of the Muslim communities there took an independent path. The autocephalous Islamic administration, the Muftiate, with the purpose of unifying Muslim congregations scattered around Poland under one representative institution and thus gaining bargaining power vis-à-vis state authorities and other faith communities, was founded in late 1925 at the convention of delegates of Muslim congregations, which took place in the north-eastern city Wilno (Vilnius) around which most of the Tatar communities lived. However, it took another decade to formally institutionalise the Muslim presence in Poland. After the Muftiate lobbied for and actively participated in its drafting, in the spring of 1936 a new law was promulgated by the Polish state governing the relationship between the local Muslim communities (nineteen at that time, scattered across territories currently belonging to Poland, Lithuania and Belarus) and the state. According to the law, communities of the Muslim Religious Union in the Republic of Poland were awarded self-rule, with the right to elect their own mullahs/imams and *muazzins*. The Muftiate was thus officially recognised by the state as the representative of Poland's Muslims, this way recognising the Tatar community as an autocephalous faith community. The interwar period is generally seen as having been very rewarding for the Polish Muslim community with both the religious and socio-cultural life of Tatars flourishing, with numerous publications on Islam and the history of the Tatars procured by the Tatar religious and secular elite.

With the communist period, however, the demographic composition of the Polish Muslim population started changing. This happened first of all with the resettlement of Polish citizens from territories seized by the USSR during the Second World War to the former German territories added to the Polish state after the war. Since there were Tatars among those resettled, western and northern parts of Poland – for example, the cities of Gdansk (formerly Danzig) and Szczecin (formerly Stettin) on the Baltic Sea or Gorzów Wielkopolski and Oleśnica – saw Muslim settlers for the first time. Gdansk even became the host of a sizeable enough Muslim Tatar community to need a mosque; one was built in the city in the late 1980s, still during the communist period.

Starting with the arrival of scores of young men in the 1970s from Muslim-majority countries, who came initially to study but subsequently settled, and continuing with more students and refugees in the 1990s, over the course of several decades the Tatar community gradually became a small, though privileged, segment of the numerically expanded Muslim community. Thus, though from a historical point of view the appearance and development of Muslim communities in Poland would warrant putting it alongside Lithuania and Belarus, not least because of demographic trends the contemporary situation of Islam in Poland clearly brings it closer to other Central European states where the majority of Muslims are of either immigrant or convert background.

Today Poland has anywhere between 25,000 and 35,000 Muslims; the exact numbers are impossible to establish as the Polish census does not include a question on religious identity. There are an estimated 4,000 ethnic Tatars, though it is not known how many among them still self-identify as Muslim. It may be remembered that only half of Lithuania's ethnic Tatars identified as Muslims in the census, a situation which to a greater or lesser degree may also be the case in Poland. Even if one presumes that all Tatars are (or at least identify themselves as) Muslims, their share is no more than a sixth of the estimated Muslim body of Poland. After Tatars, Arabs constitute the biggest linguistic group, followed, possibly, by Chechens.

The communist period put the institutional development of Muslim communities on hold; with the mufti emigrating and the formal seat of the Muftiate

– Vilnius – now outside the post-Second World War Polish borders, the Muftiate ceased to exist. However, the Muslim communities themselves were still allowed to practise Islam, albeit only within the restraints of the communist state. Compared to Soviet Lithuania and Byelorussia, in Poland the situation for religion in general and Islam in particular was much better. This meant that the Muslim Tatar community there not only survived but also were able to preserve their religious identity and traditions, enabling them to re-emerge as a much more viable religious community in the post-communist era.

The Polish Muslim Tatars proceeded with reinstating the institute of mufti and reactivating the 1936 law, which incidentally recognises the Tatar Muslim organisation (the Muslim Religious Union in the Republic of Poland) as the only representative Muslim organisation in the country, thus putting it in a privileged position vis-à-vis other (non-Tatar) Muslim religious organisations. The mufti of this organisation claims the title of the Mufti of Poland and is recognised as such by the state; however, not only are there rival aspirants to the title from non-Tatar religious congregations, but the current mufti appears to have a limited following, chiefly comprised of Tatars. Lately, however, even some of the Tatars have turned against the mufti thus further dividing the already very fragmented Muslim community in the country.

As argued by Pędziwiatr, '[u]ntil the end of 1990s the membership of the MZR was open only to Muslims with Polish citizenship which has in fact partially contributed to the creation of second major Muslim organisation in the country that had much more inclusive character' (Pędziwiatr 2011: 13). That other organisation, the Muslim League (LM), was founded in 2001 by Muslims of immigrant background and in 2004 it gained official recognition by the state as a Muslim religious organisation, even though the law of 1936, which is still in force, explicitly states that the Union is the sole representative of Islam in Poland with the ensuing understanding that the mufti of the Union is the all-Poland mufti. The LM has set up a post of mufti as the top spiritual authority in the group. The LM has chapters throughout the country and its network covers locations where there are sizeable Muslim communities (of immigrant and convert background) but the Union's structures are weak or non-existent.

Divisions in the Muslim community in Poland may be seen as running along ethnic/citizenship lines but they also run along the lines of how the contents of Islam is interpreted, with the Tatars representing the more liberal end of the spectrum and the Arabs the more conservative, even revivalist. Chechen immigrants in the Polish capital Warsaw are reported to have their own mosque and the Shi'i, Ahmadi and Sufi communities also meet separately.

Sufism, in the form of brotherhoods who maintain their lodges, has never historically been present in the Polish territory and so the Sufi groups found around the country today are a modern feature and part of a wider phenomenon of the emergence of neo-Sufi movements and groups, many of which are of

New Religious Movements type, some even denying their connection to Islam. Unlike Sufism, folk Islam was very widespread among Polish Tatar Muslims who have retained some of its features into present times.

Though Poland's Muslims are not known to have fallen for revivalist forms of Islamic religiosity, radicalisation among the immigrant segment of Muslims in the country has been observed, particularly among the Chechens, some of whom have been suspected of nurturing radical and possibly even extremist ideologies. The recent arrests of some of them on suspicions of engaging in recruitment to and otherwise aiding jihadi activities in the Middle East attest to the presence of, even if tenuous, forms of Islamic religiosity far removed from the historically locally recognisable ones.

Hungary

Though on issues pertaining to Muslim presence in its territory the modern state of Hungary shares many similarities with the Czech Republic and Slovakia (as sovereign states emerging in the aftermath of the First World War they all had no indigenous Muslim populations and their current small Muslim minorities are primarily of immigrant and, to a much lesser degree convert, background), the history of Muslim presence in its territory is, however, closer to that of the neighbouring Balkan states, like Croatia and Serbia. Aside from the Ottoman period, medieval Hungary is reported to have had a Muslim population between the eleventh and thirteenth centuries, well before the Ottoman conquest in the sixteenth century. Nonetheless, it was in the Ottoman period when Islam spread in the Hungarian lands in all its forms, including, besides legalist Islam of Ottoman officialdom, Sufi Islam and even its folk forms. There are reports of Sufi lodges, for instance, a 'Mevlevî-khana', established in the town of Pécs in the 1660s (Lelić 2006: 19), and to this day there are several *turbes* to be found around the country with probably the most famous one, that of Gul Baba, in the historical part of the capital city Budapest, on the Buda's side.

However, like many other parts of Eastern Europe that had been ruled by the Ottomans, following their retreat, with Muslims gone and practically all its symbols destroyed or converted to other uses, Islam all but disappeared from Hungarian lands. And although formally the Hungarian parliament in 1916 adopted a law recognising Islam, it was not in reaction to any increased presence of Muslims in Hungary but rather in anticipation of their arrival following the annexation of Bosnia by the Austro-Hungarian Empire, of which Hungary at the time was a constitutive part. With the defeat and subsequent collapse of the empire and emergence of nation states in its place, Hungary did not experience any significant influx of people of Muslim background, although in the interwar period it hosted a tiny Muslim population (of between 300 and 500 souls) comprised of émigrés from what by then had become Yugoslavia. Some of them aspired to organise Muslim religious and communal life in a more ordered manner and proceeded with establishing a Hungarian national Muslim organisation, which in 1931 was registered as the Independent Hungarian Autonomous Islamic Religion Community (Póczik 2016: 60).

This first Muslim organisation in Hungary did not survive the communist period but individual Muslims did continue living in communist-ruled Hungary and, like in many other parts of communist-controlled Eastern Europe, increased in number through the arrival of students of Muslim background from the Middle East and beyond. By the mid-1980s, the number of devout Muslims, composed chiefly of expatriates, had reached a critical mass to raise the need to found a more organised community. In the late 1980s, an informal Association of Muslim Students was formed to be followed, in 1988, by the Hungarian Islamic Community (HIC), founded by a small group of Muslims mainly of convert background. However, as the law at the time required the founding group to consist of no less than twenty individuals, six of the founding members were not even Muslim (Csiszár 2016: 346). So, very much like in many other countries not only in Central but also wider Eastern Europe, organised Islam appeared in Hungary just before the fall of the communist system.

Though by the end of the communist era Hungary already had a several-thousand-strong Muslim community of immigrant background, the modest but steady immigration trend continued so that by the early 2010s, the country's Muslim population was estimated to have surpassed 30,000. The official figures, unsurprisingly, like elsewhere in Eastern Europe, suggest a much lower number: the 2011 census results recorded only 5,579 Muslims living in the country at the time, of whom 4,097 (that is, almost three quarters) identified themselves as ethnic Hungarians, with 2,369 (or over 40 per cent) identifying themselves as ethnic Arabs – making the total sum significantly higher than the total number of those who self-identified as Muslims. This discrepancy was caused by the census methodology, which allowed respondents to choose several ethnic identities at once. In any case, even if all those who identified themselves as Arabs had at the same time identified themselves as also belonging to the Hungarian ethnicity, there would still be a staggering 1,728 ethnic Hungarian Muslims, presumably of convert background or children of converts. This is apparently one of the highest numbers of such a category of Muslim in all of Eastern Europe, superseded possibly only by ethnic Russian Muslims.

With a fairly liberal regime of governance of religion, post-communist Hungary witnessed a mushrooming of religious communities; by the 2010s, there were already some 300 registered 'churches' (this is how religious communities and their organisations are labelled in Hungary) in the country. Of them, three were Muslim: the already mentioned HIC; a splinter organisation, called the Organisation of Muslims in Hungary, founded in 2000; and yet another organisation, the Church of Islam, established in 2003. The three organisations would constantly see each other as rivals rather than partners until, in compliance with a new law on religions of 2012, they had to re-register. The first two successfully did so and formed the Council of Muslims, while the third went into oblivion after its founder, and the primary vehicle behind its activities, an immigrant himself, encountered problems with the security services and in the end chose to leave Hungary.

Of the two remaining Islamic administrations, the Hungarian Islamic Community represents classical normative Islam in its Sunni Hanafi tradition. As such, it has sought close relations with the Bosnian Islamic Community to the point where, in 2013, it requested to be accepted under its aegis and that the Grand Mufti of Bosnia and Herzegovina 'also become Grand Mufti of Hungary' (Csiszár 2016: 342). Instead, the Mufti of Zagreb, himself a subordinate of the BIC, was seconded to serve as the Mufti of the HIC. There are reports that, in 2015, the HIC 'renewed its intention to belong directly to the Bosnian Islamic Community' (Csiszár 2016: 343). The Hungarian Islamic Community has maintained a rather high public profile, at times bordering on political activity. For instance, its head, a Hungarian convert, is reported to have declared in 2015 that 'supporting FIDESZ [a governing coalition party] is considered a deeply sinful, forbidden act (*haram*) for all Muslims' though the organisation after a month 'withdrew this statement . . . due to "Prime Minister Orban's positive statements about Muslims of Hungary"' (Csiszár 2016: 342).

The Organisation of Muslims in Hungary (OMH), which traces its origins to the Association of Muslim Students from the 1980s though only formally established in 2000, is seen to be closer to if not revivalist, then certainly non-denominational universalist Islam. However, its membership in the pan-European Federation of Islamic Organizations in Europe may suggest its ideological affinity with the Muslim Brotherhood. In any case, the OMH has kept a much lower public profile than the HIC.

The Czech Republic and Slovakia

The two sovereign central European states of the Czech Republic and Slovakia emerged in 1993, when the constitutive parts of the hitherto country of Czechoslovakia parted ways. Unlike the disintegration of the USSR and the SFRY, which were marked by bloody conflicts, Czechs and Slovaks bid farewell to each other in the most civilised manner. To the tiny Muslim community of Czechoslovakia this meant the emergence of two national Muslim communities. In the years leading up to the split, communist Czechoslovakia hardly had any indigenous Muslims. In fact, the Czechs and Slovaks and their inhabited lands may be regarded historically to have been the least exposed to Muslim presence in all of Eastern Europe. Though the Ottoman Empire had been a menacing

neighbour, apart from what today is the southern part of Slovakia, the Czec
and Slovak lands had not experienced direct Muslim (Ottoman) rule.

Though individual Muslims would come to and settle in the Czechoslova
territories from the end of the nineteenth century – when Bosnia became pa
of the Austro-Hungarian Empire, which Czechoslovakia itself had been pa
of for several centuries – a nascent Muslim community only emerged in inte
war Czechoslovakia in 1934, formed by local converts to Islam and Musli
expatriates. However, the state authorities deliberately postponed its offici
registration so that it took place only in 1941 at the hands of the Nazi-controlle
Protectorate authorities. In the aftermath of the Second World War, howeve
the official recognition was recalled and the community's leadership eve
prosecuted for alleged collaboration with the Nazis. The Muslim communit
in communist Czechoslovakia then remained practically unorganised until la
in the communist period when devout Muslim students from the Middle Eas
joined by the few local converts, started forming nucleus congregations on un
versity campuses and in student dorms.

The emergence of two states with liberal economies and open borde
facilitated the arrival of expatriates of Muslim background to both of then
though the Czech Republic with its capital city Prague attracted the bulk of th
immigrants of Muslim background. So, while as of the end of 2016 Slovakia
Muslim population barely exceeded 5,000, (with the 2011 census recording ju
over 1,900), the Czech Republic was estimated to host an up to 20,000-stron
Muslim community, though the 2011 census results give significantly lowe
numbers – just a little over 1,900 respondents indicated Islam as their religiou
affiliation with almost 1,500 indicating their affiliation with the Headquarte
of the Muslim Communities in the Czech Republic (UMO). As the two group
plausibly overlap, and some 45 per cent of respondents did not indicate the
religious affiliation (the census questions on religious identity and affiliation wer
merely optional), it is not possible to say exactly how many inhabitants of th
Czech Republic self-identified with Islam that year.

Though in both countries the number of local converts to Islam amounts t
several hundred, they are outnumbered by Muslims of immigrant backgroun
both naturalised and not, and those born locally and with citizenship of eith
of the two countries but of mixed parentage. Though the bulk of Muslim imm
grants have come from the Middle East, there are also groups of Balkan origi
In this regard, like neighbouring Hungary and to a certain degree Sloveni
due to the demographic structure of their Muslim populations the two cou
tries stand out in an Eastern European context and more resemble Wester
European countries. But after all, they both (as Hungary and Slovenia) had bee
part of the Austro-Hungarian Empire as opposed to those states in the Balkar
that were under Ottoman rule. The physical proximity of Bratislava, the Slova
capital, to Vienna – the distance by road is just 80 kilometres – allows Slova

Muslims to maintain close relations with Islamic organisations in Austria. As Bratislava, with its estimated 2,000-strong Muslim population, has no proper mosque and prayer space is limited, Muslims from there may make use of a mosque in Hainburg an der Donau, a mere 16 kilometres from Bratislava, just on the Austrian side of the border.

As elsewhere, Muslims in both states have established religious organisations, aspiring to both unite the respective countries' communities and be representative of them vis-à-vis the state. The leading (in fact, umbrella) organisation of normative Islam in the Czech Republic, the Headquarters of the Muslim Communities in the Czech Republic, was established back in 1991. In 2004, following new legislation governing religions in the country, it succeeded in securing state registration as a 'church' and its official recognition as the representative organisation of Muslims in the country. However, its status remains of a lower grade than it aspires to: currently it may not run religious schools and may not receive public funding for its activities. In order to qualify for an upgrade in its status, UMO, inter alia, needs to prove it represents a group of over 10,000 interested persons (Muslims). But as the 2011 census results revealed, not even 1,500 respondents indicated it as their 'church' (Macháček 2016: 200) with the overwhelming majority of the country's Muslims not associating themselves with any Muslim organisation. UMO's requests to lower the threshold have reportedly been turned down by the authorities (Macháček 2014: 178) and it has put on hold its application for the upgrade in its status (Macháček 2015: 177). As an umbrella organisation, UMO gathers together regional Muslim organisations, the most active of which are the Prague- and Brno-based Islamic Foundations, which run the mosques (*masjids*) in the two cities and are the actual vehicle behind Muslim activities in the Czech Republic.

The legal situation with Islam in Slovakia is even more precarious than in the Czech Republic, as the law requires membership of 20,000 for a religious community to be officially registered. As the Muslim community is estimated (non-registered/non-recognised religious communities are not even included in the censuses) to be around 5,000, there is virtually no prospect for it to be registered by the state in the foreseeable future, even if all of the country's Muslims unite for this purpose. Therefore, the Islamic Foundation in Slovakia, founded in 1999, formally functions as an NGO though its activities are mainly religious. Without registration, however, the Foundation has limited rights to pursue religious activities publicly – it cannot build places of worship, organise religious instruction or spiritual care in public institutions, conduct valid marriages, request the state to cover the clergy's salaries, and so on. The Islamic Foundation, however, is not the sole Muslim organisation in Slovakia; there are several other if not rival, then parallel organisations.

With no indigenous historical Muslim communities in the two countries, there have never been any forms of either folk or Sufi Islam in either the Czech

Republic or Slovakia. However, recently, neo-Sufi ideas have seeped into thes countries, with Prague hosting some Sufi groups, with Naqshbandiyya repre sentatives being most visible (O'Dell 2011: 4). There are also private group catering for Turkish immigrants/expatriates, who engage in Sufi rituals (Bure 2011: 31).

Though revivalist Islam is not reported to have taken root in either of the two countries, there are reports of Salafi-leaning congregations, which run their own prayer halls (Drobný 2014: 543).

CHAPTER 7

Islam in Eastern Europe, Eastern European Islam: new faces, new challenges

What one has been observing in practically all Eastern European nation states in the post-communist era, and certainly so since 9/11, are the constant attempts by official national Muslim administrations but also some state offices to present Eastern European Muslims as 'indigenous' or 'autochthonous', in other words, as being 'of' (Eastern) Europe/Europeans. Consequently, Islam in Eastern Europe (or, put another way, Islam of Eastern Europeans) is unequivocally discursively presented as 'European' Islam, in what may be called 'indigenization of religious identity' (Kozák 2009). As Kozák argues,

> [t]he discourse of indigenization revolves around the centre piece of ethno-religious characteristics as a fundamental element in identification and categorization. The main dimensions are recounting local history (tradition), religion as personal option, symbolic religion, and ecumenism. In this discourse religious practice is shaped by local tradition meaning that cultural identification in the form of ethnoregional imagery supersedes or more precisely qualifies the religious one. (Kozák 2009: 13)

In this way, various forms of locally conditioned folk and mystical religiosity, next to normative Islam, as understood and historically practised by different Eastern European Muslim communities, are forwarded not only as 'Islam as we know it' but as Islam itself.

Such a designation of Muslims and Islam as 'European' first of all implies a (positively charged) distinction from the Middle Eastern, Asian, African, and any other possible Islam(s). The keyword 'European' is routinely meant to signal the affinity, indeed the roots, of this Islam with the European value system. In other words, in the framework of the politics of loyalty and belonging, it is argued by the advocates of this label that the 'European' Islam of (indigenous/autochthonous) Eastern European Muslims belongs in and to this part of Europe, and through it to the entire European cultural zone. But not only that – in the minds of the local Muslim leadership and mainstream political elite, it has to stay so. To this end, it calls for a double strategy – on the one hand, promotion of the image and status of local forms of Islam in Eastern Europe as 'European' Islam *par excellence*, and on the other hand, fending off other (read, alien and unacceptable) forms of Islam, usually falling under the category of 'revivalist' Islam. However, as Bougarel aptly notes, the celebration of Balkan Islam as a 'European Islam' conceals – rather than reveals – its specific characteristics, as do the concerns expressed by outside experts on the post-Communist Balkans about the 'radicalisation' of Muslim populations or the creeping 'wahhabisation' of Balkan Islam. (Bougarel 2005: 11)

This observation is also valid for other Eastern European (chiefly post-Soviet) countries with autochthonous ethnic communities of Muslim background.

There are also proponents of 'Euro-Islam', which, unlike the organic 'European' Islam of autochthonous Muslims that needs to be preserved, is to be created by integrating indigenous 'European' Islam, European values and norms and legitimate expectations of Muslims of immigrant background. So, rather than being merely Islam *in* Europe, 'Euro-Islam' would be Islam *for* Europe. The process of creation of 'Euro-Islam' in Eastern Europe differs from that in Western Europe precisely because of the perceived existence of 'European' Islam of the autochthonous Muslim communities, something that is lacking in West Europe. Therefore, arguably, the outcome of this double process would somewhat differ in the two halves of Europe, though, as shown in preceding chapters, the situation in Hungary, the Czech Republic and Slovakia, but also Estonia, Latvia and Moldova resembles that in Western Europe, as these countries have not had any significant indigenous Muslim populations as representatives of 'European' Islam.

Though one might see the emergence of it even in Western Europe, in much of Eastern Europe, as argued by Elbasani,

[g]overnment-sponsored 'official' Islam – an organizational concept, which refers to the creation of centralized religious hierarchies approved by the state – serves as yet another powerful interlocutor of transmitting politically-conceived top-down national accounts of Islam. Headed by a Chief Mufti, governed by formal statutes, and supported and monitored by the state, central hierarchies are acknowledged as the sole authority governing the respective 'national' community of believers. (Elbasani 2015: 4)

So, in many Eastern European countries the state looks forward to or, through relevant legislations, even demands that the local Muslim community become a 'church'. Arguably, in the Balkans, and in particular in the countries with Muslim majorities or at least significant minorities, this has been attained rather smoothly.

As shown in Chapters 4 and 5, the national, church-like Islamic administrations there have become elaborate bureaucratic hierarchical structures with numerous subordinate institutions, including, but not limited to, those that produce, convey, disseminate and propagate Islamic knowledge, the contents of which are in strict conformity to the idea of the official nationally endorsed 'traditional'/'European' Islam (particularly, its normative form). This can be observed in institutions of Islamic education, in the form of madrasas and university faculties of Islamic theology, which early on were made into tools to first revive and then perpetuate this 'traditional' Islam through producing and reproducing the corpus of 'correct' beliefs instilled in the young generation of *ulama* and Islamic educators. The early 1990s saw a boom in expansion of institutions of higher Islamic learning in practically all countries with a significant enough Muslim component. So, in the Balkans, the

> [o]fficial Muslim organizations, each based near centres of political power in Sarajevo, Prishtina, Tirana, Skopje, Sofia and so on, maintain organizational devices – the faculty of Islamic Studies, a network of Madrasas, as well as intellectual, publication and humanitarian activity nets – that distribute the national/traditional vision of Islam. (Elbasani 2015: 8)

This is basically true for Russia also.

Where there are church-like institutions (like in Bosnia, Albania and Montenegro, but also Macedonia, Bulgaria, Ukraine, Belarus and Russia), the state aids/supports their efforts to bring under their control parallel/alternative groups, while refusniks are ridiculed and even outlawed. To this end, the state apparatus, through its officials, academics and media,

> keep[s] defining the borders of acceptable 'traditional' Islam(s), typically framed in the context of a nation's cultural and historical particularities. Expressions of faith that do not fit into this 'fabric' are exposed to misnomers ranging from enemies of the nation to remnants of a bygone era, to odious renegades and foreign agents. The bifurcation between 'ours' and 'theirs', local and foreign, national and global, and ultimately, good and bad Islam(s) capitalizes on nation-based categories. Accordingly, national traditional Islam is portrayed as a 'moderate' – liberal, tolerant, indigenous and European version, whereas global or foreign Islam is perceived as alien, fundamentalist, and possibly intolerant and radical. (Elbasani 2015: 7)

Ultimately, the state not only puts up with the official church-like institutions' policies but actively aids them in their pursuit of their objectives, particularly those that coincide with those of the state itself. As Elbasani points out,

> [s]tate authorities and official Islamic institutions often ally together to protect the official traditional line and consequently portray competing forms of revival of faith as 'foreign' and alien to the ideas of national identity, thus antagonizing many 'born-again' Muslims. (Elbasani 2015: 6)

This way, the historical plurality of Islamic forms is brought into conformity with and under the governance of the officially recognised church-like institution espousing quazi-legalist 'European' Islam, formally or informally recognised by the state as 'traditional'. Likewise, the plurality of contemporary forms is suppressed or even rejected through legal measures by criminalising certain forms of Islamic revivalism in the name of a double preservation of the pristine and pure 'traditional' and 'European' Islam and the general security and order. As shown in the preceding chapters, there are many cases in Eastern Europe of such a pairing of the state and its officially recognised church-like Islamic institutions.

Elbasani argues that, in the case of the Balkans,

> [b]y offering particular benefits and co-opting the Islamic 'establishment', the post-Communist states continued to maintain an intricate relationship between political and Islamic structures – the sovereign has the prerogative of control and intervention, Ulamas are domesticated, religious ideas tamed, and scholarship corrected. Central structures are consequently relegated to a subordinate political role, remarkable for their support of government policies. (Elbasani 2015: 4)

Though this may be true in certain cases, one needs to also acknowledge that the democratisation and liberalisation processes in post-Cold War Eastern Europe turned local Muslim communities in many countries of the region (more so in the Balkans) into self-conscious autonomous political actors. Though religious communities could and in many cases did themselves serve as political actors or at least agents, in a number of post-communist Eastern European countries Muslims formed political parties to represent and defend their socio-religious interests, both vis-à-vis the state and other political groupings. Though, due to legal restrictions on forming parties on a religious basis, references to religion were absent in their official names, as a rule, these parties nominally represented and defended followers of 'traditional' Islam, locally presented as a form of 'European' Islam. Once in power in the parliament or government, these Muslim parties as a rule tend to be selective when it comes to religious issues – whatever is seen by them to promote 'revivalist' forms of Islamic piety is suppressed and rejected. With no revivalist (Islamist) political party having yet made it to a power position in any Eastern European country, the re-Islamisation of local Muslim populations revolves around and limits itself to re-institutionalisation of local religious customs, bordering between moderate (if not modernist) normative Islam on the one side and folk (with traces of Sufism) Islam on the other.

Another common feature in Eastern Europe, particularly in the countries with significant Muslim populations (that is, those in absolute numbers counted in hundreds of thousands or more and making up at least 10 per cent of the country's population), is the presence and participation in national, regional or at least local politics of political parties established by representatives of ethnic groups whose members are overwhelmingly of Muslim background. Though as a rule such parties do not carry any indications of their attachment to Islam, they are perceived by both the respective ethnic electorate and outsiders as representatives of ethnic groups of Muslim background. And although none of these parties may be referred to as 'Islamic', due to their rank and file and the electorate most of them may be labelled as 'Muslim' – and so not only for the reason that their members and voters are of Muslim cultural background but because often their members either are at the same time representatives of the official Islamic administrations or at least maintain close relations with such institutions. The Bosnian case, particularly in the first decade of its independence, is chrestomathic but the Serbian, Montenegrin, Macedonian, Bulgarian, Russian and Romanian cases are witnesses to this collation of politics, ethnicity and religion. Naturally, it may be expected that such 'Muslim' political parties seek to preserve what they regard as forms of Islam traditional to the country and in this way to uphold the status quo between the state and the national Muslim community. Therefore, as a rule, when in positions of power, these parties either themselves initiate or at least actively support any legislation that restricts the emergence or spread of 'non-traditional' ('non-European') forms of Islam, in other words, revivalist Islam in all its disguises.

In an age of profound changes in the demographic composition of Muslim populations caused by both in- and out-migration as well as the emergence of a small but already strong convert Muslim segment in many countries of Eastern Europe, the indigenisation of religious identity, along the ethnicisation of Islam, coupled with the drive to monopolise the Islamic domain by the leadership of national Islamic institutions, has inadvertently led to intra-communal frictions, divisions and splits along what might look like the ethnic background of Muslim groups but are at the same time along the lines delimiting the different understandings of the contents of Islam. So, for instance, in Macedonia, Croatia, Estonia and Lithuania, the sole national Islamic administrations are internally torn by these cleavages, while in Serbia, Latvia, Slovenia, Hungary, Poland, Moldova, Belarus, Ukraine, Romania and even Russia, rival Islamic administrations have emerged.

The state-sponsored, or at least state-blessed, policies of the reigning in of differing or even opposing Islamic groups, however, naturally diminishes the availability of Islamic forms on offer through *da'wa*, which is a regular endeavour among revivalists. Deprived of legal status or otherwise subjected to a double state/'church'-sought control of their bodies and minds, revivalists have resorted to less controllable means like the World Wide Web. In this way, informal, often 'digital', 'communities' have been spreading, particularly among converts and those of immigrant background, with radical ideologies contrary to 'European'/'Euro-' Islam proliferating unchecked.

Moreover, the proliferation of local institutions of Islamic learning has been somewhat offset by a wave of Muslim students from Eastern Europe who chose to pursue higher religious education outside of Europe; while the bulk of them went to Turkey, a fairly large share opted for the Arab countries and some went as far as Malaysia. Upon their return, some of these brand new professional *ulama*, particularly those returning from Saudi Arabia, posed an unexpected challenge to the local Muslim religious (and sometimes state) authorities – at times their preached Islam was evidently not 'European'. Furthermore, such *ulama*, versed in Arabic and with social capital and networks in the Middle East, sometimes became agents of 'non-European' Islam propagated by the ever-intrusive foreign Muslim actors, be it state agencies or NGOs.

Fear of religious radicalisation (read, adoption of 'non-European' Islam) leading to extremism, enabled inter alia by contemporary information technologies, has recently become a major concern for both the governments and the state-endorsed Islamic administrations. Almost all Eastern European countries were faced with a new reality, when, in the wake of the establishing of a claimed Islamic Khilafa State in the Middle East, scores of Eastern European Muslims headed in what they themselves regarded as *hijra* to the territories governed by it. In this regard, the official national Islamic administrations and the state have found themselves in the same camp and have since been acting in tandem, though for slightly different reasons: while the state is mainly security-minded, the local Muslim leadership is primarily concerned with a falling following which threatens them with their eventual marginalisation and potentially (in certain cases already actual) dwindling bargaining power vis-à-vis the state.

Foreign actors

If there has been a general trend to 'indigenise' and 'nationalise' Islam in the post-communist Eastern European countries, there is also a discernible opposite trend, that of making it trans-national. The drivers behind this trend have been, first of all, the foreign actors who made physical and other appearances in Eastern Europe immediately after the fall of the communist system. However, as Elbasani and Roy note, foreign Islamic actors may be

> divided into competing trends, mainly: (1) Salafism, either in an institutional form, largely sponsored by Saudi Arabia, or in a de-institutionalized form, driven by informal networks, including individual imams and militant missionaries; and (2) the neo-Ottoman model, sponsored by Turkish official state structures (Diyanet) or non-official institutions such as the Gülen networks. (Elbasani and Roy 2015: 465; see also Öktem 2010: 18–42)

If Salafism to a greater or lesser extent may be found in practically all post-communist Eastern European countries (and information in the preceding chapters attests to this), the attempts at re-Ottomanisation of Islam are most visible in the Central and Eastern Balkans as well as, until recently, in the Crimea, regions that had once been under Ottoman control. There, in most cases, there is a clear symbiosis between the local Islamic administrations and the Turkish faith-based organisations, be they governmental, like the Directorate for Religious Affairs (Diyanet), Turkish International Cooperation and Development Agency

(TIKA) or Yunus Emre Institute, or NGOs, like those affiliated with such neo-Sufi movements as Hizmet, Nurcus or Suleymancis (Öktem 2010: 22–42).

The Directorate for Religious Affairs, which is directly subordinate to the Prime Minister of Turkey and is the sole official Islamic administration there, has been the main governmental foreign actor in practically all of Eastern Europe, the exceptions possibly being the Czech Republic, Slovakia, Latvia and Estonia. Though its activities are most visible in the Balkans, where it 'has established close links with the Islamic religious institutions in the region, and provides them with significant material support directly or indirectly (grants for students visiting Turkish universities, funding for local imams' salaries, etc.)' (Bougarel 2005: 19), its reach has gone as far as the Baltic States, where the Diyanet has not only sponsored religious text books for local Muslim children but has been posting salaried imams in Lithuania's mosques. Across Eastern Europe, the Turkic-speaking communities (or at least of Turkic origin, like the Lithuanian, Belarusian and Polish Tatars), chiefly ethnic Turks and Tatars, have been particularly showered with the Diyanet's attention, which, in tandem with the Turkish embassies and other Turkish governmental institutions, would seek, through Turkish language and culture courses, artistic events, exhibitions, receptions and trips, to instil Turkey-friendly sentiments among the community members. The Turkish state's policy, particularly through the Diyanet but also other governmental agencies like TIKA (which is tasked with the restoration and preservation of Ottoman era heritage, foremost in the form of buildings such as *turbes*, *tekkes*, mosques, but also cemeteries and the like), counts on the expectation that Turkey is seen as a 'second homeland' among many Balkan Muslims. Though

> this is especially true for Turkish minorities, which retain strong institutional, cultural and personal ties with the country, the historical ties, cultural affinities and commercial exchanges that connect them with Turkey – and the fact that a large part of the Turkish population originates from the Balkans – explain why Turkey is also perceived as a 'second homeland' by numerous non-Turkish-speaking Muslims in Macedonia, Kosovo and Sandjak. (Bougarel 2005: 20)

Ultimately, the Turkish state-sponsored activities and efforts in Eastern Europe are generally appreciated by the local Muslim communities and in most cases welcomed by the state authorities.

Though Turkey's interest in promoting its version of Islam may be seen as a shared wish to re-Ottomanise Islam in the post-communist Eastern European context and/or cater for the religious needs of the Turkic Muslims in the region, one needs to also realise that 'Turkey is trying to exert some control over the development of Balkan Islam and counter the growing influence of the Arab world' (Bougarel 2005: 19), particularly the Gulf States, with Saudi Arabia being chief among them. Contrary to the situation with Turkey's involvement in Islamic affairs in Eastern Europe, interests of the Gulf States and activities of their faith-based state agencies and NGOs are often met with equal suspicion or at least reserve by both the Eastern European states and the local Islamic administrations.

Next to the Turkish state agencies, Fethullah Gülen's movement, known as Hizmet, is arguably the most widespread of the trans-national movements in Eastern Europe – daughter organisations, often in the form of NGOs, are to be found in practically all of the post-communist states. However, like in the case of the Diyanet, Hizmet's most visible presence is to be found in the countries with the most sizeable Muslim populations, where it runs numerous educational institutions, publishing houses and businesses. Until the mid-2010s, Hizmet at times seemed to be supplementing Diyanet and thus complimenting the Turkish state's activities in the religious (but also political) field; Turkish embassies had been working closely with and endorsing Hizmet's activities, and not only in Eastern Europe, but on a global scale. The recent parting of the ways between the Turkish government and Hizmet, with the former going so far as officially labelling the latter as a terrorist organisation, has weighed heavily on the development of Eastern European Muslim communities, particularly in the Balkans, and especially in those countries that have a sizeable Turkish population, like Bulgaria. The full scale of the fallout from this 'love gone sour' between the two Turkish actors is yet to be seen in the coming decade.

Though Elbasani and Roy divided foreign actors active in Eastern Europe into two main categories – the Salafis and Turks – there is indeed a greater variety of trans-national Islamic movements, which have put at least a foothold in post-communist Eastern Europe. The revivalist Hizb at-Tahrir has reportedly been most visible in Ukraine (and particularly Crimea), where it functions legally. In neighbouring Russia, Hizb is also known to have been very active, though there it is banned. With Crimea annexed in 2014 by Russia, Hizb at-Tahrir activities there also became illegal and its members are reported to have been harassed by the Russian authorities and even arrested. Another trans-national revivalist movement, Tablighi Jamaat, is known to have sought to attract followers in the Baltic States, something that alarmed local security services because of Jamaat's alleged ties to international terrorism. The heterodox Ahmadi community has also made attempts to squeeze into the post-communist Muslim space – for instance, in the early 1990s, it even managed to register itself in Lithuania(!) though it has never really converted any locals to Ahmadi Islam and to this day there are no Ahmadis of immigrant background in the country. However, Ahmadis have been more successful elsewhere in Eastern Europe, particularly where there are immigrant Muslims from the Indian subcontinent. Finally, there are such neo-Sufi movements as that established by Inayat Khan and his followers, which also maintain a presence in many of the Eastern European countries. Dances of Universal Peace International claims to have chapters in several Eastern European countries (Latvia, the Czech Republic, Russia) and another neo-Sufi organisation, Sufi Ruhaniat International, indicates that it has representatives in the Czech Republic. Admittedly, membership in such groups is made up of almost exclusively 'converts', many of whom do not even necessarily identify with Islam, like in the case of the Lithuanian Sufism Study Circle. In any case, such groups are not only representative of the global developments in relation to the diversification of forms of Islamic religiosity but also their coming to Eastern Europe.

Assimilation, emigration (depopulation) and immigration

Though one may rightfully talk of the re-emergence of Islam and/or re-Islamisation of Muslim communities in post-communist Eastern Europe, the double process of secularisation and assimilation of autochthonous Muslims, set in motion during the communist period if not even earlier, has continued unabated into the post-communist era and in some countries has even increased. As revealed in the preceding chapters, in a number of countries, judging by the census and poll results, ethnic groups historically identified as being exclusively Muslim show an increasing split between those who still self-identify as Muslim and those who no longer do. So, for instance, in Lithuania, only just over a half of Tatars self-identify as Muslims.

Furthermore, in some countries, the size of the ethnic groups has been (and in some cases, drastically) decreasing, with that of the Bulgarian Turks being the most notorious. However, the decrease in size of ethnic groups of Muslim background in given countries, though certainly involving assimilation, particularly where inter-ethnic and inter-confessional marriages are more common, and also negative birth rates, nonetheless owes much to the general trends of emigration of Eastern Europeans and among them those of Muslim background to Western Europe. Although the process of emigration of Muslims from Eastern Europe is nothing new – one may recall at least half a dozen waves of (forced) migration since the mid-nineteenth century – until the collapse of the communist system, the destination had been mainly the Ottoman realm and, later, Republican Turkey, with few finding their way to the West. With the fall of the Iron Curtain, the West, and chiefly Western Europe, became the primary destination for both refugees and economic migrants from among the Eastern European Muslim communities.

Muslim refugees in the 1990s, namely Bosniaks, Albanians and Chechens who had fled armed hostilities in their home regions, represent the first large groups of Muslims to appear in Western, and indeed, albeit to a much lower level, Central and Eastern Europe. However, from around the same time, other Eastern European Muslims, most of whom may be collectively regarded as economic migrants, have also been making their way to Western Europe.

With a number of Eastern European countries joining the EU in 2004, 2007 and 2013, moving across the borders and settlement in Western Europe for nationals of the new member states (Muslims among them) became easier and subsequently the numbers of migrants momentarily increased. This movement was chiefly to the UK, which has maintained its status as the number one destination for Eastern European emigrants, particularly from the Baltic States and Central Europe. Table 7.1 reveals the numbers of Eastern European Muslims who have come to England and Wales between 2001 and 2011. Though for the countries in Eastern Europe with sizeable Muslim populations the figures might look negligible, for those where the Muslim communities are estimated to be just thousands or tens of thousands (like Latvia, Lithuania, Slovakia, but also Poland, the Czech Republic and Hungary), the share of their Muslim nationals in England and Wales alone is indeed impressive. It might, however, be noted that movement and legal residence of nationals of non-EU (as opposed to EU member) Eastern European countries has been hampered by visa regimes, though the numbers of Eastern Europeans (Muslims among them) who reside illegally in the UK is certainly higher than the statistics reveal.

Finally, the so-called 'refugee crisis' of 2015 had a side effect on migration trends of Muslims from non-EU Balkan states, chiefly Albania and Kosovo, though Serbia and Macedonia had their share also. For instance, among the asylum applicants in Germany in 2015, there were almost 55,000 Albanian, 37,000 Kosovan, 27,000 Serbian and 14,000 Macedonian citizens. As there is no data on the religious identity of those who seek asylum, how many of them might have been Muslim cannot be inferred; however, it may be safely assumed that practically all Kosovars and half or so of Albanian citizens come from a Muslim background. Moreover, as Macedonia's Albanians are known to make up a large share of its emigrants, it may be safely guessed that a third of Macedonian asylum seekers in Germany in 2015 might have been of Muslim (and ethnic Albanian) background. Ultimately, over 50,000 of the asylum seekers from these three (and possibly four, if among Serbian asylum seekers there were ethnic Albanian or Bosniak Muslims) countries might have been of Muslim cultural background and Albanians by ethnicity. It needs, however, to be added that practically all asylum applications of the nationals (and not only the Muslims among them) of these four countries were rejected and they were deported back to their home countries.

In sum, the four-fold process of secularisation, assimilation and depopulation through negative birth rates and emigration of Eastern European Muslims has already led not only to the shrinkage of the indigenous populations of Muslim background in a number of Eastern European countries, but also to the emergence of an Eastern European Muslim diaspora in Western Europe, probably already numbered in the upper hundreds of thousands and possibly over a million.

Table 7.1 Eastern European Muslims in England and Wales, arriving between 2001 and 2011

Country of origin	Number in England and Wales, 2011 census	Current Muslim population in the country of origin
Albania	2,410	1,650,000–2,300,000
Belarus	44	20,000
Bosnia and Herzegovina	243	1,790,000
Bulgaria	2,375	577,000–600,000
Croatia	25	63,000
Czech Republic	299	3,400–20,000
Estonia	61	1,500–2,000
Hungary	298	5,600–32,000
Kosovo	2,791	1,750,000
Latvia	357	5,000–6,000
Lithuania	535	2,700–4,000
Macedonia, FYR of	223	660,500–730,000
Moldova	25	1,700–5,000
Montenegro	48	118,500
Poland	2,033	25,000–35,000
Romania	439	64,300–65,000
Russia	924	16,000,000–20,000,000
Serbia	203	223,000–350,000
Slovakia	360	4,000–5,000
Slovenia	27	47,500–50,000
Ukraine	134	200,000–400,000

Source: information from the UK Office for National Statistics, compiled by the author

At the same time, most of the countries under study have already received their share of Muslim immigrants from Asia and Africa, albeit, admittedly, their numbers remain rather small and in none of the Eastern European countries exceed tens of thousands – with Russia being the sole exception, where immigrants from Central Asian former Soviet republics number in the upper hundreds of thousands.

The fresh wave of migrants from Asia and Africa to Europe in 2015 has affected Eastern European states in two ways. Some of them, chiefly Macedonia, Serbia and Hungary, bore the direct brunt of the movement of migrants seeking to reach Western Europe, while the Eastern European EU member states were made to accept the European Commission apportioned quotas of asylum seekers under the EC resettlement and relocation scheme, which envisioned the distribution of 160,000 asylum seekers throughout the bloc (see Table 7.2). Though most of the EU member states, even though somewhat grudgingly, acquiesced to the scheme, the Višegrad Four – Hungary, Poland, the Czech Republic and Slovakia – rejected it. As of late 2016, only

Table 7.2 Refugee quotas according to the EU resettlement and relocation scheme from 2015

Country	Current Muslim population	Refugee quota
Bulgaria	577,000–600,000	1,600
Croatia	63,000	1,064
Czech Republic	3,400–20,000	2,978
Estonia	1,500–2,000	373
Hungary	5,600–32,000	0
Latvia	5,000–6,000	526
Lithuania	2,700–4,000	1,105
Poland	25,000–35,000	9,287
Romania	64,300–65,000	4,646
Slovakia	4,000–5,000	1,502
Slovenia	47,500–50,000	631

Compiled by the author

several thousand displaced persons have been resettled and relocated to Eastern European EU member states with scores of them having already fled to Western Europe.

Converts

Conversion of (Eastern) Europeans to Islam is not a post-communist era novelty – apart from the historical mass conversions in the Ottoman-ruled Balkans, spoken about in Chapters 4 and 5, there have been not only individual converts in many Eastern European lands in the nineteenth and the beginning of the twentieth centuries, but even nascent communities of converts, like the one in interwar Czechoslovakia. There also were some conversions to Islam during the communist period, mainly of local Eastern European women who married Middle Eastern Muslims who had come to study in Eastern Europe, but also of some local males, often to forms of mystical or heterodox Islam. However, it is the post-communist period that has seen the explosion in conversion to Islam among Eastern Europeans (see Table 7.3). Though, admittedly, so far miniscule – hovering around several hundred in most countries – the convert component within Eastern European Muslim populations is a factor to be reckoned with. And not only because their numbers since the fall of the communist system have been on the rise, in some countries (like Russia, Poland and Hungary) skyrocketing, but also because in some countries converts either are in the leading positions in national Islamic administrations (like in Hungary, the Czech Republic and Moldova) or have their own organisations (like in Russia and Romania). It is notable that in a number of Balkan countries (for instance, Macedonia, Montenegro, Albania, Bulgaria and Bosnia and Herzegovina), conversions to Islam appear to be of a low level and, when they occur, of low profile. This may be explained by the double stigmatisation of Islam as being both the religion of the former oppressor, the Ottoman Turks and of distinct local ethnic groups, chiefly Bosniaks and Albanians.

There are numerous factors facilitating conversion of Eastern Europeans to Islam, many of which are shared across all of Europe and beyond, among them such 'motivational experiences' as 'intellectual', 'mystical', 'experimental', 'affectional', 'revivalist' and 'coercive' (Lofland and Skonovd 1981: 373–85), or even 'negativist' (Lakhdar *et al.* 2007: 1–15), with, arguably 'relational', where 'conversion under these circumstances is a means to reach another aim (marriage), not an end in itself' (Allievi 2002: 1), 'discovery of Islam' and 'rational' types of conversion (Allievi 2002) predominating. For some countries, like Poland, the Czech Republic and Slovakia, there are reports that scores of women convert to Islam after having travelled as tourists to Egypt or other Arab/Muslim-majority countries, where they apparently 'stumble upon and discover' and 'fall in love with' Islam and/or Muslims.

Table 7.3 Eastern European converts to Islam, as of the mid-2010s

Country of origin[a]	Current Muslim population	Converts, estimates
Albania	1,650,000–2,300,000	100
Belarus	20,000	300
Bosnia and Herzegovina	1,790,000	100
Bulgaria	577,000–600,000	n/a
Croatia	63,000	n/a
Czech Republic	3,400–20,000	500
Estonia	1,500–2,000	200
Hungary	5,600–32,000	5,000
Kosovo	1,750,000	n/a
Latvia	5,000–6,000	300
Lithuania	2,700–4,000	700
Macedonia, FYR of	660,500–730,000	30
Moldova	1,700–5,000	200
Montenegro	118,500	n/a
Poland	25,000–35,000	5,000
Romania	64,300–65,000	500
Russia	16,000,000–20,000,000	10,000
Serbia	223,000–350,000	500
Slovakia	4,000–5,000	500
Slovenia	47,500–50,000	500
Ukraine	200,000–400,000	1,500
TOTAL		26,000

Note:
[a] Many of the Eastern European converts to Islam have settled in Western Europe with the UK purportedly hosting the largest number compared to other countries. Ireland, Germany, The Netherlands, Belgium and Spain are other popular destinations.
Sources: Scharbrodt 2016; compiled by the author

It must also be noted that converts are collectively the most mobile group among Eastern European Muslims. As argued by Alak, they 'are the ones who long to live in an "Islamic" country and feel their spiritual life would be better, if their choices and those of the people around them were limited to traditional Islamic views' (Alak 2015: 159). With such conditions arguably unavailable in their home countries, many converts opt for emigration to either Western Europe (the British 2011 census figures attest to this) or to Muslim-majority countries, chiefly in the Middle East. Therefore, the overall number of nationals of many Eastern European countries who have converted to Islam is at any time higher than that of the number of converts who remain in their motherlands.

Eastern European converts to Islam, besides being active in existing Islamic organisations, are also some of the most active participants in online *da'wa* and digital trans-border community building. In some cases, converts maintain websites and online forums in their national languages where converts and those interested in Islam residing within and outside of the home countries' borders partake in lively online exchange of ideas and experiences and engage in self-help groups with the purpose of deepening knowledge in their adopted faith (Račius 2013).

As has been indicated in preceding chapters, though some Eastern European converts are Sufism-leaning, many more converts tend to be revivalist-leaning with scores openly identifying with the Salafi trend within revivalist Islam. Some among them go all the way to adopting radical ideologies. Radicalisation of Eastern European Muslims, though, is not confined exclusively to converts. Indeed, the bulk of radicalised Muslims in Eastern Europe come from the autochthonous Muslim communities, mainly in Russia and the Central Balkans.

Radicalisation

One should establish a mental difference between what is called 'Islamic revivalism' and what may be labelled 'Islamic radicalism'. In preceding chapters, the overview of revivalist trends among Muslims in the Eastern European countries stopped short of including violent (popularly referred to as extremist) groups. This was done deliberately. Although some Islamic revivalists are prone to religiously motivated (political) violence, the overwhelming majority of revivalists are peaceful and law-abiding citizens who shun violence. On the other hand, it is the fringe groups and individuals among the revivalists who receive the bulk of the media's attention, even to the point where it might seem that all Islamic revivalism is about violence. In order to evade this potential methodological trap, it was decided to postpone the discussion on 'Islamic radicalism' till the last, more general, chapter.

In popular parlance, the terms 'Wahhabi' and 'Salafi' are routinely taken as synonyms for if not 'Muslim terrorists', then at least 'radical' Muslims.

However, as Krasniqi, reflecting on the use of these labels in the Kosovan and Macedonian contexts, reasons,

> a problem, both practical and analytical, is the use of the term 'Wahhabi' to describe anything that is different from the local tradition of religious practice. Or, even worse, the term is often used by local people to discredit opponents in occasional power struggles within the Islamic Communities in Kosovo and Macedonia. Therefore, it is essential that the whole complexity of 'Wahhabism', both as doctrine and transnational movement, be placed in the context of the globalization of Islam and its effects in various regions of the world, including the region of the Balkans. Without a critical appraisal of this complexity, long beards and niqab on the streets of Prishtina and Skopje do not tell us much about the role of Islam in everyday life and the spread of 'Wahhabism' in the Balkan region as a whole. (Krasniqi 2011: 204–5)

In other words, labelling someone a 'Wahhabi' with an implied quality of being 'radical' and potentially violent, not only obscures the much more complex reality but also blurs the dividing line between those revivalists who simply long for a more Islamic environment to live in and those who are willing to use violence, routinely called by them 'jihad', to attain such an environment. The latter may rightfully be labelled 'radicals' or even 'extremists'.

As was revealed in the preceding chapters, though it had appeared in Eastern Europe by the end of the 1980s, Islamic radicalism exploded into full blossom in the early 1990s in a direct connection with two major armed conflicts – the wars in Bosnia and Chechnya. It was then that '[t]he arrival in the Balkans of Islamic NGOs and mujahiddins linked to "Arab-Afghan" networks also gave rise to alarmist rumours about the transformation of the Balkans into a "bridge-head" for Islamic terrorism and the creeping "wahhabisation" of Balkan Islam' (Bougarel 2005: 17). This, however, never happened in either Bosnia or elsewhere in the Balkans.

On the other hand, the presence of radicalism among local Muslims was visible in the Northern Caucasus, where the initial separatist fight for a nation state of Ichkeriya (with the help of the very same 'Arab-Afghans') was soon transformed into a full-blown jihad against 'infidel' Russia with the declared aim of creating the Islamic Emirate of North Caucasus, which was to incorporate Chechnya, Daghestan, Ossetia, Ingushetia and other Muslim-inhabited regions in the Northern Caucasus and southern Russia. At the turn of the millennium, it even looked as if the Emirate was going to become a reality as large parts of Chechnya were indeed out of the hands of the Russian authorities. But not only that: the jihad had been extended by its champions all the way to Moscow, epitomised by the hostage drama in 2002 in a centrally located theatre in the Russian capital. This and other similar terrorist acts (a similar hostage crisis at a school in southern Russia in 2004, a spree of bombings in 2003 and 2004 on the Moscow metro system, at a music festival, on an aircraft and a train, to name just some, all in the name of the declared jihad) perpetrated by the Northern Caucasian jihadis aroused a decisive reaction from the Russian government, which then resorted to a brutal campaign to eliminate the threat emanating from the jihadis. And though the jihadi insurgency in the Northern Caucasus was eventually suppressed by the Russian regime, by the late-2000s, cells of radicalised Northern Caucasian Muslims continued to menace the Russian state in following years.

The collapse of nation states in the Middle East in the wake of the so-called 'Arab Spring', the subsequent emergence of armed groups of radicalised Muslims in their territories and the founding of a post-nation state formation – the Islamic Khilafa State (IKS) – in 2014, opened a new page in the evolution of radical strains of revivalist Islam in Eastern Europe. As the fighting in Syria and Iraq, but also Libya, took on a more international face, with tens of thousands of foreign fighters from all over the world joining various armed factions, Eastern Europe also sent its share. The publicly available estimates suggest that over three and a half thousand Eastern European Muslims have voluntarily relocated to the parts of Syria and Iraq under rebel control, in what they themselves con- sider *hijra* – migration to an Islamic polity. Though two thirds of these *muhajirun* were from Russia, practically all Eastern European countries had their own *muhajirun*, in the local public parlance invariably referred to as 'foreign fighters' (see Table 7.4). However, this label is rather misleading, as among the Eastern European Muslims who have moved to the Middle East, chiefly to the Islamic Khilafa State, there are numerous families with small children. And though the men may have joined the IKS 'armed forces' and thus may be labelled as 'fight- ers' or even 'jihadis', the women and children hardly meet the criteria to qualify as a 'fighter'. In result, although the 'fighters' arguably make up the bulk of the *muhajirun* from Eastern Europe, one must recognise the 'non-fighter' segment among the Eastern European Muslims who have found themselves in the ter- ritories controlled either by the IKS or other (radicalised) rebel groups.

With the revelation of their nationals moving to the Middle East to join rebel groups there, governments of many of the Eastern European states rushed to carve out legislation proscribing 'fighting in or recruiting for fighting in armed conflicts abroad'. For instance, the parliament of Bosnia and Herzegovina (with an estimated over 300 *muhajirun*) in early 2014 adopted a law penalising such activity with up to ten years in prison. The Kosovan parliament also adopted a similar law in 2014, in reaction to some 300 of the country's citizens relocating to the Middle East. Calls, similar to those in the UK and France, to strip the *muhajirun* of Kosovan citizenship were also heard. Furthermore, the Kosovo gov- ernment's concern with radicalisation of the country's Muslims translated into arrests of a number of imams in 2014, who were charged with 'incitement to commit a terrorist offence' (Morina 2015: 357). The government is also reported to have listed over sixty NGOs as 'suspicious'. Similar actions are reported for

Table 7.4 Eastern European *muhajirun* in the Middle East, beginning of 2016

Country	Muslim population	*Muhajirun*
Albania	1,650,000–2,300,000	up to 200
Belarus	20,000	n/a
Bosnia and Herzegovina	1,790,000	up to 330
Bulgaria	577,000–600,000	up to 10
Croatia	63,000	at least 4
Czech Republic	3,400–20,000	none known
Estonia	1,500–2,000	at least 4
Hungary	5,600–32,000	up to 15
Kosovo	1,750,000	up to 300
Latvia	5,000–6,000	at least 2
Lithuania	2,700–4,000	none known
Macedonia, FYR of	660,500–730,000	up to 204
Moldova	1,700–5,000	at least 1
Montenegro	118,500	up to 30
Poland	25,000–35,000	up to 40
Romania	64,300–65,000	at least 1
Russia	16,000,000–20,000,000	2,400
Serbia	223,000–350,000	up to 70
Slovakia	4,000–5,000	up to 8
Slovenia	47,500–50,000	at least 3
Ukraine	200,000–400,000	not known
TOTAL		over 3,600
TOTAL, excl. Russia		up to 1,200

Sources: Barret 2014; The Soufan Group 2015; van Ginkel and Entenmann 2016.
Compiled by the author.

several other Balkan states and also the former Soviet republics, like Moldova, where several people were reported to have been apprehended on suspicion of being involved in IKS-related activities.

Though the outflow of Muslims from Eastern Europe to the Middle East may have considerably slowed down or even stopped altogether by the end of 2016, the fate of those present in the territories once held by rebel groups may soon become very precarious if or when those territories are captured by anti-jihadi forces. Though some will have become disillusioned with the Islamic State project and might undergo the de-radicalisation process, many of the committed *muhajirun* will have no choice but to move on. And although some are probably going to look for a new 'homeland', the majority will come back to Eastern Europe, where in addition to prosecution by the state they will face stigmatisation and marginalisation not only from the non-Muslim part of their motherlands but also from the local Muslim communities. It is also likely that the radical strain within the revivalist segments of Eastern European Muslim communities will be strengthened through the return of the *muhajirun* – something that will not only further increase the prospect of securitisation of the 'Muslim issue' in the respective countries but will also raise the already simmering tensions between the Muslims and the Muslimophobically predisposed segments of the non-Muslim populations in Eastern Europe.

CHAPTER 8

Considering the other side

Though in three Eastern European countries, namely, Kosovo, Albania and Bosnia and Herzegovina, Muslims nominally make up the majorities, in the rest they live as religious (and indeed ethnic) minorities, in more than a dozen of the countries not even exceeding 1 per cent of the local population. At the same time, in three quarters of the countries under study in this book a Muslim presence in their territories dates back several hundred years. However, this co-existence of Muslim groups and non-Muslim (majority) populations in the same physical space does not by default imply their constructive engagement, either in history or at the present time. In fact, in the Eastern European context, in many settings this co-existence has historically caused uneasiness leading to tensions and even inter-communal violence and discrimination. As has been shown in the preceding chapters, Muslim communities in Eastern Europe, particularly since the formation of both the post-Ottoman and, more recently, the post-communist nation states, have often been received with open hostility, both at state and social levels. Therefore, retrospectively, one may at best talk of toleration of, let alone tolerance toward or engaged dialogue with, Muslims and their religious practices in the overwhelmingly non-Muslim Eastern European lands.

International treaties obliging national legislation to guarantee the basic rights of Muslim citizens have facilitated the steady formal increase in such rights; today, in practically all Eastern European countries Islam has been institutionally recognised through registration of Muslim representative organisations. However, the actual level of religious rights varies considerably from country to country: where Islam is officially recognised as one of the 'traditional' religions of the country, Muslims as a rule have many more rights and privileges not only compared to Muslim communities in the countries where Islam does not hold such status but also vis-à-vis other (non-Muslim) religious communities without such status. By and large, however, Muslims and Islam in Eastern Europe have historically remained the internal and, with the appearance of 'new' Muslims in the person of immigrants and converts, also the external 'Other', with all the ensuing consequences.

Forms of 'othering' leading to segregationism may take on different shapes and be referred to by different names, among them racism, supremacism, chauvinism and xenophobia. Some of them may include a religious dimension. Negative predisposition toward adherents of Islam has attained its separate label – Islamophobia. The term is quite unique in that there are no such working labels as Hindophobia, Budhophobia or Confucianophobia, not to speak of Christophobia (all such neologisms even sound artificial). Yet, there is 'Islamophobia', coined in the 1990s and since then successfully introduced into circulation in academic, media and political discourses. 'Islamophobia' as the label for a phenomenon was introduced in the UK and soon was adopted all over Western Europe, where it primarily concerned dislike or even hate-infused stances and activities vis-à-vis the immigrant populations of Muslim cultural background. The level of their actual religiosity was of little importance but the perceived impossibility of socially integrating them was of paramount concern. Thus, in the Western European context, the object of Islamophobia was perceived to be the insurmountable cultural differences of the immigrant population of Muslim background from those of the 'indigenous' host populations.

Though there have been sceptical voices about the usability of the term – the sceptics were unsure of its scope – there may be no denial that the phenomenon of dislike, if not outright fear, of Islam and its representatives, the Muslims, has been present in practically all contemporary non-Muslim-majority societies. The only discussion is then whether Islamophobia is the correct label. It has been suggested (Erdenir 2010) that 'Muslimophobia' may be a more adequate term to label the phenomenon.

In the Eastern European context, particularly in those parts where a Muslim presence is counted in hundreds of years and where there are still very few immigrants, dislike, hatred or fear of Islam and Muslims certainly have roots of a different nature from that in Western Europe. Rather than stemming from a future-oriented presumed impossibility of ever socially integrating Muslims of immigrant background (that is, a fear of the external 'Other'), Muslimophobia in Eastern Europe primarily arises from the past-oriented historical narratives of ethnocentric national evolution, where Muslims (first of all, Turks) often serve as either former 'invaders' (the historical external 'Other') or the 'misguided part of "us"' (the internal 'Other'). So, in most countries in South-eastern Europe, the national folklore and literature is sprinkled with negative attitudes toward Turks. While Bulgaria and Serbia stand out as the countries whose national folklore and writings by national(ist) poets and writers are pregnant with what one in contemporary terms would call 'hate speech', Hungarian literary heritage also contains examples of such an attitude. Even in Slovenia, which was never ruled by the Ottomans and their incursions occurred way back in the fifteenth and sixteenth centuries, there abound poems and novels deriding Turks. Though in North-eastern Europe there are significantly fewer folkloristic tropes of an anti-Muslim nature, one may still find authored works from the nineteenth or beginning of the twentieth century, particularly in Russian, in which the portrayal of Muslims is often biased, to say the least. Practically universally, such literature refers to the perceived brutal misconduct on the side of the invading

Muslims (Turks or Mongol-Tatars) and the brave resistance by the righteou local Christians. Conscription of young Christian boys to the Ottoman arm (*devširme*) where they are also (forcibly) converted to Islam receives a particula share of scornful attention. What is interesting is that sometimes such literatur (for instance, *Eclipse of the Crescent Moon*, a 1899 novel by Géza Gárdonyi, know as *The Stars of Eger* in Hungary) is included in reading lists for secondary and hig school pupils.

But Muslimophobic attitudes and actions may come from very differer sources in and segments of the state and society: the government, politic parties, non-Muslim faith communities, lay NGOs, informal civil socie groups, media, educational system (textbooks), even arts. Of all these actors sources, non-Muslim faith communities are exceptional as in their nature the are faith-based, therefore, arguably, of the same origin as Muslim religious com munities and their institutions. The dominant non-Muslim faith communities i Eastern Europe are Christian: in more than half of the countries (chiefly Centra and Eastern Balkan, and North-eastern European) under study it is Orthodc Christians, in a third, Catholic (Western Balkan, Central European), with ju two (northern-most) countries historically having had a Protestant majorit All of the Catholic- and Protestant-majority countries are incidentally membe states of the EU, which, among other things, indirectly influences governanc of religion and rights of faith communities in the member states. Only two the Orthodox-majority countries, namely, Bulgaria and Romania, are als members of the EU.

Though it may not be directly tied to a country belonging or not to the EL in those Eastern European countries that are not members of the bloc, the rol of the dominant Christian (invariably, Orthodox) church is observably distinc from that in the nominally Catholic- and Protestant-majority countries. I many of the post-Ottoman and post-communist Orthodox-majority countrie the Orthodox faith, represented by (autocephalous) Orthodox churches, tightly bound not only to the (titular) ethnicity but indeed to the very natior hood. In other words, those belonging to a (national) Orthodox church regar themselves to be by default full members of the nation. Conversely, belongin to a faith community other than the (national) Orthodox Church automaticall puts into question one's belonging to that nation.

As has been shown above, in many of the Eastern European countries, b virtue of belonging to a non-Christian faith (often coupled with belonging to non-Slavic-speaking ethnicity) Muslims have had to constantly struggle to b accepted as part of the nation and its state. However, sometimes, their effort have been offset by the antagonist reaction on the Orthodox Church's side Moldova, Serbia and Macedonia may be put forward as countries where th leadership of the majority faith communities, in this case all Christian Orthodo has openly espoused anti-Islam/anti-Muslim sentiment and even instigate acting against Muslims and their interests through public protests, boycotts, lobbying for or against relevant legislation. But it would not be fair to maintain that it has been only Orthodox communities in non-EU Eastern European states that have been exceptionally Muslimophobic. In the Czech Republic, a former top Catholic official (a cardinal) has also openly expressed unfavourable opinions about Islam and Muslims in general, and those in Europe in particular.

Because in some Eastern European (particularly Central and Eastern Balkan) countries Church and state habitually work in tandem, if not as one, often the political parties, both in government and opposition, either follow the Muslimophobic line of the (national) Church or tacitly encourage it. So, for instance, institutionalisation of Islam in Moldova that was vehemently opposed by the Orthodox Church was also derided by parts of the country's political elite, including a former president. Likewise, in Macedonia, the political elite and the Orthodox Church have on many occasions worked closely in not only advancing the 'Christian nature of the nation' but also belittling and demonising the country's Muslim population. The Macedonian President in the mid-2010s publicly vilified Muslim refugees coming to Europe and even warned the world of the prospect of a 'Balkan Caliphate'. A radical nationalist party in Bulgaria has even gone so far as to engage in physical violence against Muslims and their property.

But even in countries where there is no national church (particularly in Central Europe), there is an observable emergence and rise of populist Muslimophobic politics, with two major political parties in Hungary being the best example – though political parties probably equally Muslimophobic but less open about it may be found in most Eastern European liberal democracies. Such parties usually tie the 'Muslim question' to the perceived threats stemming from (Muslim) immigration, ranging from security, economic, social and cultural aspects, all the way to the very survival of the 'native' nations. So far, however, with the exception of Hungary, such populist Muslimophobic parties have not made it into ruling positions in their countries, though the rising tide of cultural racism and primordialism in the face of perceived and real immigration from Asia and Africa may soon catapult them into the limelight and give political dividends. Besides one Hungarian Prime Minister, a Czech President as well as a Slovak Prime Minister are also known to have expressed a manifestly Muslimophobic position.

Next to these formal and institutional actors with Muslimophobic agendas and rhetoric, there are lay non-state actors representing groups of 'concerned' citizens. The formation of secular citizen groups openly predisposed against a Muslim presence in their countries is another yardstick against which to measure the level of Muslimophobia in a given Eastern European country. PEGIDA (Patriotic Europeans Against the Islamisation of the Occident) and Stop Islamization of Europe are the two 'pan-European' initiatives but there are also a number of national or even local similar one-issue groups with easily guessable identical agendas and rhetoric. Stop Islamization of Europe has been actively spreading its ideas and seeking to gain supporters in the EU member states in Eastern Europe, and PEGIDA, for its part, has gained a following in Macedonia: a Facebook page 'PEGIDA Macedonia' was set up in 2015 and assembled 'about 1.1 million users engaged in various calls to purge Macedonia of Muslims by appropriating the language of the European right' (Rexhepi 2016: 446).

Though there are many fields and contested issues where Muslimophobia may express itself not only rhetorically but also in practice – like dress code, diet, prayer facilities, artistic and other creative expression, sports and leisure – the 'mosque issue' may probably be regarded as the most symptomatic of them all. Though as a rule a legal basis for erection of mosques and other Islamic communal buildings in Eastern European countries is in place, either through bilateral state–Islamic administration agreements or implied in laws formalising the governance of religion, the actual implementation of the right to prayer facilities is very often obstructed by interested non-Muslim actors, ranging from state institutions (like local municipal authorities) to administrative institutions of other, non-Muslim, religious communities, to NGOs and other civil society actors to, finally, 'ordinary' citizens. Though it probably would be too far-fetched to measure the level of Muslimophobia through the prism of the practical accessibility to and implementability of mosque construction, this is nonetheless a good tool to assess the level of toleration/tolerance toward a public visibility of Islam/Muslims in the land.

Arguably, post-communist Eastern Europe has witnessed an unprecedented level of construction of new and reconstruction of older destroyed, damaged or otherwise neglected mosques. One may argue that with just a few exceptions, purpose-built mosques (*jami'*) or premises converted into mosques (*masjid*) now may be found in practically all Eastern European urban settlements with a sizable enough believer community. On the other hand, the documented evidence reveals that there could have already been many more of them had there been less obstructionist activities. The same documented evidence also discloses that many of the by now standing and functioning mosques took a long time to materialise, often due to the same obstructionist activities on the side of non-Muslim actors. So-called 'mosque debates' have at one time or another occurred in practically all Eastern European countries, though their scope, depth and consequences varied widely.

If in some Balkan states (particularly in the Central and Eastern Balkans) the problem revolves around the rebuilding of mosques (for instance, in Macedonia, local non-Muslim authorities are reported to obstruct the rebuilding of historical mosques in the municipalities under their jurisdiction and at times mosques are vandalised or even destroyed by members of the local non-Muslim population),

in most other Eastern European countries, and particularly in central and northern parts, it is about obtaining permissions for building new, and in most cases
the first ever, mosques, like in the Czech Republic, Slovakia and Moldova, but
also Hungary, Poland and the Baltic States. In the ensuing debates and discussions, the opposing side as a rule advances Muslimophobic arguments like 'the
fear from increased Muslim migration, the infiltration with Islamists, terrorists,
and organized crime, the interference with the existing architectural character
and townscape, and concerns over a different and unknown religious ideology'
(Bureš 2011: 29). Though many of them may be dismissed offhand, such arguments do find a listening ear not only among the local population whose hostility
toward mosque construction is aroused but also the local authorities who often,
if they do not have grounds to reject the project outright, drag their feet for as
long as possible.

The picture painted of the reception of Islam and Muslims in Eastern
Europe, however, is only one side of the coin. The other side reveals that there
have been numerous instances of Muslim communities working together and
with not only Christian but also with local Jewish communities. In some countries, there are long-functioning inter-faith dialogue and cooperation platforms,
like the one in Poland bringing together representatives of the country's dominant Catholic faith and Muslims. There are reports of Christian communities
coming forward with assistance for Muslims in the Czech Republic, where they
have provided space for prayer. In countries where Islam, albeit a minority
religion, is recognised as a traditional faith, like Lithuania and Belarus, but also
Poland and Ukraine, the state authorities are known to have not only maintained a favourable attitude toward the local Muslim communities but have also
awarded them exclusive rights and privileges – like the Lithuanian state giving
permission to perform Islamic slaughter of domestic animals or its allocation of
an annual financial subsidy to the Muslim community of the country. And more
generally, it would be wrong to assume that Eastern European non-Muslims are
either exceptionally Muslimophobic or more so than their Western European
counterparts.

The growing closer or further apart of the Muslim and non-Muslim sections
of Eastern European societies depends on numerous factors, many of which are
of an external nature and thus hard to control. However, it is already evident
that with the changing demographic make-up of local Muslim communities,
with more and more Muslims of immigrant and convert background (and their
forms of religiosity) appearing on the scene, not only are the intra-communal
relations among Muslims bound to change but the view of Muslim populations
among non-Muslims in the respective Eastern European countries is also to
undergo a profound reassessment. It is still too early to predict what direction(s)
this reassessment may take and what its consequences may be to all concerned sides. One may only hope that it will not be in a more confrontational

(Muslimophobic) direction but rather one towards more understanding, acceptance and mutual respect, all based on more authentic and unbiased acquaintance with the spectrum of ways to be a Muslim in Eastern Europe or indeed, an Eastern European Muslim. This book was precisely designed to contribute to the spread of such acquaintance and the author's wish is for it to have succeeded in that.

Notes

Chapter 1

1. For more on normative Islam and Islamic law, see Wael B. Hallaq (2004), *The Origins and Evolution of Islamic Law*, Cambridge: Cambridge University Press.
2. For more on Sufism, see Annemarie Schimmel (1975), *The Mystical Dimensions of Islam*, Chapel Hill, NC: University of North Carolina Press.
3. For differences between normative Islam and folk Islam, and also between variants of folk Islam, see Clifford Geertz (1971), *Islam Observed: Religious Development in Morocco and Indonesia*, Chicago, IL: University of Chicago Press.
4. For more on Wahhabism, see Natana J. DeLong-Bas (2008), *Wahhabi Islam: From Revival and Reform to Global Jihad*, Oxford: Oxford University Press.
5. For more on Salafism, see Roel Meijer (ed.) (2009), *Global Salafism: Islam's New Religious Movement*, Oxford: Oxford University Press.
6. For more on Islamism, see Peter R. Demant (2006), *Islam vs. Islamism: The Dilemma of the Muslim World*, Westport, CT: Praeger.
7. For more on Hizb at-Tahrir, see Reza Pankhurst (2016), *Hizb ut-Tahrir: The Untold History of the Liberation Party*, London: Hurst.
8. For more on the Muslim Brotherhood, see Carrie Rosefsky Wickham (2013), *The Muslim Brotherhood: Evolution of an Islamist Movement*, Princeton, NJ: Princeton University Press.

Chapter 3

1. There certainly are Muslim communities on the Asian side of Russia but they are comparatively small, in total amounting to possibly less than 1 million. However, due to the geographical scope of this book, these communities are deliberately left out, though one may presume that much of what is related to the development of Muslim communities on the European side of Russia is also valid for those living on the Asian side.
2. For a general history and doctrines of the global Ahmadi community, see Simon Ross Valentine (2008), *Islam and the Ahmadiyya Jama'at: History, Belief, Practice*, London: Hurst.

Chapter 4

1. As noted by Bougarel, '[n]umerous experts are labelling this "imported Islam" as "wahhabi Islam", contrasting it with a supposedly heterodox and tolerant "local Islam". But the spectre of a "wahhabisation" of Balkan Islam conceals what is really at stake. In fact, the representatives of these new religious doctrines do not define themselves as "Wahhabis", and are sometimes openly hostile to the Saudi regime. The label "neo-Salafists" – which refers to religious movements that demand a return to the religion of the "pious ancestors" – would thus be more appropriate' (Xavier Bougarel (2005), *The role of Balkan Muslims in building a European Islam*, Brussels: European Policy Centre, Issue Paper No. 43, 18). Therefore, though the two labels, 'Wahhabi' and 'Salafi', in public discourse are uncritically used interchangeably, it would be more appropriate to apply the latter – and not only to this stream of revivalist Islam in the Balkans but also across all of Eastern Europe.

2. Although the overwhelming majority of them live in the territories west of the centre of Macedonia, particularly along the border with Kosovo and Albania, there also are small communities of Torbeshis in both Albania and Kosovo. In total, they are estimated to number between 40,000 and 100,000. Counting Torbeshis is difficult, since many among them claim to be Turks (though they do not speak Turkish), while others ethnically identify with Macedonians, and a minority even claim to be Albanians (Ali Dikici (2008), 'The Torbeshes of Macedonia: religious and national identity questions of Macedonian-speaking Muslims', *Journal of Muslim Minority Affairs*, 28: 1, 27–43).

Bibliography

General

Allievi, Stefano (2002), 'Converts and the making of European Islam', *ISIM Newsletter*, 11: 1, 26.

Barret, Richard (2014), *Foreign Fighters in Syria*, The Soufan Group, http://soufan group.com/wp-content/uploads/2014/06/TSG-Foreign-Fighters-in-Syria.pdf (last accessed 27 February 2017).

DeLong-Bas, Natana J. (2008), *Wahhabi Islam: From Revival and Reform to Global Jihad*, Oxford: Oxford University Press.

Demant, Peter R. (2006), *Islam vs. Islamism: The Dilemma of the Muslim World*, Westport, CT: Praeger.

Erdenir, Burak (2010), 'Islamophobia qua racial discrimination: Muslimophobia', in Anna Triandafyllidou (ed.), *Muslims in 21st Century Europe: Structural and Cultural Perspectives*, London: Routledge, pp. 27–44.

Gallup (2012), *Global Index of Religiosity and Atheism*, WIN-Gallup International, http://www.wingia.com/web/files/news/14/file/14.pdf (last accessed 27 February 2017).

Geertz, Clifford (1971), *Islam Observed: Religious Development in Morocco and Indonesia*, Chicago, IL: University of Chicago Press.

Gellner, Ernest (1992), *Postmodernism, Reason and Religion*, London: Routledge.

Ginkel, Bibi van, and Eva Entenmann (eds) (2016), *The Foreign Fighters Phenomenon in the European Union: Profiles, Threats and Policies*, The Hague: International Centre for Counter-Terrorism, https://www.icct.nl/wp-content/uploads/2016/03/ICCT-Report_Foreign-Fighters-Phenomenon-in-the-EU_1-April-2016_including-AnnexesLinks.pdf (last accessed 27 February 2017).

Hallaq, Wael B. (2004), *The Origins and Evolution of Islamic Law*, Cambridge: Cambridge University Press.

Koller, Markus (2012), 'Ottoman history of South-east Europe', in *European History Online* (EGO), Mainz: Leibniz Institute of European History (IEG), http://www.ieg-ego.eu/kollerm-2010-en (last accessed 27 February 2017).

Lakhdar, M., G. Vinsonneau, M. J. Apter and E. Mullet (2007), 'Conversion to Islam among French adolescents and adults: a systematic inventory of motives', *International Journal for the Psychology of Religion*, 17: 1, 1–15.

Lofland, John, and Norman Skonovd (1981), 'Conversion motifs', *Journal for the Scientific Study of Religion*, 20: 4, 373–85.

McCarthy, Justin (2000), 'Muslims in Ottoman Europe: population from 1800 to 1912', *Nationalities Papers*, 28: 1, 29–43.

Meijer, Roel (ed.) (2009), *Global Salafism: Islam's New Religious Movement*, Oxford: Oxford University Press.

Motadel, David (2014), *Islam and Nazi Germany's War*, Cambridge, MA: Belknap Press.

Pankhurst, Reza (2016), *Hizb ut-Tahrir: The Untold History of the Liberation Party*, London: Hurst.

Pew Research Center (2011), *The Future Global Muslim Population: Projections for 2010–2030*, The Pew Forum on Religion and Public Life, http://www.pewforum.org/2011/01/27/future-of-the-global-muslim-population-regional-europe/ (last accessed 27 February 2017).

Pew Research Center (2012), *The World's Muslims: Unity and Diversity*, The Pew Forum on Religion and Public Life, http://www.pewforum.org/2012/08/09/the-worlds-muslims-unity-and-diversity-executive-summary/ (last accessed 27 February 2017).

Rosefsky Wickham, Carrie (2013), *The Muslim Brotherhood: Evolution of an Islamist Movement*, Princeton, NJ: Princeton University Press.

Scharbrodt, Oliver, Jørgen S. Nielsen, Samim Akgönül, Ahmet Alibašić and Egdūnas Račius (eds) (2016), *Yearbook of Muslims in Europe*, Leiden: Brill, vol. 8.

Schimmel, Annemarie (1975), *The Mystical Dimensions of Islam*, Chapel Hill, NC: University of North Carolina Press.

The Soufan Group (2015), *Foreign Fighters: An Updated Assessment of the Flow of Foreign Fighters into Syria and Iraq*, The Soufan Group, http://soufangroup.com/wp-content/uploads/2015/12/TSG_ForeignFightersUpdate3.pdf (last accessed 27 February 2017).

Valentine, Simon Ross (2008), *Islam and the Ahmadiyya Jama'at: History, Belief, Practice*, New York, NY: Columbia University Press.

North-eastern Europe (Russia, Ukraine, Moldova, Belarus, the Baltic States)

Abiline, Toomas (2008), *Islam Eestis. Islam in Estonia. Ислам в Эстонии*, Tallinn: Huma.

Akaev, Vakhit (2015), 'The history and specifics of contemporary Islamic revival in the Chechen Republic', *Russian Social Science Review*, 56: 6, 40–62.

Akhmetova, Elmira (2010), 'Russia', in Jørgen S. Nielsen, Samim Akgönül, Ahmet Alibašić, Brigitte Maréchal and Christian Moe (eds), *Yearbook of Muslims in Europe*, Leiden: Brill, vol. 2, pp. 435–56.

Balodis, Ringolds (2010), 'The constitutional and administrative aspects of state and Church regulation in the Republic of Latvia', in J. Martínez-Torrón and W. C. Durham (eds), *Religion and the Secular State*, Provo, UT: International Center for Law and Religion Studies, Brigham Young University, pp. 475–92.

Braginskaia, Ekaterina (2012), 'Domestication or representation? Russia and the institutionalisation of Islam in comparative perspective', *Europe-Asia Studies*, 64: 3, 597–620.

Bulatov, Ayder (2014), 'Salafism as an ideological and political movement in the Muslim Ummah Crimea', *Anthropology & Archeology of Eurasia*, 53: 3, 66–71.

Crews, Robert D. (2006), *For Prophet and Tsar: Islam and empire in Russia and Central Asia*, Cambridge, MA: Harvard University Press.

Erşahin, Seyfettin (2005), 'The official interpretation of Islam under the Soviet regime: a base for understanding of contemporary Central Asian Islam', *Journal of Religious Culture*, 77: 1–19.

Kouts, Natalya, and Elmira Muratova (2014), 'The past, present, and future of the Crimean Tatars in the discourse of the Muslim community of Crimea', *Anthropology & Archeology of Eurasia*, 53: 3, 25–65.

Kričinskis, Stanislovas (1993), *Lietuvos totoriai*, Vilnius: Mokslo ir enciklopediju leidykla.

Malashenko, Alexei V. (2009), 'Islam in Russia', *Social Research*, 76: 1, 321–58.

Motadel, David (2013), 'Islam and Germany's war in the Soviet borderlands, 1941–5', *Journal of Contemporary History*, 48: 4, 784–820.

Muratova, Elmira (2015), 'Islamic groups of Crimea: discourses and politics', *Russian Social Science Review*, 56: 6, 24–39.

Nurullina, Roza (2015), 'The revival of Muslim communities in Russia's regions based on sociological research materials in the Republic of Tatarstan', *Russian Social Science Review*, 56: 6, 3–23.

Račius, Egdūnas (2013), 'A "virtual club" of Lithuanian converts to Islam', in Göran Larsson and Thomas Hoffman (eds), *Muslims and the New Information and Communication Technologies*, Berlin: Springer Verlag, pp. 31–47.

Račius, Egdūnas, and Vaida Norvilaitė (2014), 'Features of Salafism among Lithuanian converts to Islam', *Nordic Journal of Religion and Society*, 27: 1, 39–57.

Shikhsaidov, Amri (2009), 'Ancient mosques of Daghestan', in Moshe Gammer (ed.), *Islam and Sufism in Daghestan*, Helsinki: Finnish Academy of Sciences and Letters, pp. 15–28.

Yarlykapov, Akhmet (2010), '"Folk Islam" and Muslim youth of the Central and Northwest Caucasus', in Marjorie Mandelstam Balzer (ed.), *Religion and Politics in Russia – A Reader*, London: Routledge.

Yemelianova, Galina M. (2002), *Russia and Islam: a Historical Survey*, Basingstoke: Palgrave.

Yemelianova, Galina (2003), 'Russia's umma and its muftis', *Religion, State and Society*, 31: 2, 139–50.

In Russian:

[Arapov] Арапов, Дмитрий Юрьевич (2001), *Ислам в Российской империи (законодательные акты, описания, статистика)*, Москва: Академкнига.

[Brylov] Брилев, Денис (2016), 'История ислама в Украине', А. А. Аулин (ed.), *Мусульманское сообщество Украины: институционализация и развитие*, Вінниця: Консоль, pp. 194–201.

[Bogomolov *et al.*] Богомолов, А. В., С. И. Данилов, И. Н. Семиволос, Г. М. Яворская (2006), *Исламская идентичность в Украине*, Киев: Издательский дом «Стилос».

[Guseva] Гусева, Ю. Н. (2013), 'Суфийские братства, «бродячие муллы» и «святые места» Среднего Поволжья в 1950–1960-е годы как проявления «неофициального ислама»', *Исламоведение*, 2, 35–43.

[Korolev] Королев, А. А. (2007), 'Советские мусульмане Поволжья (вторая половина 1940-х – 1980-е гг.', *Известия Алтайского государственного университета*, 4: 2, 82–90.

[Kubanova] Кубанова, Ф. М. (2008), 'Советский период истории ислама в России', *Научные проблемы гуманитарных исследований*, 13, 1–8 (49–61).

[Muratova] Муратова, Э. С. (2009), *Крымские мусульмане: взгляд изнутри (результаты социологического исследования)*, Симферополь: ЧП «Элиньо».

[Nurullina] Нуруллина, Роза Вагизовна (2014), 'Проблемы и перспективы возрождения мусульманских общин глазами имамов Татарстана', *Мониторинг общественного мнения: экономические и социальные перемены*, 1: 119, 160–7.

Successor states of Yugoslavia (Bosnia and Herzegovina, Kosovo, Serbia, Montenegro and FYROM, Slovenia and Croatia)

Abazović, Dino (2007), 'Bosnian Muslims and country in transition', in Dragoljub B. Đorđević, Dragan Todorović and Ljubiša Mitrović (eds), *Islam at the Balkans in the Past, Today and in the Future*, Niš: Yugoslav Society for the Scientific Study of Religion, Yearbook 14, pp. 51–6.

Alibašić, Ahmet (2005), 'Globalisation and its impact on Bosnian Muslims practices', paper read at the conference *Democracy and Global Islam, University of California, Berkeley*.

Alibašić, Ahmet (2014), 'Bosnia and Herzegovina', in Jocelyne Cesari (ed.), *The Oxford Handbook of European Islam*, Oxford: Oxford University Press.

Banac, Ivo (1996), 'Bosnian Muslims: from religious community to socialist nationhood and postcommunist statehood, 1918–1992', in Mark Pinson (ed.), *The Muslims of Bosnia-Herzegovina*, Cambridge, MA: Harvard University Press, pp. 129–53.

Barišić, Srđan (2007), 'Muslims in the Balkans: problems of (re)institutionalization and transformation of identity', in Dragoljub B. Đorđević, Dragan Todorović and Ljubiša Mitrović (eds.), *Islam at the Balkans in the Past, Today and in the Future*, Niš: Yugoslav Society for the Scientific Study of Religion, Yearbook 14, pp. 29–42.

Bougarel, Xavier (2005), *The role of Balkan Muslims in building a European Islam*, Brussels: European Policy Centre, Issue Paper No. 43.

Bringa, Tone (1996), *Being Muslim the Bosnian Way: Identity and Community in a Central Bosnian Village*, Princeton, NJ: Princeton University Press.

Császár, Zsuzsa M. (2010), 'The political, social and cultural aspects of the Islam in the Balkans', *Eurolimes*, 10, 62–76.

Dikici, Ali (2008), 'The Torbeshes of Macedonia: religious and national identity questions of Macedonian-speaking Muslims', *Journal of Muslim Minority Affairs*, 28: 1, 27–43.

Đorđević, Dragoljub B., and Dragan Todorović (2007), 'Tekkias, Tarikats and Sheiks of Niš Romas', in Dragoljub B. Đorđević, Dragan Todorović and Ljubiša Mitrović (eds), *Islam at the Balkans in the Past, Today and in the Future*, Niš: Yugoslav Society for the Scientific Study of Religion, Yearbook 14, pp. 87–104.

Elbasani, Arolda (2015), 'Introduction: nation, state and faith in the post-Communist era', in Arolda Elbasani and Olivier Roy (eds), *The Revival of Islam in the Balkans: From Identity to Religiosity*, Basingstoke: Palgrave Macmillan, pp. 1–19.

Elbasani, Arolda, and Olivier Roy (2015), 'Islam in the post-Communist Balkans: alternative pathways to God', *Southeast European and Black Sea Studies*, 15: 4, 457–71.

Ismaili, Besa (2014), 'Kosovo', in Jørgen S. Nielsen, Samim Akgönül, Ahmet Alibašić and Egdūnas Račius (eds), *Yearbook of Muslims in Europe*, Leiden: Brill, vol. 6, pp. 352–63.

Izetbegović, Alija (1990), *The Islamic Declaration: a Programme for the Islamization of Muslims and the Muslim Peoples*, Sarajevo, http://profkaminskisreadings.yolasite.com/resources/Alija%20Izetbegovic-%20The%20Islamic-Declaration%20(1990).pdf (last accessed 23 February 2017).

Jahja, Muharem (2014), 'Macedonia', in Jørgen S. Nielsen, Samim Akgönül, Ahmet Alibašić and Egdūnas Račius (eds), *Yearbook of Muslims in Europe*, Leiden: Brill, vol. 6, pp. 398–408.

Karčić, Fikret (1997), 'The office of Rais al-Ulama among the Bosniaks', *Intellectual Discourse*, 5: 2, 109–20.

Karčić, Fikret (2006), *What is 'Islamic Tradition of Bosniaks'?* (translated from Bosnian by Djermana Šeta), *Preporod*, http://cns.ba/wp-content/uploads/2014/03/what_is_islamic_tradition_of_bosniaks.pdf (last accessed 10 November 2016).

Karčić, Fikret (2015), *The Other European Muslims: a Bosnian Experience*, Sarajevo: Center for Advanced Studies.

Kostić, Ivan Ejub (2015), 'Serbia', in Oliver Scharbrodt, Jørgen S. Nielsen, Samim Akgönül, Ahmet Alibašić and Egdūnas Račius (eds), *Yearbook of Muslims in Europe*, Leiden: Brill, vol. 7, pp. 503–14.

Krasniqi, Gëzim (2011), 'The "forbidden fruit": Islam and politics of identity in Kosovo and Macedonia', *Southeast European and Black Sea Studies*, 11: 2, 191–207.

Lelić, Emin (2006), *Reading Rumi in Sarajevo: the Mevlevi Tradition in the Balkans*, Chicago, IL: Babagân Books.

Li, Darryl (2014), *Expert Opinion on Foreign Fighters in the Bosnian Jihad*, prepared for US v. Bahar Ahmad and US v. Syed Talha Ahsan, https://www.academia.edu/28287134/Expert_Opinion_on_Foreign_Fighters_in_the_Bosnian_Jihad (last accessed 23 February 2017).

Mehmeti, Jeton (2015), 'Faith and politics in Kosovo: the status of religious communities in a secular country', in Arolda Elbasani and Olivier Roy (eds), *The Revival of*

Islam in the Balkans: From Identity to Religiosity, Basingstoke: Palgrave Macmillan, pp. 62–80.

Merdjanova, Ina (2013), *Rediscovering the* Umma: *Muslims in the Balkans between Nationalism and Transnationalism*, Oxford: Oxford University Press.

Moe, Christian (2015), 'Slovenia', in Oliver Scharbrodt, Jørgen S. Nielsen, Samim Akgönül, Ahmet Alibašić and Egdūnas Račius (eds), *Yearbook of Muslims in Europe*, Leiden: Brill, vol. 7, pp. 523–33.

Morina, Driton (2015), 'Kosovo', in Oliver Scharbrodt, Jørgen S. Nielsen, Samim Akgönül, Ahmet Alibašić and Egdūnas Račius (eds), *Yearbook of Muslims in Europe*, Leiden: Brill, vol. 7, pp. 353–63.

Mujadzevic, Dino (2013), *Croatian Muslims or Bosniak Diaspora? Two Competing Identities in Contemporary Islamic Community in Croatia*, Akademie der Diözese Rottenburg-Stuttgart, https://www.academia.edu/6258994/Croatian_Muslims_or_Bosniak_Diaspora_Two_Competing_Identities_in_Contemporary_Islamic_Community_in_Croatia (last accessed 28 February 2017).

Mujadzevic, Dino (2014), 'Croatia', in Jørgen S. Nielsen, Samim Akgönül, Ahmet Alibašić and Egdūnas Račius (eds), *Yearbook of Muslims in Europe*, Leiden: Brill, vol. 6, pp. 144–52.

Öktem, Kerem (2010), *New Islamic Actors after the Wahhabi Intermezzo: Turkey's Return to the Muslim Balkans*, Oxford: University of Oxford, https://wikileaks.org/gifiles/attach/126/126845_Oktem-Balkan-Muslims.pdf (last accessed 24 February 2017).

Öktem, Kerem (2011), 'Between emigration, de-Islamization and the nation-state: Muslim communities in the Balkans today', *Southeast European and Black Sea Studies*, 11: 2, 155–71.

Pačariz, Sabina (2016), *The Migrations of Bosniaks to Turkey from 1945 to 1974: the Case of Sandžak*, Sarajevo: Center for Advanced Studies.

Pramenković, Almir (2014), 'Serbia', in Jørgen S. Nielsen, Samim Akgönül, Ahmet Alibašić and Egdūnas Račius (eds), *Yearbook of Muslims in Europe*, Leiden: Brill, vol. 6, pp. 529–39.

Rexhepi, Piro (2016), 'Macedonia', in Oliver Scharbrodt, Jørgen S. Nielsen, Samim Akgönül, Ahmet Alibašić and Egdūnas Račius (eds), *Yearbook of Muslims in Europe*, Leiden: Brill, vol. 8, pp. 441–55.

Smajić, Aid (2014), 'Bosnia and Herzegovina', in Jørgen S. Nielsen, Samim Akgönül, Ahmet Alibašić and Egdūnas Račius (eds), *Yearbook of Muslims in Europe*, Leiden: Brill, vol. 6, pp. 108–25.

Smajić, Aid, and Muhamed Fazlović (2015), 'Bosnia and Herzegovina', in Oliver Scharbrodt, Jørgen S. Nielsen, Samim Akgönül, Ahmet Alibašić and Egdūnas Račius (eds), *Yearbook of Muslims in Europe*, Leiden: Brill, vol. 7, pp. 114–29.

Sorabji, Cornelia (1989), 'Muslim Identity and Islamic Faith in Sarajevo', PhD thesis, University of Cambridge, Cambridge, UK.

Stoyanov, Yuri (2013), *Between Middle Eastern Heterodoxy, Indigenization and Modern Shiʿism: Competing Identities among the Balkan Alevi and Bektashi Communities in the post-Ottoman*

Period, http://ef.huji.ac.il/publications/Ottoman%20Legacies/Yuri%20Stoyanov _Between%20Middle%20Eastern%20Heterodoxy.pdf (last accessed 10 August 2016).

Vukomanović, Milan (2007), 'Dervishes in Belgrade: the Belgrade tekkes, tariqas, shaikhs', in Dragoljub B. Đorđević, Dragan Todorović and Ljubiša Mitrović (eds), *Islam at the Balkans in the Past, Today and in the Future*, Niš: Yugoslav Society for the Scientific Study of Religion, Yearbook 14, pp. 83–6.

Zdravkovski, Aleksander (2014), 'Islam and politics in the Serbian Sandžak: institutionalization and feuds', in Sabrina P. Ramet (ed.), *Religion and Politics in Post-Socialist Central and Southeastern Europe: Challenges since 1989*, Basingstoke: Palgrave, pp. 212–39.

Zhelyazkova, Antonina (2002), 'Islamization in the Balkans as an historiographical problem: the Southeast-European perspective', in Fikret Adanır and, Suraiya Faroqhi (eds), *The Ottomans and the Balkans: a Discussion of Historiography*, Leiden: Brill, pp. 223–66.

South-eastern Europe (Albania, Bulgaria, Romania)

Alak, Alina Isac (2015), 'Types of religious identities within Romanian Muslim communities', in *Journal for the Study of Religions and Ideologies*, 14: 41, 148–73.

Clayer, Nathalie (2010), 'Adapting Islam to Europe: the Albanian example', in Christian Voss and Jordanka Telbizova-Sack (eds), *Islam und Muslime in (Südost) Europa im Kontext von Transformation und EU-Erweiterung*, München: Otto Sagner, pp. 53–69.

Clayer, Nathalie (2012), 'The Bektashi Institutions in Southeastern Europe: alternative Muslim official structures and their limits', *Die Welt des Islams*, 52: 2, 183–203.

Eminov, Ali (2000), 'Turks and Tatars in Bulgaria and the Balkans', *Nationalities Papers*, 28: 1, 129–64.

Erolova, Yelis (2016), 'Contemporary development of the Akyazili Baba Tekke/St. Athanasius in Bulgaria', in Ekaterina Anastasova and Mare Kõiva (eds), *Current Cultural Studies*, Tartu: Estonian Literary Museum Scholarly Press, pp. 50–69.

Ghodsee, Kristen (2010), *Muslim Lives in Eastern Europe: Gender, Ethnicity, and the Transformation of Islam in Postsocialist Bulgaria*, Princeton, NJ: Princeton University Press.

Grigore, George (1999), 'Muslims in Romania', *ISIM Newsletter*, 3, p. 34.

Jazehxi, Olsi (2016), 'Albania', in Oliver Scharbrodt, Jørgen S. Nielsen, Samim Akgönül, Ahmet Alibašić and Egdūnas Račius (eds), *Yearbook of Muslims in Europe*, Leiden: Brill, vol. 8, pp. 19–33.

Kozák, Gyula (2009), *Muslims in Romania: Integration Models, Categorization and Social Distance*, Working Papers in Romanian Minority Studies, no. 18, Cluj-Napoca: Romanian Institute For Research On National Minorities.

Maeva, Mila (2015), 'Turkish religious identity in Bulgaria in the last twenty four years (1989–2013)', in Ekaterina Anastasova and Mare Kõiva (eds), *Balkan and Baltic*

States, and Post-Soviet Studies, Tartu: Estonian Literary Museum Scholarly Press, pp. 82–106.

Marushiakova, Elena, and Vesselin Popov (2004), *Muslim Minorities in Bulgaria*, http:// www.islamawareness.net/Europe/Bulgaria/bulgaria_article0003.pdf (last accessed 28 February 2017).

Nitzova, Petya (1994), 'Islam in Bulgaria: a historical reappraisal', *Religion, State and Society*, 22: 1, 97–102.

Osterman, Laura Olson (2013), *Islamic Revival and Folk Revival among Rural Bulgarian Muslims in the Post-Communist Period*, http://researchfellowships.americancouncils. org/sites/researchfellowships.americancouncils.org/files/Osterman_Final_ Report.pdf (last accessed 28 February 2017).

Shakir, Aziz (2016), 'Bulgaria', in Oliver Scharbrodt, Jørgen S. Nielsen, Samim Akgönül, Ahmet Alibašić and Egdūnas Račius (eds), *Yearbook of Muslims in Europe*, Leiden: Brill, vol. 8, pp. 143–60.

Vainovski-Mihai, Irina (2016), 'Romania', in Oliver Scharbrodt, Jørgen S. Nielsen, Samim Akgönül, Ahmet Alibašić and Egdūnas Račius (eds), *Yearbook of Muslims in Europe*, Leiden: Brill, vol. 8, pp. 562–77.

In Bulgarian:
[Gramatikova] Граматикова, Невена (2011), *Неортодоксалният ислям в българските земи*, Гутенберг.

Central Europe (Poland, the Czech Republic, Slovakia, Hungary)

Berend, Nora (2001), *At the Gate of Christendom: Jews, Muslims and 'Pagans' in Medieval Hungary c.1000–c.1300*, Cambridge: Cambridge University Press.

Berend, Nora (2014), 'A note on the end of Islam in medieval Hungary: old mistakes and some new results', *Journal of Islamic Studies*, 25: 2, 201–6.

Bureš, Jaroslav (2011), 'Muslims in the Czech Republic: integration into the closed society', in Visegrad Fund, *Muslims in Visegrad*, Prague: Institute of International Relations, pp. 25–38.

Csiszár, Esztella (2016), 'Hungary', in Oliver Scharbrodt, Jørgen S. Nielsen, Samim Akgönül, Ahmet Alibašić and Egdūnas Račius (eds), *Yearbook of Muslims in Europe*, Leiden: Brill, vol. 8, pp. 337–51.

Drobný, Jaroslav (2014), 'Slovakia', in Jørgen S. Nielsen, Samim Akgönül, Ahmet Alibašić, Egdūnas Račius (eds), *Yearbook of Muslims in Europe*, Leiden: Brill, vol. 6, pp. 540–6.

Górak-Sosnowska, Katarzyna (ed.) (2011), *Muslims in Poland and Eastern Europe. Widening the European Discourse on Islam*, Warsaw: University of Warsaw Press.

Hannova, Daniela (2014), 'Arab students inside the Soviet Bloc: a case study on Czechoslovakia during the 1950s and 60s', *European Scientific Journal*, 2, 371–9.

Macháček, Štěpán (2014), 'Czech Republic', in Jørgen S. Nielsen, Samim Akgönül,

Ahmet Alibašić and Egdūnas Račius (eds), *Yearbook of Muslims in Europe*, Leiden: Brill, vol. 6, pp. 176–88.

Macháček, Štěpán (2015), 'Czech Republic', in Oliver Scharbrodt, Jørgen S. Nielsen, Samim Akgönül, Ahmet Alibašić and Egdūnas Račius (eds), *Yearbook of Muslims in Europe*, Leiden: Brill, vol. 7, pp. 174–81.

Macháček, Štěpán (2016), 'Czech Republic', in Oliver Scharbrodt, Jørgen S. Nielsen, Samim Akgönül, Ahmet Alibašić and Egdūnas Račius (eds), *Yearbook of Muslims in Europe*, Leiden: Brill, vol. 8, pp. 194–202.

Mendel, Miloš (1998), 'The Islamic religious community in Bohemia and Moravia (1934–1945)', *Archív Orientální* (Quarterly Journal of African and Asian Studies), 66: 2, 127–41.

O'Dell, Emily Jane (2011), *Islam in the Czech & Slovak Republics: an Invisible Minority Becomes Visible*, Scholar Research Brief, IREX, https://www.irex.org/sites/default/files/ODell%20Scholar%20Research%20Brief%202010-2011.pdf (last accessed 10 August 2016).

Pędziwiatr, Konrad (2011), 'Muslims in contemporary Poland', in Visegrad Fund, *Muslims in Visegrad*, Prague: Institute of International Relations, pp. 10–24.

Póczik, Szilveszter (2016), 'Foreign fighters from the Balkans and Hungary in the Middle East', *Defence Review* (The Central Journal of the Hungarian Defence Forces), 144: 1, 52–70.

Rozsa, Erszebet (2013), 'The exceptionality of Central Europe: the Muslim minorities', in Kinga Dévényi (ed.), *Studies on Political Islam and Islamic Political Thought*, Budapest: Corvinus University, pp. 219–63.

Stojkovski, Boris (2010), 'Legal position of Muslims in medieval Hungary' [in Serbian], *Зборник радова Правног факултета у Новом Саду*, 1, 171–9.

Štulrajterova, Katarina (2013), 'Convivenza, Convenienza and Conversion: Islam in medieval Hungary (1000–1400 ce)', *Journal of Islamic Studies*, 24: 2, 175–98.

Index